Implementing International Economic Law

# Nijhoff International Trade Law Series



VOLUME 6

*The titles published in this series are listed at brill.nl/nint.*

# Implementing International Economic Law

## Through Dispute Settlement Mechanisms

*Edited by*
Yusuf Aksar

MARTINUS NIJHOFF PUBLISHERS

LEIDEN • BOSTON
2011

This book is printed on acid-free paper.

Library of Congress Cataloging-in-Publication Data

Implementing international economic law : through dispute settlement mechanisms / edited by Yusuf Aksar.
p. cm. -- (Nijhoff international trade law series ; v. 6)
Includes bibliographical references.
ISBN 978-90-04-20383-9 (hardback : alk. paper) 1. International economic relations. 2. Dispute resolution (Law) 3. International finance--Law and legislation. 4. Investments, Foreign--Law and legislation. I. Aksar, Yusuf, 1972- II. Title. III. Series.

K3820.I48 2011
343'.07--dc23

2011021166

ISSN 1877-7392
ISBN 978 90 04 20383 9

*To my sons,*

*Ahmet Talha Aksar and Mehmet Emin Aksar*

CONTENTS

# FOREWORD

It is a great pleasure for me to introduce *Implementing International Economic Law: Through Dispute Settlement Mechanisms* as one of the first titles of The Nijhoff International Trade Law Series. International economic law is rapidly becoming one of the most important areas of law. It is an interdisciplinary area of law, both within the law where jurists with different backgrounds in domestic and international law make their contributions and with a close relationship to economics and other social sciences. International economic law is often divided into three sub disciplines: international finance law, international trade law, and international investment law. They give rise to similar issues of enforcement and dispute resolution but the response to these is different. The response depends on the treaty base and institutional structure that has been established in the respective field. The focus of the current book on the dispute settlement mechanisms allows the authors to say something about their significance and contribution to international economic law. The book demonstrates that the practice of the international institutions such as the dispute settlement panels and the Appellate Body of the World Trade Organisation, and arbitration panels of the system under the International Centre for the Settlement of Investment Disputes, have gone beyond narrowly interpreting and applying the rules of international economic law. The authors contend that this activity has included formulating new rules when needed, turning the judicial institutions of international economic law into important law makers.

The authors are all well-known scholars, based in the UK and Turkey, and with practical experience in public international law, private international law, international trade law, international finance law, and international investment law.

The book has five main chapters. Chapter 1, "International Economic Law", is written by Yusuf Aksar and provides an overall framework for the analysis of international law and international economic law and the dispute settlement mechanisms. This chapter deals with the nature and role of international economic law, its relationship with other branches of law like public international law, private international law, international business law, the European Union law, international environment law, and domestic law. Chapter 2, "New Challenges and Issues in International Finance Law", is by Ilias Bantekas and focuses on international finance law. The universal institutions of the international financial system, the latest global financial crisis and its impact on the international economic system, as well as possible solutions are discussed in detail. Chapter 3, "Dispute Settlement in International Trade

Law", is written by Pınar Karacan Baklacı and deals with the dispute settlement mechanisms in international trade law. The Dispute Settlement System of the WTO with the practice of the panels and the Appellate Body of the WTO, their contribution to international economic law, alternative methods in settling disputes, the use of the WTO system by developing countries, and the proposals for changes on the shortcomings of the system are the main points of this chapter. Chapter 4, "Dispute Settlement in International Investment Law", is written by Yusuf Çalışkan and examines the dispute settlement mechanism in international investment law. Bilateral Investment Treaties, the main aspects of ICSID arbitration proceedings, amendments of the ICSID rules demonstrating the impact of previous ICSID tribunals' decisions on the new rules, transparency issue, and third party participation in ICSID arbitration are discussed and the case for accepting amicus curiae submissions is forcefully stated. The protection of shareholder rights through ICSID arbitration and the issue of contract claims versus treaty claims, sovereign immunity, the main substantive principles of international law such as most favoured nation, fair and equitable treatment, and non-precluded measures are also discussed.

In a final concluding part with some general conclusions an agenda for future research is set out. The authors emphasise the relationship between public international law and international economic law. This is a two-way street: due account has to be taken of general principles and methods of international law in the different treaty regimes. Then customary international law and its general principles have to take account of the law developing in particular in the dispute settlement bodies of international economic law.

The Nijhoff International Trade Law Series is a forum for important and original research. It moves across the boundaries that have divided the law and includes studies of trade law subjects that would fall within the fields of public and private international and comparative law. Comparative law is increasingly used as a tool in the making of law at national, regional, and international levels. Private international law is now often affected by international conventions, and the issues faced by classical conflict rules are dealt with by substantive harmonization of law under international auspices. Mixed international arbitrations, especially those involving state economic activity, raise questions of public and private international law, while in many fields (such as the protection of human rights and democratic standards, investment guarantees) international and national systems interact. National constitutional arrangements relating to 'foreign affairs', and to the implementation of international norms, are a focus of attention. The focus is on scholarly monographs, with a particular emphasis on those which are interdisciplinary in nature, both in relation to legal disciplines and the humanities and social sciences. Edited collections of essays will also be included where they are appropriate. The series is wide in scope and aims to cover studies of particular areas of substantive and of institutional law, economic and historical works, theoretical studies, and analyses of current debates.

*Mads Andenas*
General Editor

# PREFACE AND ACKNOWLEDGEMENTS

The book aims to examine the relationship between international law and one of its sub-branches called international economic law. Chapter 1 provides general information relating to the interdisciplinary nature of international economic law, its relationship with other branches of law, its sources and the reasons why international economic law does work. The substantive content of the discipline by limiting it to international finance law, international trade law and international investment law is examined in Chapters 2-4 respectively. However, the main focus in the work is the dispute settlement mechanisms of international economic law. In particular, the WTO Dispute Settlement System and the ICSID (International Centre for the Settlement of Investment Disputes) are taken into consideration as tools which are used for the implementation of international economic law. Throughout the work it becomes clear that international law in terms of its sources and its mechanisms plays a crucial role in providing guidance for international judicial institutions operating in the field of international economic law. The principles upon which international economic law was built such as the most favoured nation treatment and fair and equitable treatment can meet the needs of the international community and provide solutions to the challenges of the 21st century when they are interpreted and applied in accordance with the rules of international law like Articles 31 and 32 of the Vienna Convention on the Law of Treaties. Through which international judicial institutions can contribute to the creation of global judicial settlement mechanisms which are inevitable in achieving a global and secure market for the 21 century.

The present book is the product of the Project sponsored by the Turkish Academy of Sciences since 2007. On a personal note, I would like to express my gratitude to the Turkish Academy of Sciences for its generous financial support which made possible the preparation of this work. I am greatly indebted to Professor Ilias Bantekas, Assistant Professor Pınar Karacan Baklaci and Associate Professor Yusuf Caliskan, all those who agreed to contribute chapters to the work. I am most indebted to Professor Malcolm D. Evans, who personally has strengthened my interest in and understanding of international law since my PhD study in the School of Law at Bristol University. Professor Evan's high intellectual capacity provided me with much personal inspiration for which I will always be grateful. I would also like to express my special thanks to Faruk Ekmekci who provided me with invaluable assistance in the process of editing of the project. I wish to express my gratitude to those at Martinus Nijhoff Publishers for their role in the production of the book.

Finally, and most importantly, I should like to thank my wife, Ilknur Ozkan Aksar and my sons, Ahmet Talha Aksar and Mehmet Emin Aksar for their encouragements and moral supports throughout all stages of the production of the work.

*Yusuf Aksar*
*Professor of International Law*
*Maltepe University Law Faculty, Istanbul*
*2011*

## NOTES ON CONTRIBUTORS

**Yusuf Aksar,** LLB (Ankara), LLM (Ankara), LLM (Sheffield), PhD (Bristol), is Professor of International Law at Maltepe University Law Faculty in Istanbul, Turkey. After graduating from Ankara University Law Faculty, he practised as a public prosecutor and judge candidate for the Ministry of Justice. He was awarded with LL.M. by both Ankara University Law Faculty and Sheffield University Law Faculty in 1996 and 1997 respectively and received his Ph.D. from Bristol University Law Faculty in 2000. He is member of the European Society of International Law and of International Law Association. He was also awarded by the Turkish Academy of Sciences as one of the Honourable Youngest Scientists of 2007. His principal publications include *Implementing International Humanitarian Law From the Ad Hoc Tribunals to a Permanent International Criminal Court* (Routledge, 2004) and *Evrensel Yargı Kuruluşları (Universal Judicial Institutions)* (Seckin, 2007).

**Ilias Bantekas,** LLB (Athens), LLM (Liverpool), Ph.D. (Liverpool), Dip. Theology (Cambridge), is Professor of International Law at Brunel University School of Law. From 1998–2006 he was an Associate Professor and Director of the International Law Unit at Westminster Law School and during 2003–04 he was a Fellow at Harvard Law School. He is Head of International Law & Arbitration at Mourgelas and Associates Law Firm (Athens). He was a Senior Fellow at IALS and a Visiting Professor at SOAS, University of London in 2009. His publications include: *Principles of Individual Criminal Responsibility in International Humanitarian Law* (Manchester UP, 2002); *International Criminal Law* (Hart, 4th edition, 2010); *Trust Funds in International Law: Trustee Obligations of the United Nations and the World Bank* (Asser/Cambridge UP, 2009). He has published widely in leading international journals, including the American Journal of International Law, ICLQ, British Yearbook of International Law and others.

**Yusuf Caliskan,** LLB (Ankara), LLM (USA), JSD (USA), is Associate Professor of International Law and teaches Private International Law, International Investment Law and International Commercial Law at Kocaeli University School of Law. He studied Law at Ankara University School of Law, Case Western Reserve University School of Law (LL.M) and Washington University in St Louis School of Law (JSD). His JSD dissertation is entitled "The Development of International Investment Law: Lessons from the OECD MAI Negotiations and Their Application to a Possible Multilateral Agreement on Investment". He has written Articles and books on private international law, international investment law and arbitration. He is also a member of the ICSID Panel of Conciliators and Arbitrators, designated by Republic of Turkey.

**Pınar Karacan Baklaci**, LLB (Izmir), LLM (USA), SJD (USA), is Assistant Professor of International Law and teaches Private International Law, International Commercial Law and International Trade Law at Dokuz Eylul University, Izmir-Turkey. She was awarded with LLM by the University of Iowa, College of Lawand and SJD by the University of Wisconsin, Law School. Her research interests include private international law, international trade law, competition law, EU law and international investment law. Her recent publications include subject areas such as: "Most Favored Nation Treatment in International Investment Law", "Energy Charter Treaty and Dispute Settlement" and Bilateral Investment Treaties.

## LIST OF ABBREVIATIONS

| | |
|---|---|
| AB | Appellate Body |
| ACWL | Advisory Centre for WTO Law |
| ADB | Asian Development Bank |
| AfDB | African Development Bank |
| AU | African Union |
| BIS | Bank for International Settlements |
| BITs | Bilateral Investment Treaties |
| DDA | Doha Development Agenda |
| DSB | Dispute Settlement Body |
| DSU | Dispute Settlement Understanding |
| EC | European Community |
| ECJ | European Court of Justice |
| ECR | European Court Reports |
| EEC | European Economic Community |
| ESF | Exogenous Shocks Facility |
| EU | European Union |
| FET | Fair and Equitable Treatment |
| FAO | Food and Agriculture Organisation |
| FATF | Financial Action Task Force |
| FDI | Foreign Direct Investment |
| FSB | Financial Stability Board |
| FSF | Financial Stability Forum |
| GAB | General Agreements to Borrow |
| GATS | General Agreement on Trade in Services |
| GATT | General Agreement on Tariffs and Trade |
| GDP | Gross Domestic Product |
| HIPC | Heavily Indebted Poor Countries |
| IBRD | International Bank for Reconstruction and Development, usually known as the World Bank |
| ICJ | International Court of Justice |
| ICSID | International Centre for the Settlement of Investment Disputes |
| IDA | International Development Agency |
| IFC | International Finance Corporation |
| ILM | International Legal Materials |
| IMF | International Monetary Fund |
| IOSCO | International Organisation for Securities Commissions |

| | |
|---|---|
| ITU | International Telecommunications Union |
| MDBs | Multilateral Development Banks |
| MDRI-I Trust | Multilateral Debt Relief Initiative-I |
| MERCOSUR | *Mercado Comun del Sur*, which means Common Market of the South |
| MFN | Most Favoured Nation (Treatment) |
| MIGA | Multilateral Investment Guarantee Agency |
| NAB | New Arrangements to Borrow |
| NAFTA | North American Free Trade Agreement |
| NGOs | Non-Governmental Organisations |
| NPM | Non-Precluded Measures |
| OECD | Organisation for Economic Co-operation and Development |
| OIC | Organisation of the Islamic Conference |
| PCIJ | Permanent Court of International Justice |
| PRGF | Poverty Reduction and Growth Facility |
| SAF | Structural Adjustment Facility |
| SDRs | Special Drawing Rights |
| TRIPS | Agreement on Trade-Related Aspects of Intellectual Property Rights |
| UK | United Kingdom |
| UN | United Nations |
| UNCITRAL | United Nations Commission on International Trade Law |
| UNCTAD | UN Conference on Trade and Development |
| UNDP | UN Development Program |
| UNGA | United Nations General Assembly |
| UNTS | United Nations Treaty Series |
| US | United States |
| USA | United States of America |
| WIPO | World Intellectual Property Organisation |
| WHO | World Health Organisation |
| WTO | World Trade Organisation |

# TABLE OF CASES

INTRODUCTORY REMARKS

# IMPLEMENTING INTERNATIONAL ECONOMIC LAW THROUGH DISPUTE SETTLEMENT MECHANISMS

Yusuf Aksar

As one of the branches of international law, international economic law is very likely to be one of the most significant areas of law throughout the 21st century. As it can be inferred from its name, international economic law is an inter-disciplinary area of law which has close relationship with both public international law and international economics. The rules and principles constituting international economic law have been basically created by international conventions (treaties, agreements), which are the main sources of international law. In cases of disputes or cases arising out of the practice of international community with regard to international economic law matters, international conventions will provide necessary principles for resolving the disputes. The fundamental principles concerning the interpretation and application of treaties of international law will play central role in settling such disputes. In the same vein, the significance of economics cannot be denied because it would not be possible to understand the national and international law regulations without insights from economics. Moreover, the effects of politics, history and geography on international economic law should also be considered.

International economic law covers very broad and different fields since it deals with all economic aspects of relations among the subjects of international law. However, the common practice among the scholars in the field is to limit field to three different areas of law, namely, international finance law, international trade law and international investment law.

Those three fields of international law have been the central pillars of international economic law particularly since the end of the Cold-War. In today's world, the relations among the subjects of international law (States, international organisations, individuals and companies) have dramatically intensified and consequently the borders separating the States from one another have increasingly lost their significance, if not disappeared. In order to create a stable and secure global economy, it is a *sine qua non* requirement that the disputes among the subjects of the international law or cases deriving from the application of the principles of international economic law must be solved by the dispute settlement mechanisms which are established by the international community. Such mechanisms in settling disputes are crucial both for the protection of international peace and security in general and for the implementation of international economic law in particular.

For the aforementioned reasons the work entitled "Implementing International Economic Law Through Dispute Settlement Mechanisms" will focus on the dispute settlement mechanisms and their significance and contribution to international economic law. This book will demonstrate that the practice of the international institutions such as the panels, the Appellate Body of the World Trade Organisation (the WTO), and the International Centre for the Settlement of Investment Disputes (the ICSID) went beyond merely interpreting and applying the rules of international economic law and included formulating new rules when needed. In other words, international judicial institutions in the field of international economic law have become "law-makers" by way of applying the law. This is the point that sources of international law may provide the necessary guidance for the international adjudicative bodies.

In accordance with limiting international economic law to international finance law, international trade law and international investment law and the related dispute settlement mechanisms in this regard the book consists of following Chapters:

Chapter 1 "International Economic Law" written by Yusuf Aksar aims to provide an overall framework for thinking about international law and international economic law and how they interrelate as long as the dispute settlement mechanisms and the interpretation and application of rules are taken into consideration in this respect. The nature and role of international economic law; its relationship with other branches of law like public international law, private international law, international business law, the European Union law, international environment law, and domestic law; its sources and substantive content are the main topics covered in this chapter.

Chapter 2 "New Challenges and Issues in International Finance Law" written by Ilias Bantekas focuses on international finance law. The universal institutions of the international financial system, the latest global financial crisis and its impact on international economic system, and possible solutions will be discussed in detail.

Chapter 3 "Dispute Settlement in International Trade Law" written by Pınar Karacan Baklacı specifically deals with the dispute settlement mechanisms in international trade law. The Dispute Settlement System of the WTO in accordance with the practice of the panels and the Appellate Body of the WTO and their contribution to international economic law, alternative methods in settling disputes, the use of the WTO system by developing countries and the proposals for changes on the shortcomings of the system are discussed in detail.

Chapter 4 "Dispute Settlement in International Investment Law" written by Yusuf Çalışkan examines the dispute settlement mechanism in international investment law. Bilateral Investment Treaties (BITs), the main aspects of

ICSID arbitration proceedings, in particular, amendments of the ICSID rules demonstrating the previous ICSID tribunals' decisions impact on the new rules, transparency issue and third party participation in ICSID arbitration will be discussed through giving some case examples for accepting amicus curiae submissions. Furthermore, the protection of shareholder rights through ICSID arbitration and the issue of contract claims v treaty claims, sovereign immunity, the main substantive principles of international law such as most favoured nation, fair and equitable treatment and non-precluded measures will be discussed in more detail.

Finally, in the Conclusion section, the book draws some general conclusions and provides certain suggestions for future research and practice in the field of international economic law.

CHAPTER ONE

# INTERNATIONAL ECONOMIC LAW

Yusuf Aksar

## 1.1. *Introduction*

International law is a system of rules and principles that govern international relations of the subjects of international law namely; sovereign States, international organisations, the entities which do not have the full requirements of statehood and individuals. Throughout the historical development of international law some legal commentators and jurists have questioned the ever existence of rules and principles which qualify as being called "international law". To support such an idea they wrongly compared the institutions of international law to those of domestic law, whereby they referred to the lack of institutions for law-making, executing and enforcing the rules and principles at the international level. However, it should be indicated that the international legal system is completely different from the national legal system and it basically governs the relationship between sovereign and equal subjects of international law. And, in today's world there is no doubt that international law as a legal system plays a central role for affecting and regulating the attitudes of the members of the international community.[1]

The same sceptical arguments can also be put against the concept of international economic law. As will be discussed in detail below, despite the lack of a clear definition of international economic law, in the widest sense, international economic law may be defined as the rules and principles which govern all economic aspects of relations among the subjects of international law.

During the last decades of 20th century the international community has witnessed the globalisation of almost everything. The creation of a truly global economy is only one of these processes. As a result, from the point of view of international economic relations, the subjects of international law have become much more interdependent than ever before. Some of the reasons for the growing extent of international economic interdependence can be indicated as follows: a) the technological advancements in communication

[1] For a brief discussion on the nature of international law and the international system, *see* M. Dixon, *Textbook on International Law*, Oxford: Oxford University Press, 6th edn., 2007, pp. 1–22.

and transportation and the use of internet making possible instant and cyber transactions; b) creation of an economic climate that is favourable to principles of market economics through conclusion of regional and universal treaties which reduce governmental barriers to trade; d) the effect of globalisation in a way of influencing the competition in production and services; e) the relative peace in the world.[2]

The global economy is one of the reflections of globalisation and has not been created by law. Legal rules and principles on the one hand and the legal institutions on the other are crucial in helping economic activities[3] and providing stability to the global economy. This is where the concept of international economic law as an independent branch of international law derives from.

Although this study focuses on dispute settlement mechanisms in international economic law as a means of implementing the rules and principles of international law, in this Chapter it is necessary to look at some of the important fundamental issues such as the nature of international economic law, its role, its relationship with other branches of law, its sources, and its substantive content.

## 1.2. *The Concept of International Economic Law*

### 1.2.1. *Defining International Economic Law*

In understanding the concept of international economic law it would be appropriate to start with an anecdote from Zamora:

> *When asked what kind of law I teach, I usually reply "international economic law." After the inevitable pause, I offer the necessary explanation: "I teach and write about the legal aspects of international trade, international business, international banking, and other subjects that involve economic relations between nations, as well as between private parties." Another pause. "You know, NAFTA and stuff like that."*[4]

As it can be understood from this expression, there are some problems relating to the definition and the content of international economic law. Both in theory and in practice it is not possible to find a clear definition of international economic law. That is why international economic law is not an easy

---

[2] J. H. Jackson, "Global Economics and International Economic Law", (1998) 1 *Journal of International Economic Law*, p.1.

[3] C. R. Reitz, "International Economic Law", (1996) 17 *University of Pennsylvania Journal of International Economic Law*, p. 29.

[4] S. Zamora, "International Economic Law", "International Economic Law", (1996) 17 *University of Pennsylvania Journal of International Economic Law*, p. 63.

task to be defined since it covers very broad range of topics among the subjects of international law.

In general terms, international economic law can be explained or evaluated in a broader or narrower manner. In the broadest sense, international economic law could be defined as the law including all legal subjects that have both international and economic components.[5] In the narrower sense, international economic law is defined as "international law rules dealing with some of the *economic conduct* of international law subjects, and with some of their *economic relations* inter se."[6] In this sense, international economic law is considered as a branch of international law and also be referred to as 'international law of the economy'.[7]

However, both the wider and the narrower definitions do not reflect the real nature and scope of international economic law. As will be discussed later, one of the fundamental characteristics of international economic law is to be an interdisciplinary field of law. So, any definition concerning international economic law must reflect this fact. Some of the definitions, in this context, can be noted as follows:

According to Petersmann, international economic law "presents itself as a conglomerate of private law (including 'law merchant' and 'transnational commercial law'), state law (including 'conflict of laws') and public international law (including supranational integration law as in the EEC) with a bewildering array of multilateral and bilateral treaties, executive agreements, 'secondary law' enacted by international organisations, 'gentlemen's agreements' central bank arrangements, declarations of principles, resolutions, recommendations, customary law, general principles of law, de facto-orders, parliamentary acts, governments decrees, judicial decisions, private contracts or commercial usages."[8]

Jackson defines international economic law as covering "a very broad inventory of subjects: embracing the law of economic transactions; government regulation of economic matters; and related legal relations including litigation and international institutions for economic relations."[9]

Zamaro offers the following definition: "International economic law comprises a broad collection of laws and customary practices that govern

[5] G. Loibl, "International Economic Law", in Malcolm D. Evans (ed.), *International Law*, Oxford: Oxford University Press, 2003, p. 689.

[6] F. Ortino and M. Ortino, "Law of the Global Economy: In Need of a New Methodological Approach", in C. B. Picker, I. D. Bunn, D. W. Arner (eds.), *International Economic Law The State and Future of the Discipline*, Oxford and Portland, Oregon: Hart Publishing, 2008, p. 92.

[7] Ibid.

[8] E.-U. Petersmann, "International Economic Theory and International Economic Law: On the Tasks of a Legal Theory of International Economic Order", in R. St. J. MacDonald & D. M. Johnston (eds.), *The Structure and Process of International Law: Essays in Legal Philosophy Doctrine and Theory*, (1983), 251.

[9] Jackson, p. 8.

economic relations between actors in different nations. It includes the examination of both law and policy issues on multiple levels, including private law, local law, national law, and international law."[10]

According to Schwarzenberger, international economic law could be defined by enumerating the fields which constitute this branch of law: a) the exploitation of natural resources; b) the production and distribution of goods; c) invisible economic or financial transactions; d) currency and finance; e) related services; and f) status and organisation of those engaged in such activities.[11]

Vagts defines "international economic law as the international law regulating trans-border transactions in goods, services, currency, investment, and intellectual property."[12]

What we can infer from different definitions is that international economic law embraces too many areas including the law of economic transactions, the law of economic institutions, the law of economic integration, the law of investment, the law relating to finance and currency, the law of intellectual property. It is even possible to extend the list to include the protection of human rights and the environment in the context of economic development.

According to Jackson, in general terms, the areas or subjects embraced by international economic law can be divided into two main categories: Transactional International Economic Law and Regulatory International Economic Law.[13]

The first category deals with transactions carried out in the context of international trade or other economic activities and mainly focuses on parties (particularly, private entrepreneurs) taking part in such activities.[14] Through mechanisms or regulations of Transactional International Economic Law, cross-border transactions between parties located in different nations are being facilitated. One of the best examples of such regulations is the Convention on International Contracts for the Sale of Goods.[15]

The second category deals with the role of government institutions (national, local, or international). There is no doubt that the international trade transaction leads all other private transactions in terms of the effect of government in regulating the activity in question (e.g. customs declaration).

---

[10] S. Zamora, "International Economic Law", (1996) 17 *University of Pennsylvania Journal of International Econonomic Law*, pp. 63–64, (footnotes omitted).

[11] G. Schwarzenberger, "The Principles and Standards of International Economic Law", (1966) 117 *Receuil Des Cours D'Académie de Droit International* I, 1, p. 17.

[12] D. F. Vagts, "International Economic Law and the American Journal of International Law", (2006) 100 *American Journal of International Law*, p. 769.

[13] Jackson, pp. 8–9.; J. H. Jackson, *Sovereignty, the WTO and Changing Fundamentals of International Law*, Cambridge: Cambridge University Press, 2006, p. 47. (hereinafter, Jackson, *Sovereignty, the WTO …*).

[14] Jackson, p. 9.

[15] Reitz, p. 30.

However, the international community needs to look at international economic law as "regulatory law", similar to national subjects like labour, tax, anti-trust or other regulatory topics in order to understand international economic law and its effect on governments and private citizens' lives.[16]

In addition to two general categorisation of international economic law, one other approach is to divide the concept into three different legal parts, namely, transactional law, international investment (enterprise) law and constitutional or institutional law.[17] In a similar fashion, the literature in international economic law usually examines the notion as limiting the areas of international economic law to international financial issues (International Finance Law), international trade (International Trade Law) and issues concerning foreign investment (International Investment Law). The legal justification for such division is the fact that the rules and principles of international economic law governing the relations between subjects of international law are taken into account.[18]

From the standpoint of international lawyers, I think, this should be the best way to understand the scope and nature of international economic law. At least, this is the method that an international lawyer should adopt and follow when he/she wants to conduct any research in the field at present.

### 1.2.2. *Historical Development of International Economic Law*

Although international economic law is not a new phenomenon the phrase or the name is relatively new. Despite the fact that international law has inevitably consisted of economic content, as witnessed in the practice of international law jurisprudence throughout the centuries devoted to various economic subjects including trade, investment, commerce and navigation the real and rapid development of the rules and principles governing international economic activities have taken place after World War II.[19] Based on these facts it would be convenient to examine the development of international economic law by dividing into four stages:

a) The Pre-1914 Period
b) The Inter-War Period
c) The Bretton Woods Era (World War II and the Post-Bretton Woods Conference)
d) The Post-Marrakesh Period (the Age of Globalisation).[20]

---

[16] Jackson, p. 9.
[17] Reitz, p. 29.
[18] Loibl, p. 690.
[19] J. H. Jackson, "International Economic Law: Complexity and Puzzles", (2007) 10/1 *Journal of International Economic Law*, p. 3. (hereinafter Jackson, "International Economic Law ...").
[20] Vagts, p. 770.

1.2.2.1. *The Pre-1914 Period*

When the attitude of the international community is examined it can be seen that before World War I international law almost did not pay any attention to economic activities. Throughout the 19th century, the policy of *laissez faire* was the basic principle followed by many States in their internal economies and so, there was little control of commercial and financial transactions in relation to foreigners. The control was provided through domestic law regulations which employed customs and import restrictions.[21] In other words, it was the period of international economic law that was governed by the principle of faith and free from government intervention. International payments used to be made by gold standard. Although there were differences from one State to another, tariffs were too low providing the possibility of free exports and imports. Workers were free to find jobs in different places without facing major barriers/impediments. The contemporary function of international law, which is to limit economic activities by way of State interferences with economic flows, was hardly existent before 1914.[22]

In accordance with our earlier limitation of the concept of international economic law to international trade law, international financial law and international investment law, the main features of this period can be summarised as follows:

Concerning international trade law in the pre-1914 period, we can surprisingly examine the fact that liberal international trade, which was known as a post-World War II phenomenon, was common as an international trade policy among States.[23] During the nineteenth century, States such as Britain, France and Germany negotiated and concluded bilateral international treaties particularly dealing with customs amongst themselves and with other European States.[24] The main regulations in those treaties were mainly relating to the application of the principle of most favoured nation treatment and lower duties on certain commodities.[25]

In the pre-1914 period, it would not be wrong to say that there was no international financial law and the States were setting the terms of their own currencies. It should be noted that the British pound become a benchmark for other countries' currencies.[26] The only surprising development was the creation of two international monetary unions or conclusions of standardizing

[21] T. Hillier, *Principles of Public International Law*, London, Sydney: Cavendish Publishing, 2nd edn. 1999, p. 305.

[22] Vagts, pp. 770–1.

[23] M. Trebilcock and M. Fishbein, "International Trade: Barriers to Trade", in A. T. Guzman and A. O. Sykes (eds.), *Research Handbook in International Economic Law*, Celtenham, UK. and Northampton, MA. USA: Edward Elgar, 2007, p. 5.

[24] Ibid. p. 6.

[25] Vagts, p. 771.

[26] Ibid. pp. 771–2.

agreements in Europe: The Latin Monetary Union established by France, Italy, Belgium, Switzerland, and Greece in 1865 and the Scandinavian Monetary Convention created by Denmark, Norway, and Sweden in 1873.[27]

The development of international investment law followed the same path as other branches of international economic law, that is to say, it followed the increase in trans-border economic activities among the States. The rules, which were basically customary rules of international law, were concerning the protection and treatment of aliens on foreign territory as part of the law of State responsibility.[28] Though the rules were including standards of treatment of aliens as regards their life, security and property in general,[29] in the field of international investment law, the main issue, in particular, was the expropriation of the property of foreigners throughout the pre-1914 period. A great deal of case law has well established the principle that a State could not expropriate or nationalise the property of foreigners without paying compensation.[30]

#### 1.2.2.2. *The Inter-War Period*

The inter-war period took the concept of international economic law to a very different stage. The international community witnessed the expanded role of governments in the governance of domestic economy that inevitably affected international economic relations, too.[31] The real impetus was the creation of the USSR (the Union of Soviet Socialist Republics) in 1917. A new economic system, which was based on the State ownership of the means of production, was introduced by the Soviet Union. Implementation of such a system required the expropriation of foreign owned properties[32] that was clearly affecting the international economic field.

One other significant result of World War I was the creation of the League of Nations which played some important roles concerning international trade law. First of all, the Covenant on the League of Nations tried to eliminate discrimination practices between nations. Secondly, the League itself conducted studies dealing with international trade law. The Agreement on the Abolition of Import and Export Prohibitions and Restrictions[33] and the International Convention Relating to Simplification of Customs Formalities[34] can be viewed

---

[27] Ibid. p. 772.

[28] S. W. Schill, *The Multilateralization of International Investment Law*, Cambridge: Cambridge University Press, 2009, p. 25.

[29] Schill, p. 25.

[30] Vagts, p. 773.

[31] Ibid. p. 774.

[32] Hillier, p. 305.

[33] Agreement on the Abolition of Import and Export Prohibitions and Restrictions, (8 November 1927), 46 Stat. 2461, 2 Bevans 651.

[34] International Convention Relating to Simplification of Customs Formalities, (3 November 1923), 30 *LNTS* 372.

as outcomes of such studies.[35] As it could be inferred from these two Conventions, the main feature of this period was the increase in trade barriers on both imports and exports. The negative effect of trade barriers on international trade law was tried to be eased by means of concluding bilateral agreements which reciprocally reduced barriers.[36] A major example to reciprocal tariff reductions, the establishment of the *Austro-German Customs Union* through an agreement between Germany and Austria could be seen as one of the possible solution to the problem of trade barriers during this period. The creation of the Austro-German Customs Union and its legality in international law were challenged before the Permanent Court of International Justice, which was the judicial organ of the League of Nations. According to Article 88 of the Treaty of Saint-Germain (1919), Austria was under the obligation of abstaining from any act that might directly or indirectly compromise its independence, unless it obtained the consent of the League of Nations. Since Austria did not get such consent, the League of Nations had to get an advisory opinion concerning the issue whether the Austro-German Customs Union violated the provisions of the peace treaty from the Permanent Court of International Justice. In its advisory opinion the Court found that the establishment of the Austro-German Customs Union was against the regulations of peace treaty, so the Union was unlawful.[37] However, the attempt of both States in creating such Customs Union should be evaluated as a significant step in the development of international trade law of today's world.

During the inter-war period, the situation concerning international financial law was not very promising. World War I caused some of the most important changes in the international financial law field. The significance of pound sterling dramatically decreased while the USA dollar was becoming a major player in the international money market. However, throughout the following years, the Great Depression of in 1929 destroyed the entire monetary system. So, the USA had to go off the gold standard, which was the decision that rocked confidence in the dollar. Foreign exchange controls and revaluations were the main issues to be solved by national courts. Revaluations had also affected the obligations of the States.[38] As a result, the Permanent Court of International Justice at the international level had to deal with these problems as was the case in the *Brazilian*[39] and *Serbian Loans* cases.[40]

---

[35] Vagts, p. 774.
[36] Ibid. p. 775.
[37] *Austro-German Customs Union Case,* Advisory Opinion, *PCIJ Reports,* Series A/B, No. 41, (1931).
[38] Vagts, p. 776.
[39] *Brazilian Loans Case, (France v. Brazil), PCIJ Reports,* Series A, No. 21, (1929). The case was relating to the interpretation of certain Brazilian Government loans, some of bonds of which were held by French nationals. The governing law was the Brazilian law. Thus, the Permanent Court of International Justice had to interpret municipal law in solving the dispute before it.
[40] *Serbian Loans Case, PCIJ Reports,* Series A, No. 20, (1929).

The response of the international community to the problems occurred in the international monetary field during this period can be examined in two ways both of which may be regarded as a precursor to the institutions set up after World War II. The first one is the conclusion of stabilizing agreements, according to which a State commits itself to support the currency of another State in times of crisis. The so-called sterling bloc connecting Great Britain, the Scandinavian countries, and some of the dominions is one of the best examples of such practice.[41] The second one is the establishment of the Bank for International Settlements whose seat was in Basel, Switzerland. The main reason for the creation of the Bank was to facilitate the fulfilment of the Young Plan for the payment of German reparations and the related indebtedness of other States.[42]

The inter-war period should be viewed as one of the worst times as long as international investment law is concerned. As indicated above, the Soviet Union introduced new economic policies in that period. One of the fundamental features of the new system was the attack on the very notion of private property, which directly affected foreign investors. The view taken by the Soviet Union was the denial of any owning to foreign investors. The same approach was also deployed by Mexico in a way of nationalising landholdings and oil properties.[43]

The major contribution of the inter-war period to international investment law can be examined in the creation of conditions concerning the expropriation of foreign property. Actually, this was one of the main issues to be resolved by the Permanent Court of Justice in the *Chorzow Factory Case*,[44] which was considered as representing the practice of the international community in cases of expropriation of foreign investment and according to which, it is necessary to pay a prompt, adequate, and effective compensation in the case of expropriation.[45]

#### 1.2.2.3. *The Bretton Woods Era (World War II and the Post-Bretton Woods Conference)*

The real development of international economic law took place after the end of the Second World War. In light of the problems faced before World War II, the international economic order had to be arranged in a way that would regulate international trade, international finance, and international investment on a multilateral level. The present international economic order was created in the Bretton Woods Conference in 1944. One of the major purposes of the

[41] Vagts, p. 776.
[42] Ibid. p. 777.
[43] Ibid.
[44] *Chorzow Factory Case (Merits), (Germany v. Poland), PCIJ Reports,* Series A, No. 17, (1928).
[45] Ibid. p. 48.

Conference was to prevent the international community from the monetary disorders of the inter-war period and to facilitate international trade.[46] To do so, two international organisations were created: the International Monetary Fund (IMF) and the International Bank for Reconstruction and Development (IBRD, usually known as the World Bank). The General Agreement on Tariffs and Trade (GATT)[47] was also signed after a few years.

From the point of view of international trade law, the conclusion of GATT has a special place since it eventually led to the creation of another important international institution, the World Trade Organisation, in 1995. The GATT basically introduced two fundamental principles: The first one was the agreement on not increasing tariffs that the parties to the GATT had negotiated and bound.[48] The second one was the agreement to give the benefit of such bindings to all other contracting parties, the principle of most-favoured-nation. In addition to these principles, it should also be noted that the GATT system outlawed quotas and discrimination against imported goods and introduced limitations to subsidies.[49]

The weakest point of the GATT system was that it was not able to create an international organisation. Actually, the creation of an International Trade Organisation was on the agenda in 1947 and for this reason, the Havana Charter of 1947 was adopted by 53 States establishing the Organisation. However, the Charter could not enter into force.[50] To witness the presence of such an international institution, the international community had to wait until the establishment of the WTO in 1995, which remedied the main gap in the GATT system.

In the field of international finance law, the main developments were the establishment of the IMF and the World Bank in the Bretton Woods Conference. While the IMF played a regulatory role in solving currency crisis of the members of the international community the World Bank undertook a banking role in providing loans that would be used for major developmental projects.[51]

Throughout this period, particularly during the 1950s and 1960s, a great number of newly independent States took their places in the international

---

[46] Jackson, "International Economic Law …", p. 3.; Loibl, p. 690.

[47] The General Agreement on Tariffs and Trade was opened for signature on 30 October 1947, and entered into force on 1 January 1948. The GATT lasted until 1994, when it was replaced by the International Trade Organisation in 1995. The original GATT text, subject to the modifications of GATT 1994 is still in effect under the WTO law. Full text available online at: http://www.wto.org/english/docs_e/legal_e/06-gatt_e.htm. For the detailed explanation concerning the evolution of the GATT and GATT law, *see* A. F. Lowenfeld, *International Economic Law*, Oxford and New York: Oxford University Press, 2002, pp. 45–67.

[48] Lowenfeld, p. 29.; Vagts, p. 779.

[49] Lowenfeld, pp. 28–9.; Vagts, p. 779.

[50] Hillier, p. 306.

[51] Vagts, p. 779.

arena. They became members to the United Nations and started to reshape the international economic legal order. The reflections of such development on international investment law can be summarised as follows:

A number of newly independent and developing States strongly opposed to the rules on expropriation. They claimed that foreign companies had the control of important local industries and therefore adopted policies concerning expropriation. As a result, the first UN Conference on Trade and Development (UNCTAD) was held with the participation of majority of States in 1964. The Resolutions adopted by the Conference provided guiding principles governing the law in relation to economic development. The establishment of UNCTAD as one of its permanent institutions by the UN General Assembly followed this movement.[52] The General Assembly Resolution on Permanent Sovereignty over Natural Resources of 1962[53] and the Charter of Economic Rights and Duties of States of 1974[54] proclaimed the sovereignty of States over their natural resources and their right to nationalise them when needed.

The way of handling international investment during the mentioned period was the conclusion of bilateral investment treaties, which were providing guarantees for the investors of capital-exporting States abroad and threatening retaliation against expropriators.[55] Custom as a source of international investment law had little significance on the ground that States have entered into bilateral treaties in order to fulfil gaps or limitations in the protection provided by the customary rules of international law in the field of the treatment of aliens leading to the concepts of State responsibility and of diplomatic protection.[56] Since 1945, the attempts to conclude multilateral investment treaties governing relations between foreign investors and the host State repeatedly failed. The reasons for such a situation was the creation of newly independent States strongly opposing to foreign investors and the ideological difference between the West and the East over the governance of economic activities during the Cold War era.[57] As examples of the failed attempts, the Havana Charter in 1948 and the OECD Draft Convention on the Protection of Foreign Property of 1967 may be indicated here.[58] Only two of the multilateral investment treaties, the Convention on the Settlement of Investment Disputes between States and Nationals of Other States of 1965 (the ICSID Convention,

[52] Hillier, p. 306.

[53] UNGA Res. 1803 (XVII) (1962).

[54] UNGA Res. 3281 (XXIX) (1974).

[55] A. B. Zampetti and P. Sauve, "International Investment", in A. T. Guzman and A. O. Sykes (eds.), *Research Handbook in International Economic Law*, Celtenham, UK and Northampton, MA, USA: Edward Elgar, 2007, pp. 215, 217, 225.; Vagts, 780.

[56] C. Mclachlan QC, L. Shore and M. Weiniger, *International Investment Arbitration Substantive Principles*, Oxford: Oxford University Press, 2008, p. 17.

[57] Schill, pp. 23, 61–2.

[58] For detailed information, *see* Schill, pp. 31–40.

entered into force on 14 October 1966)[59] and the Convention Establishing the Multilateral Investment Guarantee Agency of 1985 (the MIGA Convention, entered into force on 12 April 1988)[60] were successful and enjoyed broad support by both developed and developing countries.[61]

1.2.2.4. *The Post-Marrakesh Period (The Age of Globalisation)*
One of the most important turning points in the development of international economic law is the adoption of World Trade Organisation Agreements at Marrakesh in 1994. Undoubtedly, the agreements were the starting point of the age of globalisation in international economic law.[62] As one of the results of the Agreements, the WTO was created as an international institution and it became operational on 1 January 1995. The establishment of the WTO fulfilled one of the deficiencies in international economic legal order since it had the power to deliver binding adjudications in the field.

The WTO was built on four main pillars:

a. GATT 1994, which supplemented GATT 1947 by a number of understandings of interpretation and decisions;
b. the General Agreement on Trade in Services (GATS, which provides for a liberalization of trade in services);
c. the Agreement on Trade-Related Aspects of Intellectual Property Rights (TRIPS, which provides for the application of the principle of national treatment and the most-favoured-nation treatment and sets standards concerning the availability, scope, and use of intellectual property rights);
d. the Dispute Settlement Understanding (DSU, which was built on the experience of GATT 1947 and strengthened the rule of law in international trade law by providing binding adjudications).[63]

It should be noted here that the multilateral agreements such as GATS and TRIPS have also addressed international investment law problems in search of creating a favourable investment environment.

Though the establishment of the WTO and its practice, in particular the practice of the dispute settlement mechanisms,[64] are major achievements of

[59] The Convention on the Settlement of Investment Disputes between States and Nationals of Other States, 575 *UNTS* 159.

[60] The Convention Establishing the Multilateral Investment Guarantee Agency, 1508 *UNTS* 99.

[61] Schill, pp.44–9.

[62] Vagts, p. 781.

[63] Loibl, pp. 700–1.

[64] For detailed examination *see infra* Chapter 3 entitled Dispute Settlement in International Trade Law. For an evaluation of the literature on the dispute settlement mechanisms of the GATT and the WTO during the last decade, *see* H. Horn and P. C. Mavroidis, "International Trade: Dispute Settlement", in A. T. Guzman and A. O. Sykes (eds.) *Research*

the international community there are several pending issues that have yet to be resolved. Some of these issues can be indicated as: those relating to the sovereignty of nation States, trade regulation and other non-protectionists and legitimate policy goals, the protection of human rights and of environment, and the relationship of WTO agreements to other international agreements.[65]

Concerning the international finance law, at the age of globalisation, the international community has seen one of the worst financial crises in Autumn 2008. Although there have been many crisis either in national or regional levels, the financial institutions the World Bank and the IMF were sufficient to overcome crisis. Unfortunately, those institutions failed to forecast and to prevent the 2008 crisis of the developed countries that led the global economy into recession.[66] To prevent the reoccurrence of such a situation, governments have to take necessary measures. The 2008 crisis made clear that the Bretton Woods Institutions were not, on their own, sufficient to meet the challenges of international economic law during the 21st century.[67] Therefore, the group of 20 leading economies meeting in November 2008 "pledged to improve transparency, enhancing sound regulation and integrity of markets, reinforcing international cooperation and reforming international financial institutions in the coming months and years."[68]

In the field of international investment law, because of the success of the ICSID and MIGA Conventions as well as the proliferation of bilateral treaties after the end of the Cold War, developed countries are encouraged to continue to make attempts to conclude multilateral investment treaties governing the treatment of foreign investors by host States.[69] These efforts could be examined within different negotiation rounds of the GATT/WTO and in the OECD.[70] Moreover, the latest efforts to launch negotiations of multilateral investment rules within the WTO in the new millennium did not produce any concrete results.[71] However, in contrast to the failure of the conclusion of

---

*Handbook in International Economic Law*, Cheltenham, UK and Northampton, MA, USA: Edward Elgar, 2007, pp. 177–210.

65 T. Cottier, "Challenges ahead in International Economic Law", (2009) 12/1 *Journal of International Economic Law*, p. 4.

66 Ibid. p. 7.

67 For a work suggesting solutions by way of applying justice criteria to the IMF and the World Banks, *see* F. J. Garcia, "Global Justice and the Bretton Woods Institutions", in W. J. Davey and J. Jackson (eds.), *The Future of International Economic Law*, Oxford: Oxford University Press, 2008, pp. 23–43.; Also *see* H. R. Torres, "Reforming the International Monetary Fund – Why Its Legitimacy is at Stake?", in W. J. Davey and J. Jackson (eds.), *The Future of International Economic Law*, Oxford: Oxford University Press, 2008, pp. 5–22.

68 Cottier, p. 7.; For the detailed examination of reforming international financial institutions, *see infra* Chapter 2 entitled New Challenges and Issues in International Finance Law.

69 Schill, p. 49.

70 Ibid. pp. 49–50. For the detailed explanation of the process, *see* pp. 50–8.

71 Zampetti and Sauve, pp. 248–9.; Schill, p. 50. For the detailed explanation of the process, *see* pp. 58–60.

multilateral investment treaties, the number of bilateral investment treaties has reached to more than 2.500, and additionally, some other international treaties concerning international trade and economic cooperation provided substantive rules on the protection of foreign investment.[72] Actually, when those bilateral investment treaties are closely examined it can be seen that the substantive content of bilateral investment treaties are not much different from the content of the proposed conventions texts at the multilateral level.[73] On this ground, it would not be wrong to conclude that "international investment law only formally developed on the basis of bilateral treaties while in substance these treaties remained multilateral in creating uniform rules for the protection of foreign investment on the basis of general principles".[74]

### 1.3. *International Economic Law—Its Relationship with Other Branches of Law*

The latest financial crisis may also be regarded as the crisis of social sciences, in particular, of law, economics, and international relations theory. It shows the failures of strictly disciplinary tradition of fragmentation and specialisation, and the lack of truly interdisciplinary research and study.[75] At this point, once more the significance of international economic law and its role in improving the global economic system should be noted since one of the main features of international economic law is to be an interdisciplinary field. In this context, some other areas of law that have interdependence with international economic law and their connections could be briefly explained.

#### 1.3.1. *Public International Law—International Economic Law*

International economic law has features of different branches of social sciences in general and of law in particular. Amongst, public international law deserves to be number one in the sequence since almost 90 per cent of international law covers more or less international economic law features.[76] In a sense, public international law is an economic law. For example, the law of the sea, the law of permanent sovereignty of natural resources, environmental law, and the reason of war are all linked to economic interests and they are inseparable from economic law.[77] Certainly, some subjects of international law may not have any relation to international economic law, such as the use of force,

---

[72] Schill, p. 61.
[73] Ibid.
[74] Ibid. p. 63.
[75] Cottier, p. 12.
[76] Jackson, p. 8.
[77] Cottier, p. 13.

humanitarian intervention, etc. However, some fields of international law such as the law of treaties[78] are the branches of international law upon which the international economic law was built. Treaties and other agreements concluded between States /or international organisations establishing international institutions and their activities like the GATT/WTO, IMF and the World Bank are just examples confirming this point.[79]

The mentioned fact became clearer in the field of international trade law since the conclusion of the Uruguay Round and the entry into force of the WTO Agreements in 1995. The unprecedented practice and the case law of the panels and the Appellate Body of the WTO moved the notion of international economic law into centre stage in public international law.[80] Furthermore, it is possible to find the approach that the WTO law is a part of public international law and there is no way around it on the ground that it is based on the law of treaties, which is central to the interpretation of WTO rights and obligations.[81]

Additionally, the relationship of international economic law with other branches of international law, particularly human rights and environmental law has broadened perspectives and helped bring trade regulation fully into the realm of public international law.[82]

In conclusion, it would be true to say that as one of the facts and impacts of globalisation, international economic law has become one of the most important sub-subjects of international law, like many other subjects.[83]

### 1.3.2. *Private International Law—International Economic Law*

Traditionally, private international law means that it is a branch of law dealing with "the range of legal issues deriving from the fact that private relations cross jurisdictional boundaries, and different jurisdictions implicate different legal systems".[84] The conflict of laws, in particular, falls within the realm of private international law. The fundamental problem that the conflict of laws should solve is which State will have the legal power or which State's law will be applied to the specific situation in question. As it can be figured out, in fact,

---

78 Jackson, p. 8.

79 K. W. Abbott, "International Economic Law: Implications for Scholarship", (1996) 17 *University Pennsylvania Journal of International Economic Law*, p. 507.

80 Cottier, p. 3.

81 E. Voyiakis, "Of Foxes and Hedgehogs: Some Thoughts About the Relationship Between WTO Law and General International Law", in C. P. Bicker, I. D. Bunn, D. W. Arner (eds.), *International Economic Law: The State and Future of the Discipline*, Oxford and Portland, Oregon: Hart Publishing, 2008, p. 107.

82 Cottier, p. 3.

83 Jackson, Sovereignty, *the WTO* ... pp. 46–7.

84 J. P. Trachtman, "The International Economic Law Revolution", (1996) 17 *University Pennsylvania Journal of International Economic Law*, p. 40.

private international law is within the realm of public international law since the State authority or power is the fundamental issue.[85]

Though the difference between private and public international law is not very much important in the field of international law, it is still necessary to look at what makes the law private or public: while public international law takes into account persons from the perspective of being a subject and object of the law, and of the direct effect of law on individuals, private international law governs the relationship of private persons/individuals with regard to property, contracts, civil wrongs or any other issues in which individuals involved in directly to one another.[86] Private international law is also different from other international law fields. This is because, it is enforced by domestic courts backed by the full power of the State. In this sense, it enjoys a domestic law status, too.[87]

### 1.3.3. *International Business Law—International Economic Law*

As far as international economic law as an interdisciplinary field of international law is concerned, economics, business, and law are interrelated. In general terms, while economics is usually dealt with the allocation of resources through markets with the government acting as optimising for the aggregate of society rather than for the individual or firm, business is concerned with sales, marketing, accounting, and human relations, topics conventionally not covered by economics and focused on the individual or firm.[88]

The similar relationship by way of indicating the difference between transactions and trade can be witnessed between international business law and international economic law. In this context, it should be noted that transactions take place between private persons or public persons acting more or less as private persons on the one hand, and trade is an issue of public policy and mercantilism or protectionism on the other. Thus, the conclusion that the activity at the individual or firm level is transactional while the activity at the State or higher level is economic should not be wrong.[89]

Sales of goods, licensing of intellectual property, and foreign direct investment fall within the meaning of international business transactions, but the tariffs and nontariff barriers affecting these transactions do not.[90] However, from the perspective of international economic law both in theory and practice these issues are inseparable for the following reasons: "Sales cannot be made without considering tariff and nontariff barriers to export transactions

[85] Ibid. p. 40.
[86] Ibid. pp. 41–2.
[87] Ibid. pp. 42–3.
[88] Ibid. pp. 37–8.
[89] Ibid. p. 38.
[90] Ibid. p. 39.

and their international legality. Intellectual property cannot be licensed without considering local laws protecting intellectual property, which have been recognised in the Uruguay Round to be importantly related to trade, and which are disciplined under the Agreement on Trade-Related Aspects of Intellectual Property Rights, Including Trade in Counterfeit Good ("TRIPS"). Foreign investment decisions cannot be made separately from issues of tariffs, antidumping duties, and rules of origin, and from issues of protection against mistreatment that may be possible, for example, under bilateral investment treaties".[91]

### 1.3.4. *European Union Law—International Economic Law*

The legal base for the creation of the European Union is the Treaty of Rome establishing the European Economic Community (EEC) concluded by the six original Member States, namely, Germany, the Netherlands, Belgium, France, Italy, and Luxembourg in 1957. The EU consisting of 27 Member States is a regional international organisation and has international personality. The EU has also created its own legal system which is substantially different from the traditional understanding of international law. In a sense, the EU should be seen as "a new order of international law" on the ground that the concepts of sovereignty and the State, international economic order, and the relations between different legal orders are quite different from the traditional assumptions of international law.[92] For example, most of EU legal rules or instruments do have both direct and indirect effect at the national level without any further national implementation such as being subject to the ratification or acceptance of the Government or Parliament. In this sense, the practice of the judicial institution of the EU, the European Court of Justice (ECJ), is impressive in terms of creating the EU legal system. Only two doctrines, the doctrines of direct effect[93] and the supremacy of EU law[94] over domestic law are sufficient to prove this point.[95] Today, no one can question the vital role of the ECJ in implementing and also creating a regime specific law in Europe.[96]

So long as the economic integration part of the EU is concerned, it would not be wrong to conclude that the region of EU is the place where

[91] Ibid.

[92] F. G. Jacobs, "The State of International Economic Law: Re-Thinking Sovereignty in Europe", (2008) *Journal of International Economic Law*, p. 40.

[93] *Van Gend en Loos v. Nederlandse Administratie der Belastingen*, Case 26/62, (1963), *ECR*, p. 1.

[94] *Costa v. ENEL*, Case 6/64, (1964) *ECR*, p. 585.

[95] For the detailed information of the supremacy of the EU law and the direct effect doctrine, *see* J. Steiner, L. Woods and C. Twigg-Flesner, *EU Law*, Oxford: Oxford University Press, 9th edn., 2006, pp. 69–144.

[96] J. E. Alvarez, *International Organizations as Law-makers*, Oxford: Oxford University Press, 2005, pp. 465–6.

international economic law has been successfully implemented. One other impressive regional practice, the NAFTA, should also be indicated here. In addition to the successful implementations of international economic law at the regional levels, the WTO as a universal organisation, which, in a sense, is the equivalent of the United Nations for the world trading system, became operational in 1995. When the practice of the EU on the one hand and the WTO on the other are examined, we can witness different interpretations and applications at the regional and international level. That is why international economic law has to create mechanisms through which regional and international systems can operate side by side.[97]

### 1.3.5. *International Environmental Law—International Economic Law*

International environmental law is one of the more recent fields of public international law and provides a precautionary approach to environmental issues of global scale like the biodiversity conservation and the climate change. The concept of international environmental law has not become an independent branch of law or discipline. In a sense, it is similar to other fields such as the law of the sea, human rights and international economic law. But, it is less-developed than those areas of law: For example, while the universal or global institutions like the International Tribunal for the Law of the Sea in the Law of the Sea Convention and the World Trade Organisation and Dispute Settlement Body of the WTO in the WTO Agreements are available there is no such global environmental organisation having jurisdiction over environmental matters at the international level.[98] In this regard, it should be noted that the creation of an International Court for the Environment was proposed.[99]

Having indicated the general feature of international environmental law, from the perspective of this study, it is necessary to look at the relationship between international environmental law and international economic law.[100] As will be examined in detail below, one of the most important branches of international economic law is international trade law. That is exactly the place in where international trade and protection of environment seems to be

---

[97] For a detailed paper on the legal relationship between the NAFTA and the WTO, *see* F. M. Abbott, "The North American Integration Regime and Its Implications for the World Trading System", in J.H.H. Weiler (ed.), *The EU, The WTO and the NAFTA Towards a Common Law of International Trade*, Oxford: Oxford University Press, 2005, pp. 169–99.: For the practice of the European Court of Justice and the WTO, *see* J. H. J. Bourgeois, "The European Court of Justice and the WTO: Problems and Challenges", in J.H.H. Weiler (ed.), *The EU, The WTO and the NAFTA Towards a Common Law of International Trade*, Oxford: Oxford University Press, 2005, pp. 71–123.

[98] C. Redgwell, "International Environmental Law, in M. D. Evans (ed.), *International Law*, Oxford: Oxford University Press, 2003, pp. 657–8.

[99] Alvarez, p. 404.

[100] For a detailed explanation on the evolution of environment and international economic law, *see* Lowenfeld, pp. 297–339.

conflicting[101] because of the demands of international trade and the protection of environment is often contradictory in real life situations. This is because international trade or trade in general is concerned with economic growth that may result in the depletion or degradation of natural resources. In a sense, more trade means more harm to the environment.[102]

However, from the point of view of international economic law and international trade in particular, such an understanding may not be supported since the future of environment, humanity and the planet is in question. In today's world there is no other option but to regard international trade and protection of the environment as complementary values.[103] Economic growth and environmental protection are not mutually exclusive, but mutually supportive. That is why an environment policy cannot be created without taking into account of the effects of economic activity, the feasibility of economic approaches to regulation, and the implications of the policy for economic development or *vice versa*.[104]

The institutions acting in the field of international economic law should interpret and apply the rules of international law in a way of establishing a balance between the free international trade and the protection of environment. Although, the first practice of the GATT panel in the *Tuna Dolphin Case* completely ignored the environmental values,[105] later in the *Shrimp/Turtle Case* and the *EC-Asbestos Case*[106], the Appellate Body of the WTO adopted a more balanced approach to trade and environment.[107] Such an approach was adopted by the European Court of Justice as early as 1985, though this was not stipulated at all by the founding treaty of the European Community. When the European Court faced with the environmental issue in the *ADBHU Case*[108], it followed an interventionist approach by stating that the protection of environment was one of the Community's essential goals.[109]

---

[101] F. G. Jacobs, "The State of International Economic Law: Re-Thinking Sovereignty in Europe", (2008) *Journal of International Economic Law*, p. 30.

[102] For a detailed study indicating the contradiction between the WTO and the protection of environment, *see* L. Wallach and M. Sforza, *The WTO: Five Years of Reasons to Resist Corporate Globalization*, New York: Seven Stories Press, 1999.

[103] Jacobs, p. 29.

[104] K. W. Abbott, "International Economic Law: Implications for Scholarship", (1996) 17 *University of Pennsylvania Journal of International Economic Law*, p. 509.

[105] J. P. Trachtman, "The International Economic Law Revolution", (1996) 17 *University of Pennsylvania Journal of International Economic Law*, pp. 54–5.

[106] *EC-Asbestos*, (Appellate Body Report, *European Communities-Measures Affecting Asbestos and Asbestos-Containing Products*, WT/DS135/AB/R, adopted 5 April 2001).

[107] M. Matsushita, T. J. Schoenbaum and P. C. Mavroidis, *The World Trade Organization: Law, Practice, and Policy*, Oxford: Oxford University Press, 2006, pp. 799–803.; Alvarez, pp. 469–72.

[108] *ADBHU Case*, (Procureur de la République v ADBHU, Case 240/83 ADBHU (1985) *ECR* 531).

[109] F. G. Jacobs, "The State of International Economic Law: Re-Thinking Sovereignty in Europe", (2008) *Journal of International Economic Law*, pp.30–2.

### 1.3.6. *International Human Rights Law—International Economic Law*

International human rights law, as similar to international environment law and international economic law, is a recent branch of public international law and governs the relations between States and individuals who are seeking protection of their rights, particularly, against States.

The relationship between international human rights law and international economic law has been one of the key subjects of general international law since at least the end of the Cold War. Although human rights concept can be examined from the different aspects of international economic law such as the link between human rights and international investment law and/or international finance law, the prominent interface is witnessed between international human rights law and international trade law:

Certainly, the development of international human rights law has affected the evolution of international trade law as well. Human rights are considered providing a legitimate tool used for determining among the competing trade policy choices, according to which States or governments do not implement certain trade policies constituting violations of their human rights obligations.[110] The human rights movements by way of focusing on some certain issues like the impact of trade policy on levels of poverty, access to food, on the livelihoods of the rural poor, on the rights of women and other vulnerable groups and on the health of children has provided new substantive knowledge or new normative insights into what contemporary trade policy ought to be.[111] The policy-makers and international institutions have no other choice but to take human rights regime into consideration while engaging in global economic activities.[112]

### 1.3.7. *National Law—International Economic Law*

There are two important theories explaining the relationship between national law and international law: Monism and Dualism.

The monist theory considers that "international law and national law are simply two components of a single body of knowledge called 'law'. 'Law' is

[110] A. T.F. Lang, "Re-Righting International Trade: Some Critical Thoughts on the Contemporary Trade and Human Rights Literature", in W. Shan, P. Simons and D. Singh (eds.), *Redefining Sovereignty in International Economic Law*, Oxford and Portland, Oregon: Hart Publishing, 2008, p. 394.

[111] Ibid. p. 396.

[112] For an example analysing the right to adequate food and the WTO regime, *see* P. Simons, "Binding the Hand that Feeds Them: The Agreement on Agriculture, Transnational Corporations and the Right to Adequate Food in Developing Countries", in W. Shan, P. Simons and D. Singh (eds.), *Redefining Sovereignty in International Economic Law*, Oxford and Portland, Oregon: Hart Publishing, 2008, p. 399.

seen as a single entity of which the 'national' and 'international' versions are merely particular manifestations."[113]

The dualist theory does not accept the fact that "international and national law operate in the same sphere, although it does accept that they deal with the same subject matter."[114]

However, neither the monist nor the dualist approach is sufficient to explain the relationship between national and international law on the ground that the relations among the subjects of international law have become more interdependent and that the rapidly increasing number of inter-State activities has been the daily routines of the international community. The main feature of the contemporary State practice concerning the relationship between national and international law is to combine the monist and dualist views.[115] As far as international economic law is taken into consideration, the same criticism is also true. Some of the reasons may be indicated as follows:

Firstly, as mentioned above, international economic law is based on treaties. In a sense, it is a treaty law. One of the most important features of treaty law is that treaties can only bind the parties to them. In other words, treaties cannot bind third parties without their consent.[116] Once a State becomes a party to a treaty, the State will be under obligation to follow the provisions of that treaty. States cannot be excused on the grounds that treaty law conflicts with national law or domestic law is somehow deficient.[117] In accordance with this fact, States or international organisations that are party to treaties are under obligation to make their domestic regulations in conformity with the provisions of the treaty. However, the problem is whether and when they comply with those treaties in practice.[118]

Second, the States certainly have the power to determine whether international law will have direct effect on national law. There are some States who accepted the monist approach according to which there may not be any further implementation legislation for international treaties to be interpreted and

---

113 Dixon, p. 88.

114 Ibid. p. 89.

115 Matsushita, Schoenbaum and Mavroidis, p. 90.

116 Article 34 of the Vienna Convention on the Law of Treaties of 1969 provides: "A treaty does not create either obligations or rights for a third State without its consent." There are exceptions to such a rule: treaties establishing objectives regimes such as the Antarctic Treaty of 1959 and the provisions of a treaty which are regarded as customary rules of international law bind third parties regardless of being a party to treaty.

117 Matsushita, Schoenbaum and Mavroidis, p. 90. Article 27 of the Vienna Convention on the Law of Treaties of 1969 provides: "A party may not invoke the provisions of its internal law as justification for its failure to perform a treaty."

118 Concerning the implementation of investment treaties by States, *see* M. Hirsch, "Compliance with Investment Treaties: When are States More Likely to Breach or Comply with Investment Treaties?", in C. Binder, U. Kriebaum, A. Reinisch, S. Wittich (eds.), *International Investment Law For the 21st Century Essays in Honour of Christoph Schreuer*, Oxford: Oxford University Press, 2009, pp. 865–76.

applied at the domestic level. However, when the interests of the State constitutionally accepting the monist view are in question it is common to witness the domestic courts favouring the implementation of the dualist approach.[119] The practice of the European Court of Justice, as one other example of such an implementation at the regional level, may be noted: while the Court has developed the doctrine of direct effect[120] for some certain international agreements concluded by the European Union it has not extended the application of the doctrine to the WTO agreements which are legally binding upon both the European Union and its member States.[121] The European Court of Justice in the *Portuguese Textiles Case (Portugal v. Council)* clearly indicated this point as follows: "...'by its nature, the Agreement establishing the World Trade Organization, including the Annexes thereto, is not susceptible to being directly invoked in Community or Member State courts.'"[122]

In conclusion, both the States and international organisations adopt different legal approaches in different issues. Based on the fact that the interests of the subjects of international law prevail all other factors it would not be, at least for the near future, possible to deploy a uniform model in implementing the rules of international economic law.

### 1.4. *The Significance of International Economic Law*

At the age of globalisation, the boundaries between sovereign States have lost their significance and the subjects of international law have been engaging in economic activities at unprecedented levels. The traditional understanding of international law, in a way that having international rules in different fields and applying them independent from one to another is not sufficient to meet the needs of the international society any more.

As it can be understood from the explanation indicating the relationship of international economic law to other branches of law, different fields of law and different subjects of international law are highly interdependent and there is

---

[119] For the Japanese practice relating to the WTO law, *see* Matsushita, Schoenbaum and Mavroidis, pp. 99–102.

[120] For the direct effect doctrine, *see* J. Steiner, L. Woods and C. Twigg-Flesner, *EU Law*, Oxford: Oxford University Press, 9th edn., 2006, pp. 89–114.

[121] For the practice of the European Court of Justice, *see* P. Graig and G. de Burca, *EU Law Text, Cases, and Materials*, Oxford: Oxford University Press, 4th edn., 2008, pp. 206–13.; J. H. J. Bourgeois, "The European Court of Justice and the WTO: Problems and Challenges", in J.H.H. Weiler (ed.), *The EU, The WTO and the NAFTA, Towards a Common Law of International Trade*, Oxford: Oxford University Press, 2005, pp. 71–123.; Matsushita, Schoenbaum and Mavroidis, pp. 95–9.

[122] *Portuguese Textiles Case, (Portugal v. Council)*, Case C-149/96, (1999) *ECR*-I8395. The text of the decision is also available:http://eur-lex.europa.eu/LexUriServ/LexUriServ.do?uri=CELEX:61996J0149:EN:HTML.

no way to find a proper solution to a problem without taking all the related fields and factors into account at the same time. For example, the protection of marine life or natural resources and the depletion of resources of high seas/ oceans cannot be saved by only adopting the Law of the Sea Convention and establishing the Deep Sea Bed Authority. The WTO related subsidies to the fishing industry should be considered, too. Similarly, the health issues that the international society facing with and dealt with by the World Health Organisation (WHO) cannot be understood without taking into account the WTO law, particularly intellectual property rights and the World Intellectual Property Organisation (WIPO).[123] International trade and economic growth cannot be thought without considering the protection of environment, in particular the natural resources. Moreover, the latest financial crisis proved that mainstream economic models in financial and monetary affairs are not capable of providing adequate solutions to the today's complicated problems. The practice of leaving matters to unregulated markets has to be reconsidered. To avoid similar crisis, it is necessary to develop a more comprehensive and broader global economic system, which should be regulated by law.[124]

To do so, each situation/issue should be evaluated in an interdisciplinary manner. At this point, due to being an interdisciplinary field, the role of international economic law becomes more visible. Through which for a specific case at least, from the perspectives of economics, international law, trade law, investment law and finance law will be evaluated at the same time. Such a view would hopefully help the international community not to witness any other major financial crisis.

To conclude that international economic law and its mechanisms will play a vital role in providing solutions to the complicated problems of international community at the globalisation age would not be wrong.

### 1.5. *The Sources of International Economic Law*

Though the term "source" was not used in Article 38 of the Statute of the International Court of Justice (ICJ), it is the tradition in international law to start with Article 38 when the sources of international law are to be indicated. Article 38 states:

1. The Court, whose function is to decide in accordance with international law such disputes as are submitted to it, shall apply:
   a. international conventions, whether general or particular, establishing rules expressly recognised by the contesting States;

[123] Cottier, p. 13.
[124] Ibid. p. 12.

b. international custom, as evidence of a general practice accepted as law;
c. the general principles of law recognised by civilised nations;
d. subject to the provisions of Article 59, judicial decisions and the teachings of the most highly qualified publicists of the various nations, as subsidiary means for the determination of rules of law.

2. This provision shall not prejudice the power of the Court to decide a case *ex aequo et bono,* if the parties agree thereto.

The aim of Article 38 of the ICJ Statute is not to list the sources of international law. It purports to provide a guideline to the Court empowering it to take into account different materials when settling disputes brought before it.[125] The practice of the ICJ apparently shows that the members of the Court did not feel themselves to literally follow the wordings of the Statute; they went beyond the literal meaning of the Statute and applied other international materials (to be possibly regarded as sources of law) in providing a solution to the disputes such as the resolutions of the UN General Assembly and the unilateral declarations of States (e.g. Ihlen Declaration in *the Legal Status of Eastern Greenland Case*[126] and the French Declaration in the *Nuclear Test Cases*[127]).[128] The view taken by the ICJ should be considered as in compliance with the needs and development of international law. The fact that the Statute of the ICJ was drafted as similar to the Statute of the Permanent Court of International Justice (PCIJ) created in 1920 should also be noted as providing another evidence proving the correctness of the ICJ practice on the ground that the international legal system governing the relations among the subjects of international law and the activities of the members of the international community have become more complicated and interdependent than ever. Thus, it would not be right to say that all sources of international law are explicitly indicated in Article 38 of the ICJ Statute.

Actually, there is no consensus among international lawyers as to what constitutes a source of law and how these sources should be classified.[129] The same criticism goes for the sources of international economic law as well. In understanding the sources of international economic law, the best way is to follow the traditional method used to explain the sources of international law. In other words, it is necessary to look at international conventions (treaties), international custom, general principles of law, judicial decisions and the doctrine in accordance with the provisions of Article 38 of the ICJ Statute, *but* from the point of view of international economic law.

---

[125] Dixon, p. 23.

[126] *Legal Status of Eastern Greenland Case, (Denmark v. Norway),* (1933) *PCIJ Reports*, Series A/B, No. 53.

[127] *Nuclear Test Cases, (Australia v. France; New Zealand v. France*), (1974) *ICJ Reports* 253.

[128] Matsushita, Schoenbaum and Mavroidis, p. 21.

[129] Ibid. p. 21.

1.5.1. *International Conventions (Treaties)*

Certainly, international conventions/treaties are the most important sources of international law. Their significance has particularly increased after World War II. The main reason for such a case lies on the fact that a number of newly independent States did not want to accept the customary rules of international law since they did not play any role in State practice, which is one of the main requirements in creating a customary rule of international law. In addition to their general importance in international law, treaties have become even vital when they govern economic relations between different subjects of international law. This is because, international economic law is obviously different from other areas of international law in particular, from the perspective of customary rules they may play a far more limited role in this field.[130]

In general, treaties concerning international economic law can be divided into three categories: The first one concern the treaties establishing regional or universal bodies with powers relating to the international economy like the Treaty of Rome of 1957 creating the European Economic Community (today's EU) and the WTO Agreement of 1994 establishing the WTO. The second one concerns the multilateral treaties such as the Bretton Woods Agreements and different international commodity agreements. The third one concerns the bilateral treaties which include the bulk of the rules governing international economic relations. Treaties dealing with export and import trade, foreign investment and banking between the States may be indicated as examples of this category.[131] Bilateral treaties are particularly important for the development of international investment law on the ground that the international community failed to conclude a multilateral international investment treaty establishing general rules or principles in governing the relationship between foreign investors and the host States.[132]

So long as the interpretation and application of the sources of international economic law by international judicial institutions in the field is in question, it should be kept in mind that they firstly apply the sources of law which may be called as "the regime-specific sources of law".[133] This is the exact place where treaties comes first when compared to the rest of the sources of international law in terms of application by the dispute settlement mechanisms. For instance, the WTO Agreement in international trade law clearly introduces a "regime-specific sources of law", which will be in the first place applied by the WTO adjudicating bodies. Even the customary rules of international law

[130] Hillier, p. 307.

[131] Ibid.

[132] The ICSID and MIGA Conventions are the exceptions of such multilateral treaties in the field. For an excellent work on this subject, *see* S. W. Schill, *The Multilateralization of International Investment Law*, Cambridge: Cambridge University Press, 2009.

[133] Matsushita, Schoenbaum and Mavroidis, p. 22.

other than those codified in the WTO Agreement may not have any significant role to play for the settlement of disputes in international economic law.[134]

The notion of regime specific sources of law in the field of international economic law should not lead us to the conclusion that all other sources of international law have no meaning for the following reasoning: As is well known from the practice of international judicial institutions in the field of public international law, in particular the ICJ, customary rules of international law and general principles of law may prevail international conventions when either of the disputant is not a party to the treaty. However, the same approach would not be convenient for the settlement of disputes in international economic law. Instead, the best way to provide a general guidance in international economic law is to first indicate the regime specific sources of law for each individual branches of law (e.g. main treaties establishing the IMF and the World Bank in international finance law; the WTO Agreements in international trade law etc.). Second, to look at the other sources of international law regardless of whether they are indicated in Article 38 of the Statute of the ICJ, such as customary rules of international law, general principles of law, judicial decisions and resolutions of international organisations and so on.

Actually, the method indicated above was, in a different way, applied by the WTO adjudicating bodies. They identified a number of interpretative elements, in fact each of which may be treated as a source of international law, while interpreting the WTO Agreements. Some of the interpretative elements are as follows: GATT panel reports, WTO panel reports and Appellate Body reports, decisions and recommendations by various WTO organs, international agreements not reflected in the WTO Agreement, acts adopted by various international organisations, decisions by international courts, domestic law and practice, unilateral declarations by WTO Members, customary international law, general principles of law and doctrine.[135]

Based on the fact that international law, with its own sources, is a legal system including international economic law, the method used by the WTO agents should not be regarded as consistent with the implementation of the sources of law in international legal system. The basic reasons for such a view will be discussed in greater detail while explaining other related sources of international economic law below.

### 1.5.2. *Customary International Law*

Article 38 1 (b) of the ICJ Statute defines international custom "as evidence of a general practice accepted as law". In the case of the ICJ being unable to solve a dispute by reference to treaty law, Article 38 1 (b) provides that customary

[134] Ibid. p. 23.
[135] Ibid. p. 25.

rules of international law shall be applied. Customary international law is a source of law which was created by the practice of subjects of international law (mainly State practice, but the practice of international organisations is important, too). To be a customary rule of international law, the practice of the States or of international organisations must be supported by a belief that the practice is obligatory (*opinion juris*, which is the second requirement for the creation of a customary international law rule). Despite the fact that the importance of international conventions has increased in providing solutions to disputes, customary rules of international law have still significant role, in particular, in the field of public international law. This is because, for instance, when a State is not a party to a treaty, one of the effective ways to make the State in question acting in accordance with international law is to enforce customary rules against it. Moreover, it should not be forgotten that some of the fundamental rules of customary international law are the peremptory norms of international law (*jus cogens* rules), which cannot be changed by the conclusion of a treaty. As Article 53 of the Vienna Convention on the Law of the Treaties states that the treaty at the time of its conclusion conflicting with the peremptory norm of international law will be null and void.

However, the role of customary international law is too limited in the field of international economic law. The basic reason for such a limitation lies in the fact that there are major differences in the practice of the members of the international community though almost all States follow the practice of capitalist form of economics and support the idea of free market and free trade. The majority of rules concerning international trade, international banking, and foreign investment between States are to be found in bilateral treaties. Despite the fact that many of these bilateral treaties share common features, they cannot be considered as a body of State practice and *opinion juris* sufficient to form a binding customary rule of international law.[136] Even one of the most known principles, the most favoured nation principle, cannot be regarded as a customary law in the field of international economic law.[137] This is because, in any event, States or parties to treaties look for an express agreement in order to get rights or to be under obligations. So, the most favoured nation rule must be in the treaty rather than custom.[138]

On the other hand, the aforementioned situation should not lead us to conclude that customary international law has nothing to do with the international economic law. Firstly, it is well-known that most of customary rules of international law have been codified by the conclusion of international conventions such as the 1969 Vienna Convention on the Law of Treaties and the

[136] Hillier, p. 307.
[137] Matsushita, Schoenbaum and Mavroidis, p. 23.
[138] Mclachlan, Shore and Weiniger, p. 17.

1982 UN Convention on the Law of the Sea. Furthermore, the practice of the International Court of Justice in the *North Sea Continental Shelf Cases*[139] indicated that a customary rule of international law from the provisions of a treaty could be created under certain conditions; the treaty provision must be a new norm-creating character, State practice concerning the relevant provision of the treaty and the *opinion juris* in this context.[140] The same effect is truly valid for the multilateral treaties of international economic law like the WTO Agreements.

Secondly, in terms of implementing international economic law by way of dispute settlement mechanisms, customary international law has a special role to play in different branches of international economic law, namely international investment law and international trade law. As is well known, international investment law, together with other branches of international economic law, developed in accordance with the increase in trans-border economic activities of the States. The milestone rules of international investment law derived from general international law were dealing with the protection and treatment of aliens. Undoubtedly, these rules constitute a primary part of customary international law.[141] That is why it would be true to say that the creation of international investment law was started with customary rules of international law. Additionally, the fact that customary international law is particularly relevant for the practice of investment arbitration with regard to the rules dealing with the concepts of attribution and of damages may be indicated at this point. The number of cases in the field of international investment law has indeed led to a situation in which some general rules of international law, here customary rules of international law in question, find their main practical expression in investment law.[142]

Customary international law and its importance in international trade law may well be examined in the WTO system. As has been indicated in Article 3 (2) of the Dispute Settlement Understanding, the WTO dispute settlement system is "a central element in providing security and predictability to the multilateral trading system." Moreover, Article 3 (2) of the Dispute Settlement Understanding provides that the purpose of dispute settlement is to clarify the provisions of the WTO Agreements in accordance with customary rules of interpretation of public international law. This provision has inevitably led GATT panels and the Dispute Settlement Body of the WTO to Articles 31 and 32 of the Vienna Convention on the Law of Treaties, which provided basic

---

[139] *North Sea Continental Shelf Cases, (Federal Republic of Germany v. Denmark and the Netherlands)*, (1969) *ICJ Reports* 3.

[140] Ibid. paras. 71–2.

[141] Schill, pp. 25–8.

[142] R. Dolzer and C. Schreuer, *Principles of International Investment Law*, Oxford: Oxford University Press, 2008, p. 24.

principles to be taken into account in treaty interpretation.[143] In a sense, customary rules of international law relating to the interpretation of treaties are treated as a tool used to provide security and predictability in international trade law.

The practice of the WTO Dispute Settlement Bodies even went beyond the limited understanding of the customary rules in the WTO legal system. In other words, customary rules should not necessarily be related to the rules of interpretation. In this context, the impressive part of the panel report on *Korea-Procurement*[144] may be quoted as follows:

> *We take note that Article 3.2 of the DSU requires that we seek within the context of a particular dispute to clarify the existing provisions of the WTO agreements in accordance with customary rules of interpretation of public international law. However, the relationship of the WTO Agreements to customary international law is broader than this. Customary international law applies generally to the economic relations between the WTO Members. Such international law applies to the extent that the WTO treaty agreements do not "contract out" from it. To put it another way, to the extent there is no conflict or inconsistency, or an expression in a covered WTO agreement that implies differently, we are of the view that the customary rules of international law apply to the WTO treaties and to the process of treaty formation under the WTO.*[145]

### 1.5.3. *General Principles of Law*

Article 38 1 (c) of the ICJ Statute empowers the Court to take into account "the general principles of law recognised by civilised nations" where there is no treaty and customary rules of international law to be applied to the dispute brought before it. General principles of law are so significant at least for the following two reasons: Firstly, they fulfil the gaps when there is no treaty or customary rules of international law applicable to the case before international courts. Secondly, they are considered as an appropriate tool for the interpretation of treaties or any other sources of international law.

Although there are problems relating to the exact content of general principles of law some of the most important ones may be briefly examined as follows:

#### 1.5.3.1. *The Doctrine of Estoppel*

The concept of *estoppel* is a well-known principle both in national legal systems and the international legal system. International judicial institutions

---

143 Alvarez, pp. 490–1.

144 *Korea-Measures Affecting Government Procurement*, WTO Doc. WT/DS163/R, (1 May 2000). Report of the Panel is available at http://www.wto.org/english/tratop_e/dispu_e/cases_e/ds163_e.htm (visited on 26 September 2009). (hereinafter *Korea-Procurement*).

145 *Korea-Procurement*, para. 7.96.

have used the doctrine of estoppels as a legal base for their decisions. In this context, the clearest example can be found in the ICJ practice in the *Temple Case.*[146] The Case was between Thailand (formerly known as Siam) and Cambodia (formerly part of French Indo-China). The dispute was over a part of the frontier, specifically, which State has the territory in where the Temple was. The Cambodian side depended on a map which was produced by the French authorities in 1907 as a result of the request of the Siamese government. According to the map, the Temple area was inside the borders of the French Indo-China. At that time the attitude of the Siamese authorities was not against the map, and borders. Even, they thanked to the French for preparing the map. Furthermore, a Siamese prince visited the disputed area and welcomed by the French officials in 1930. Based on these facts, the Court decided that the acts of Thailand were far from denying the frontier indicated on the map.[147]

To some extent, by way of the practice of international adjudicating bodies in the field the application or the reference to the *estoppel* principle can be seen in international economic law. Here, we can mention the *US-Softwood Lumber II*[148]*case* in which the detailed discussion of *estoppel* to be witnessed. The reason for examining the presence of *estoppel* in the dispute was the conclusion of a memorandum of understanding (MOU) between Canada and the USA. The issue before the panel was to decide whether the parties by way of signing the MOU had waived their rights under the Agreement and had stopped from any other action. Despite the fact that the panel did not provide a clear answer to those questions[149] it did not, at least, concluded that the principle of *estoppel* had nothing to do with the GATT law, or with international trade law.

In addition to the GATT law, the WTO adjudicating bodies have to deal with the doctrine of *estoppel* in different cases. Some of these cases and their significance may be indicated as follows: The Panel Report on *Guatemala-Cement II*[150] made it clear that the deferral of the initial application of Mexico to establish a panel by the Dispute Settlement Body (DSB) could not be

[146] *Temple of Preah Vihear Case*, (Cambodia v. Thailand), (1962) *ICJ Reports*, p. 6, pp. 26–7.

[147] Hillier, p. 29.

[148] GATT Panel Report, Panel on *United States-Measures Affecting Imports of Softwood Lumber from Canada*, GATT Doc. BISD 40S/358, SCM 162, (adopted on 27 October 1993), (hereinafter *US-Softwood Lumber II*). The Panel report is available at :http://www.worldtradelaw.net/reports/gattpanels/uslumbercvdII.pdf (visited on 4 November 2009).

[149] *US-Softwood Lumber II*, paras. 308–25.

[150] Panel Report, *Guatemala-Definitive Anti-Dumping Measures on Grey Portland Cement from Mexico*, WTO/DS156/R, (adopted on 17 November 2000). (hereinafter *Guatemala-Cement II*). The Panel Report is available at: http://www.wto.org/english/tratop_e/dispu_e/cases_e/ds156_e.htm (visited on 4 November 2009). The dispute was between Mexico and Guatemala, and it was relating to definitive anti-dumping duties imposed by the authorities of Guatemala on imports of grey Portland cement from Mexico.

regarded as Mexico was stopped from requesting the DSB to set up a new panel on the ground that the principle of *estoppel* is only possible when the consent to a particular behaviour was obviously reflected.[151] Similarly, the Panel Report on *Argentina-Poultry Anti-Dumping Duties*[152] discussed the *estoppel* principle based on the Argentina's argument that was to say that, Brazil was *estopped* from bringing the dispute before the WTO adjudicating bodies, since the very same problem had already been decided by a regional integration scheme to which both Argentina and Brazil participate, known as a MERCOSUR[153] panel. The view of the Panel was clearly refusing the argument in question. The reasoning of the Panel was based on the fact that the Panel was not under the obligation to follow the decisions of any other adjudicating bodies. It should also be noted that the Panel is not even bound by the earlier reports/decisions of the previous panel.[154]

Actually, the view taken by the GATT panel report and WTO's adjudicating bodies in relation to the arguments of the parties to the disputes in question may be considered as the application of the principle of *ne bis in idem.*

---

[151] *Guatemala-Cement II*, para. 8.24.

[152] *Argentina-Poultry Anti-Dumping Duties*, (Panel Report, Argentina-Definitive Anti-Dumping Duties on Poultry from Brazil, WT/DS241/R, adopted 19 May 2003), (hereinafter *Argentina-Poultry Anti-Dumping Duties*). The report is available at: http://docsonline.wto.org/GEN_highLightParent.asp?qu=%28%40meta%5FSymbol+WT%FCDS241%FCR%2A+and+not+RW%2A%29&doc=D%3A%2FDDFDOCUMENTS%2FT%2FWT%2FDS%2F241R%2D00%2EDOC%2EHTM&curdoc=3&popTitle=WT%2FDS241%2FR (visited on 4 November 2009).

[153] The MERCUSOR is a regional trade organisation formed in 1991 to establish a common market and common trade policy in Latin America. The name derives from the Spanish phrase Mercado Comun del Sur, which means Common Market of the South. The parties to the organisation are: Argentina, Brazil, Uruguay, Paraguay, Venezuela, Chile, Bolivia, Peru, Columbia and Ecuador. Clearly, although the MERCUSOR was established as a custom union, consisting of Argentina, Brazil, Paraguay and Uruguay in 1991, today it became the third largest economic integration, right after the EU and the NAFTA. For the constitutional treaty establishing this integration, *see* Treaty Establishing a Common Market between the Argentine Republic, the Federal Republic of Brazil, the Republic of Paraguay and the Republic of Uruguay (26 March 1991), 30 *ILM* 1041.

[154] *Argentina-Poultry Anti-Dumping Duties*, para. 7.41. The related part of the Panel Report may be quoted as follows: "We note that Article 3.2 of the DSU is concerned with international rules of treaty interpretation. Article 31.3(c) of the Vienna Convention is similarly concerned with treaty interpretation. However, Argentina has not sought to rely on any law providing that, in respect of relations between Argentina and Brazil, the WTO agreements should be interpreted in a particular way. In particular, Argentina has not relied on any statement or finding in the MERCOSUR Tribunal ruling to suggest that we should interpret specific provisions of the WTO agreements in a particular way. Rather than concerning itself with the interpretation of the WTO agreements, Argentina actually argues that the earlier MERCOSUR Tribunal ruling requires us to rule in a particular way. In other words, Argentina would have us apply the relevant WTO provisions in a particular way, rather than interpret them in a particular way. However, there is no basis in Article 3.2 of the DSU, or any other provision, to suggest that we are bound to rule in a particular way, or apply the relevant WTO provisions in a particular way. We note that we are not even bound to follow rulings contained in adopted WTO panel reports…, so we see no reason at all why we should be bound by the rulings of non-WTO dispute settlement bodies. Accordingly, we reject Argentina's alternative arguments regarding Article 31.3(c) of the Vienna Convention."

However, it is necessary to note that the *estoppel* doctrine is different from *ne bis in idem*. Although the *estoppel* may be the result of *ne bis in idem*, it covers situations/circumstances other than *ne bis in idem*.[155] In light of the explanation made above, it could be concluded that the implementation of the doctrine of *estoppel* by the international judicial institutions in the field of international economic law has not reached the level practiced in public international law.[156]

1.5.3.2. *Good Faith*

The principle of good faith is a main column over which both national and international legal systems are built on. It is a fundamental political principle governing international relations as well. It has taken its place both in international legal documents and in the practice of judicial institutions:

According to Article 2 (2) of the UN Charter, all Member States are under the obligation to fulfil their obligations in accordance with the principle of good faith. Moreover, the UN General Assembly in its Resolution namely *the Declaration on Principles Concerning Friendly Relations and Co-operation among States*[157] indicates that States should undertake their international obligations in good faith. The International Court of Justice in its decisions has often noted the significance of the principle of good faith in governing the creation and performance of legal obligations.[158]

Certainly, the principle of good faith is also taken into account by the adjudicating bodies operating in the field of international economic law:

Following the rule of good faith is particularly pertinent to the international investment law. That is why tribunals dealing with foreign investment disputes have had recourse to this principle.[159] The nature of foreign investment law and its distinctive features impel the tribunals to observe the presence of good faith. As is known from the comparison of international investment law to trade law, the previous one carries the long-term risk while the latter does not. In other words, international investment law regulates the long term relationship between the investor and the host State and the investor provides most of

---

[155] Matsushita, Schoenbaum and Mavroidis, p. 82.

[156] Ibid. p. 83.

[157] UN GA Resolution, 2625 (XXV) (1970).

[158] As an example, the *Nuclear Test Cases* of 1974 may be noted here. The related part of the Judgement may be quoted as follows: "One of the basic principles governing the creation and performance of legal obligations, whatever their source, is the principle of good faith. Trust and confidence are inherent in international co-operation, in particular in an age when this co-operation in many fields is becoming increasingly essential. Just as the very rule of pacta sunt servanda in the law of treaties is based on good faith, so also is the binding character of an international obligation assumed by unilateral declaration. Thus interested States may take cognizance of unilateral declarations and place confidence in them, and are entitled to require that the obligation thus created be respected." *(Nuclear Test Case (Australia v. France), Judgement,* (1974), *ICJ Reports*, p. 253, at para. 46).

[159] Dolzer and Schreuer, p. 5.

the resources at the outset of the project and expects to receive a fair return in a stable relationship within the legal order of the host State. Once the investor fulfilled its obligations the power clearly shifts in favour of the host State. The distinctive nature of the foreign investment law– the long-term risk/ relationship, in a sense, directs tribunals to apply the principle of good faith.[160]

When the practice of arbitral tribunals is examined, it can easily be noted that the rule of good faith is regarded as inherent in the Fair and Equitable Treatment Standard. For example in *Tecmed,* the Tribunal while interpreting the fair and equitable standard referred to the *bone fide* principle recognised in international law as an expression of it.[161] Similarly, the tribunal in *Waste Management* held that the obligation to act in accordance with the rule of good faith was a basic obligation under the Fair and Equitable Treatment Standard.[162] In defining the Fair and Equitable Treatment Standard, the tribunal, in *Saluka v. Czech Republic,* focused on the requirement of good faith.[163]

The adjudicating body operating in international trade law, namely the Panel Report, referred to the principle of good faith on the *Korea-Procerement Dispute* in the sense that it should be taken into consideration in interpreting treaty provisions and in fulfilling obligations deriving from being a party to the WTO Agreement. One of the places the Report that contains reference to the principle may be quoted as follows: "It seems clear that good faith performance has been agreed by the WTO Members to include subsequent actions which might nullify or impair the benefits reasonably expected to accrue to other parties to the negotiations in question."[164]

According to the Appellate Body considered the dispute known as *US-Offset Act (Byrd Amendment),*[165] the only violation of WTO Agreement is not sufficient to prove that the member violated the principle of good faith. The related

---

160 Ibid.

161 *Tecmed v. Mexico Case (AF),* (*Técnicas Medioambientales Tecmed, S.A. v. United Mexican States,* Award, 29 May 2003, (2004) 43 ILM 133). (hereinafter *Tecmed v. Mexico Case (AF),* at para. 154.

162 *Waste Management v. Mexico II Case (AF),* (*Waste Management, Inc. v. United Mexican States,* Case No. ARB(AF)/00/3 Final Award, 30 April 2004, (2004) 43 ILM 967), at paras. 137–40.

163 The related part of the findings is as follows: "A foreign investor protected by the Treaty may in any case properly expect that the Czech Republic implements its policies bona fide by conduct that is, as far as it affects the investors' investment, reasonably justifiable by public policies and that such conduct does not manifestly violate the requirements of consistency, transparency, even-handedness and non- discrimination." (*Saluka v. Czech Republic,* Partial Award, (17 March 2006), para. 307).

164 *Korea-Procurement,* para. 7.94.

165 United States-Continued Dumping and Subsidy Offset Act of 2000, WTO Doc. WT/DS217/AB/R and WT/DS234/AB/R, (16 January 2003), (hereinafter *US-Offset Act).* The text is available at: http://docsonline.wto.org/GEN_highLightParent.asp?qu=%28%40meta%5FSymbol+WT%FCDS234%FCAB%FCR%2A+and+not+RW%2A%29&doc=D%3A%2FDDFDOCUMENTS%2FT%2FWT%2FDS%2F234ABR%2EDOC%2EHTM&curdoc=3&popTitle=WT%2FDS217%2FAB%2FR%3Cbr%3EWT%2FDS234%2FAB%2FR (visited on 5 November 2009).

part of the Report of the Appellate Body indicates this fact as follows: "Nothing, however, in the covered agreements supports the conclusion that simply because a WTO Member is found to have violated a substantive treaty provision, it has therefore not acted in good faith. In our view, it would be necessary to prove more than mere violation to support such a conclusion."[166]

In sum, the principle of good faith has been continuing to find its places in the interpretation and implementation of the rights and obligations of Member States deriving from international economic law documents like the WTO Agreement. Similar to any other branches of law, its content and application will undoubtedly be made clearer through the practice of international judicial institutions.[167]

1.5.3.3. Res Judicata

*Res judicata* is a general principle of law that can be invoked, under certain conditions by the judicial bodies operating either in the field of public international law or in international economic law. The principle has taken its place in the WTO legal system and the WTO adjudicating bodies made its requirements clear to be applied to a specific situation.

The Panel Report on *India-Autos*[168] defines the principle of *res judicata* as follows: "In international jurisdictions where it is applicable, the doctrine is generally understood to mean that an issue that has been decided on in a final adjudication, that is, after exhaustion of any available appeal rights, must be considered as a settled matter between the parties to the dispute."[169] And the conditions for a possible application of the doctrine set out by the Panel may be quoted as follows: "The Panel therefore considers that for *res judicata* to have any possible role in WTO dispute settlement, there should, at the very least, be in essence identity between the matter previously ruled on and that submitted to the subsequent panel. This requires identity between both the measures and the claims pertaining to them. There is also, for the purposes of *res judicata*, a requirement of identity of parties..."[170]

1.5.4. *Judicial Decisions*

Article 38 (1) (d) of the ICJ Statute states that "judicial decisions and the teachings of the most highly qualified publicists of the various nations" shall be applied "as subsidiary means for the determination of rules of law."

---

[166] *US-Offset Act*, para. 298.

[167] Matsushita, Schoenbaum and Mavroidis, p. 84.

[168] *India-Autos,* (Appellate Body Report, *India-Measures Affecting the Automotive Sector,* WT/DS/146AB/R and WT/DS/175/R, adopted 5 April 2002),(hereinafter *India-Autos*).

[169] *India-Autos*, para. 7.62.

[170] Ibid. para. 7.66.

Judicial decisions may be taken into account by the ICJ when there was no solution to the dispute by reference to international convention, international custom or general principles of law. Judicial decisions and the doctrine in the practice of the ICJ are treated as the secondary sources of international law. In other words, while treaty, custom and general principles of law are regarded as binding sources of international law, judicial decisions and the doctrine are considered as among the non-binding sources of international law. Such an understanding and the practice by the ICJ is also consonant with the provisions of Article 59 of the Statute of the ICJ, which provides: "The decision of the court has no binding force except between the parties and in respect of that particular case". Although there is no *stare decisis* in international law it is necessary for an international or national judicial institution to look at earlier decisions and take them into account in order to create a credible jurisprudence or judicial consistency.

When the practice of adjudicating bodies in the field of international economic law is assessed in light of the implementation of ICJ it can clearly be seen that it is in compliance with the general international law. One of the best example indicating the fact that there is no *stare decisis* in international economic law is to be found in the practice of the WTO adjudicating bodies: The Panel Report on *Argentina-Poultry Anti-Dumping Duties* made it clear that it was not bound by the decisions of any other judicial institutions and even not bound by the earlier decisions or rulings of panels. The explanation of the Panel was:

> *... However, there is no basis in Article 3.2 of the DSU, or any other provision, to suggest that we are bound to rule in a particular way, or apply the relevant WTO provisions in a particular way. We note that we are not even bound to follow rulings contained in adopted WTO panel reports..., so we see no reason at all why we should be bound by the rulings of non-WTO dispute settlement bodies. Accordingly, we reject Argentina's alternative arguments regarding Article 31.3(c) of the Vienna Convention.*[171]

Moreover, the Appellate Body of the WTO also adopted the same approach in its Report on *Japan-Alcoholic Beverages.*[172]

---

171 *Argentina-Poultry Anti-Dumping Duties*, para. 7.41.

172 "Adopted panel reports are an important part of the GATT acquis. They are often considered by subsequent panels. They create legitimate expectations among WTO Members, and, therefore, should be taken into account where they are relevant to any dispute. However, they are not binding, except with respect to resolving the particular dispute between the parties to that dispute. ... In short, their character and their legal status have not been changed by the coming into force of the WTO Agreement." "It is worth noting that the Statute of the International Court of Justice has an explicit provision, Article 59, to the same effect. This has not inhibited the development by that Court (and its predecessor) of a body of case law in which considerable reliance on the value of previous decisions is readily discernible." (*Japan-Taxes on Alcoholic Beverages*, WT/DS8/AB/R, WT/DS10/AB/R and WT/DS11/AB/R, 4 October 1996), (fotnote 30 and accompanying text of the Report).

### 1.5.5. *The Doctrine*

Article 38 (1) (d) of the Statute of the ICJ refers to the teachings of the most highly qualified publicists of the various nations (the doctrine) as subsidiary means for the determination of rules of law. In the field of international law the writings and teachings of international lawyers have played a central role for the development of international law. As long as the sources of international law in general and international economic law in particular, the doctrine is considered as a non-binding source of international law. The parties to a dispute often referred to the writings of academicians in their pleadings before international judicial institutions. The adjudicating bodies have basically regarded the doctrine as a supplementary means of their interpretation.

### 1.5.6. *Soft Law*

In accordance with the development in the study of sources of international law, it is possible to say that in terms of their legal binding, the rules of international law can be divided into two groups: hard law and soft law.

Hard law may be defined as those rules, usually contained in treaties, which constitute positive obligations and objectively binding the States or other subjects of international law.[173] Since customary rules of international law and general principles of law have the same binding effect for the legal persons to whom they are addressed they also fall within the concept of hard law.

Soft law, on the other hand, may be defined as "written instruments that spell out rules of conduct that are not intended to be legally binding, so that they are not subject to the law of treaties and do not generate the *opinion juris* required for them to be state practice contributing to custom."[174] Though not binding the subjects of international law in the manner of hard law documents, they can constitute normative claims and provide standards or targets to be achieved. Such international instruments may have significant impact on the behaviour of States. In a sense, they cannot be ignored by the legal persons, just because they are not legally binding.[175] In public international law, some of the most important examples of soft law include the Final Act of the Conference on Security and Co-operation in Europe 1975, the OECD Guidelines for Multinational Enterprises, the Bonn Declaration on International Terrorism 1978 and the Rio Declaration on Environmental and Development 1992.

Having indicated the general nature of the concept of soft law in public international law in general, it is necessary to look at it briefly from the point

---

[173] Hillier, p. 37.

[174] D. J. Harris, *Cases and Materials on International Law*, London: Sweet & Maxwell, 2004, 6th edn., p. 62.

[175] Harris, p. 62.; Hillier, p. 37.

of view of international economic law. One of the most important contributions of soft law can be witnessed in the field of international economic law since it provides a tool overcoming deadlocks occurring between legal persons pursuing conflicting interests or economic aims.[176]

As is well known from the practice of the international community, monetary policies are basically exercised based on discretion and within international networks. Thus, in the field of international finance law it is very difficult to find any kind of hard law. Financial services are mainly governed by domestic law amounting to one of the most dense and specialised areas of regulation. However, there is too little international law dealing with the subject.[177] And the documents trying to fulfil this gap in international finance law are often soft law. The Basle Accords on International Convergence of Capital Measurement and Capital Standards (known as the Basle Accords) may be indicated as a key example of such law and were "praised as an alternative to law in bringing about international cooperation."[178] Although the Basle Accords were not binding law, they were implemented by more than 100 countries.[179] Such a case would be sufficient to prove the importance of soft law in international finance law.

In addition to the implementation of the soft law documents of international finance law at the domestic law level, the real contribution of soft law can be witnessed both in international trade law and international investment law in providing guidance to the interpretation and application of arbitral tribunals:

The WTO adjudicating bodies clearly referred to some of the documents adopted by various international organisations. In this context, the arbitrators report on *US-FSC (Article 22.6-US*[180]*)* referring to the report on State Responsibility, a report prepared by the International Law Commission and voted and adopted as the UN resolution; the report on *Mexico-Telecoms*[181] depending on a series of regulations and recommendations by the International Telecommunications Union (ITU) and the panel report on *Mexico-Telecoms*[182] relying on the *Organisation of Cooperation and Development Guidelines* (OECD Guidelines) should be noted. The documents indicated in

---

[176] Harris, p. 62.

[177] Cottier, p. 6.

[178] Ibid.

[179] For a detailed study explaining the reasons why countries implement soft law documents, *see* D. E. Ho, "Compliance and International Soft Law: Why Do Countries Implement the Basle Accord?", (2002) 5/3 *Journal of International Economic Law*, pp. 647–88.

[180] United States-Tax Treatment for "foreign Sales Corporations", Recourse to arbitration by the United States under Article 22.6 of the DSU and Article 4.11 of the SCM Agreement, WTO Doc.WT/DS108/ARB, 30 August 2002. (At the footnote 52 of the Panel Report).

[181] *Mexico-Measures Affecting Telecommunications Services*, WTO Doc. WT/DS204/R, 2 April 2004. (at paras. 7.129–7.136).

[182] Ibid. at para. 7.236.

bold character were treated as supplementary means of interpretation by the WTO organs.[183] So long as the sources of international law are taken into account, the mentioned UN Resolution, regulations and recommendations of ITU and the OECD Guidelines can be treated as the best fitting soft law instruments in international law.

The main role of soft law documents in the sense that they guide the interpretative choices of arbitral tribunals may also be examined in the field of international investment law. As one of the leading examples of such situation, the OECD National Treatment Instrument forming part of the OECD Declaration on International Investment and Multinational Enterprises together with an OECD Council Decision obliging adhering States to notify their exceptions to the Instrument should be indicated here. Despite the fact that the National Treatment Instrument did not have a binding effect, in the sense that the violation of it would not give rise to justiciable disputes, it has had a broader impact than it was thought.[184] The OECD National Treatment Instrument and its contribution to international investment law can be, at least at this point, noted in the following situations: Firstly, it provides a guideline indicating the common understanding of the OECD and of other interested States of the scope of the national treatment protection. Secondly, and most importantly, the OECD National Treatment Instrument has taken its place in a number of Investor-State cases as a tool used for the interpretative choices of arbitral tribunals.[185] The arbitral tribunals while explaining the term "like situations" in *SD Myers, Inc. v. Canada*[186] and the notion of national treatment in *Pope & Talbot Inc v. Canada*[187] explicitly referred to the OECD Instrument. These are just two examples that confirm our proposition.

---

[183] Matsushita, Schoenbaum and Mavroidis, pp. 71–2.

[184] A. van Aaken and J. Kurtz, "Prudence or Discrimination? Emergency Measures, The Global Financial Crisis and International Economic Law", (2009) 12/4 *Journal of International Economic Law*, pp. 881–2.

[185] Ibid. p. 882.

[186] *SD Myers, Inc.v. Canada*, UNCITRAL Award under the NAFTA, (13 November 2000). The text is available on line at: http://ita.law.uvic.ca/documents/SDMeyers-1stPartialAward.pdf (visited on 19 February 2010). The related part of the case (para. 248) can be quoted as follows: ".... all three NAFTA partners belong to the OECD. OECD practice suggests that an evaluation of "like situations" in the investment context should take into account policy objectives in determining whether enterprises are in like circumstances. The OECD Declaration on International and Multinational Enterprises, issued on June 21, 1976, states that investors and investments should receive treatment that is ...no less favourable than that accorded in like situations to domestic enterprises. In 1993 the OECD reviewed the "like situation" test in the following terms:
As regards the expression 'in like situations', the comparison between foreign-controlled enterprises is only valid if it is made between firms operating in the same sector. More general considerations, such as the policy objectives of Member countries could be taken into account to define the circumstances in which comparison between foreign-controlled and domestic enterprises is permissible inasmuch as those objectives are not contrary to the principle of national treatment."

[187] *Pope & Talbot Inc. v. Canada*, UNCITRAL Award under the NAFTA, (10 April 2001). For the text visit: http://www.naftaclaims.com/Disputes/Canada/Pope/PopeFinalMeritsAward.pdf

### 1.6. *The Substantive Content of International Economic Law*

In a parallel fashion with globalisation, international law has been developing and advancing in order to meet the needs of the international community. International economic law has now become an important aspect of globalisation on the ground that it provides legal rules in establishing a global social order. As have been indicated above, international economic law is an interdisciplinary field and for that reason it is very difficult to provide a definition which is covering all aspects of the discipline.[188] While examining the relationship between different branches of law on the one hand and the international economic law on the other, it was clearly indicated that international economic law could cover other areas which could be regarded as part of international economic law. Some of the examples could include economic development, international environmental protection, international business law, and private international law.[189]

The substantive content of international economic law, for the purpose of this work, is limited to the areas of international economic law which govern the relations between the subjects of international law: International Finance Law, International Trade Law, and International Investment Law.[190] Since each branch of international economic law will be examined in detail in the following chapters (Chapter 2: New Challenges and Issues in International Finance Law, Chapter 3: Dispute Settlement in International Trade Law and Chapter 4: Dispute Settlement in International Investment Law) it is not necessary to discuss the main features of those fields here. However, the main reasons why international economic law is to be limited to the mentioned fields should be briefly elaborated:

Firstly, being basically developed from general international law, the subjects of international law, and the governance of economic relations among them are taken into account. In other words, the concept of international economic law is examined from the more general international law perspective. In particular, the dispute settlement mechanisms concerning disputes occurring among the States or between foreign investors and the State provided at the international level constitute the landmark of the mentioned limitation.

Secondly, though each sub-branches of international economic law establishes its own legal regimes and institutions that enable and enhance international economic activities, a functioning international economic law may

---

(visited on 19 February 2010). The arbitral tribunal in its award in para. 78 discusses the national treatment and as an evidence of its argument in the same paragraph by way of footnote 73 depends on the OECD National Treatment Instrument.

[188] *See supra* title 1.2.1. Defining International Economic Law.

[189] For deatailed information, *see supra title* 1.3. International Economic Law- Its Relationship with Other Branches of Law.

[190] Loibl, p. 690.

become possible when international finance law, international trade law, and international investment law work together. For instance, international trade law under the World Trade Organisation system implements the principles of non-discrimination and anti-protectionism that enable competition which is the first requirement for a global market to function. At the same time, international finance law with the leading organisation of the International Monetary Fund in the field tries to stabilise exchange rates in achieving monetary stability as a basis for international transactions and capital markets.[191] Similarly, international investment law requires international cooperation not only for the element of trans-border flows of investment, but also for the involvement of the host State as a sovereign actor,[192] which is still the most important subject of international law.

## 1.7. *Why Does International Economic Law Work?*

As the practice of the international community proves, the majority of the rules of international economic law are implemented. The normal practice is to follow the rules of international economic law. In this section it would be useful to examine some of the reasons why international economic law is so effective or why it really works well.

### 1.7.1. *The Common Good*

In general, there cannot be any doubt on the fact that the first and the most practical reason for the effectiveness of international economic law is that it is based on common good and necessity.[193] Since the end of World War II inter-State economic activities has been increasing and the trend has reached the highest level at the age of globalisation. International community is more interdependent than ever. Clearly, international economic law is only one of the facts and impacts of globalisation and international economic law and its institutions are vital in order to facilitate and to govern the trillions of trans-border activities for the common good.[194] At this point, international economic law provides legal rules or principles creating a stable and global market which is a fundamental need of the international community. Certainly, compliance with those legal rules serves to the protection of the self-interests of each member of the international community. For example, the implementation of the principle of non-discrimination in the field of international trade law is very important for the creation of a free trade in a global market.

---

[191] Schill, p. 2.
[192] Ibid. p. 3.
[193] For the significance of the common good in international law, *see* Dixon, pp. 10–1.
[194] Jackson, *Sovereignty, the WTO* ... p. 47.

Likewise, the interpretation and application of the principle of fair and equitable treatment and other major rules in international investment law is vital for both capital-exporting States and developing States.

### 1.7.2. *The Practice of International Economic Law*

International economic law has become an inevitable part of the international society. It is practised on a daily basis both at the national and international level. States and related governmental organs have to take into consideration the rules of international economic law when they are engaged in any inter-State economic activities. Similarly, international organisations should follow the requirements of international economic law. The World Trade Organisation, the International Monetary Fund, and the World Bank are particularly important in the sense that the very reason for their creation is international economic law itself. They are the main international organisations where international economic law is practised at the highest level.

### 1.7.3. *The Teaching of International Economic Law*

International economic law has become an independent and interdisciplinary branch of international law. It has taken its place in general international law textbooks in providing general information about the features of the discipline as similar to the law of treaties, international human rights law, international law of the sea, international criminal law, and law of armed conflicts. Moreover, international economic law has been thought both at the under-graduate and graduate courses in law schools. Even sub-branches of the discipline like international finance law, international trade law, and international investment law are taken their places as individual programs at certain universities and institutions.[195] That means that the practitioners such as the members of international court or arbitral tribunals, members of national courts, legal practitioners at the different international organisations such as the World Trade Organisation, the World Bank, and the International Monetary Fund have been trained in the domestic law of their own countries. They all know the discipline and respect for international economic law.[196]

---

[195] For a detailed work on the teaching of international economic law in the USA, *see* K. E. Bravo, "International Economic Law in the US Law Schools: Evaluating Its Pedagogy and Identifying Future Challenges", in C. B. Picker, I. D. Bunn and D. Warner (eds.), *International Economic Law The State and Future of the Discipline*, Oxford and Portland, Oregon: Hart Publishing, 2008, p. 135.; A. Porges, "The Future of International Economic Law Practice", in C. B. Picker, I. D. Bunn and D. Warner (eds.), *International Economic Law The State and Future of the Discipline*, Oxford and Portland, Oregon: Hart Publishing, 2008, p. 241.

[196] For the same effect on international law, *see* Dixon, p. 11.

### 1.7.4. *The Flexible Nature of International Economic Law*

This is the exact point in where the relationship between general international law and international economic law clearly occurs. While examining the sources of international law above, we indicated that rules of international law are created by the subjects of international law and particularly by States. In general, rules of international law are so flexible and subjects of international law have chance to choose from a range of policies, all of which will be legal.[197] As will be seen in the following chapters, general principles of law such as the principle of good faith, non-discrimination, the principle of equity and so on are flexible in their nature. That is why dispute settlement mechanisms in international economic law are under obligation to carefully interpret and apply those rules to specific cases brought before them. If not, the result could be destructive.[198]

### 1.7.5. *Providing Dispute Settlement Mechanisms*

One of the most important features of international economic law is that it provides dispute settlement mechanisms at the international level. In implementing international economic law, the organs resolving disputed questions of fact and law occurring among the subjects of international law plays a central role. This is because, once a State becomes party to a treaty in the field of international economic law, that State will be responsible to resolve its disputes through the mechanisms provided in the treaty in question. For example, the WTO Agreement introduces for the parties to resolve their disputes through the Dispute Settlement Understanding which is in Annex 2 to the Agreement.[199] At this point, the Panels and Appellate Body at the WTO should be noted here. In addition to the practice of the Panels and the Appellate Body of the WTO, the ICSID at the World Bank should not be forgotten. As will be explained in the following Chapters in detail, their practice and contribution to international economic law is invaluable so long as the development of the discipline is concerned.

### 1.7.6. *Loss of Legal Rights and Privileges*

As with the public international law, one of the effective ways of implementing international economic law rules is to ensure that any violation of law results in the loss of corresponding legal rights and privileges.[200] As has been

---

[197] Dixon, pp. 11–2.

[198] Jackson, *Sovereignty, the WTO* ... pp. 262–3.

[199] J. G. Merrills, *International Dispute Settlement*, Cambridge: Cambridge University Press, 3rd edn., 1998, p. 218.

[200] Dixon, p. 8.

indicated above, globalisation and the economic developments are the main reasons for the development of international economic law and also for a new type of international economic law practice, according to which, treaty rights deriving from the major legal documents such as the WTO Agreement in international trade law and the bilateral investment treaties in international investment law are used to address market access problems and to remedy discrimination or takings of property.[201] In a sense, treaty rights are the tools which can be used in protecting legal rights and protection against other members of the international community. The loss of such rights or privileges by way of violating such treaties may result in a greater practical effect than any other enforcement mechanisms, which is particularly true for today's highly interdependent international society.[202]

### 1.7.7. *Sanctions*

One of the weakest points of international law is not to have enforcement mechanisms known from domestic law applications. Since being a completely different legal system from municipal law, the international legal system has its own enforcement mechanisms and sanctions.

At the broadest sense, the UN Security Council is primarily responsible for the protection and maintenance of peace. In accordance with the UN Charter, the UN Security Council may take enforcement actions against a state or any other subjects of international law, even against a non-state entity like the Al-Qaida, when it poses a threat to the peace or has committed an act of aggression or breach of the peace.[203]

The enforcement actions or sanctions imposed by the UN Security Council in accordance with Articles 41 and 42 of the UN Charter may include both non-military and military measures.[204] The non-military measures indicated in Article 41 of the Charter may include complete or partial interruption of economic relations and of rail, sea, air, postal, telegraphic,

---

[201] A. Porges, "The Future of International Economic Law Practice", in C. B. Picker, I. D. Bunn and D. Warner (eds.), *International Economic Law The State and Future of the Discipline*, Oxford and Portland, Oregon: Hart Publishing, 2008, p. 242.

[202] Dixon, p. 8.

[203] Article 39 of the UN Charter.

[204] Article 41 of the UN Charter provides: "The Security Council may decide what measures not involving the use of armed force are to be employed to give effect to its decisions, and it may call upon the Members of the United Nations to apply such measures. These may include complete or partial interruption of economic relations and of rail, sea, air, postal, telegraphic, radio, and other means of communication, and the severance of diplomatic relations."

Article 42 of the UN Charter provides: "Should the Security Council consider that measures provided for in Article 41 would be inadequate or have proved to be inadequate, it may take such action by air, sea, or land forces as may be necessary to maintain or restore international peace and security. Such action may include demonstrations, blockade, and other operations by air, sea, or land forces of Members of the United Nations."

radio, and other means of communication, and the severance of diplomatic relations."

From the point of view of international economic law, the concept of "economic sanctions"[205] plays a central role in ensuring that the regulations of law are obeyed. Economic sanctions can be used by individual countries[206] and international organisations either universal or regional. As an example of international organisations the UN practice should be briefly indicated here. Although the economic sanctions imposed by the UN Security Council were rare until the end of the Cold War era, the situation has completely changed since then. The Security Council has adopted economic sanctions ranging from complete embargo on exports and imports to arms embargoes. Prohibitions on financial transactions and restrictions on air and sea transportation should also be indicated as different deployment of economic sanctions.[207]

## 1.8. *Conclusions*

International economic law and its institutions have been playing major role in order to meet the needs of the international community of the 21st century. Since World War II, particularly after the end of the 'cold war era', the rapid increase in the number of international economic activities and of international treaties raises a number of legal, economic and political issues. In the early days of the 21st century, it became clear that the institutions created right after World War II was not sufficient to deal with the problems or crisis that the international community has faced. The 2008 financial crisis in general and the ongoing crisis in the European Union (in Greece, Spain, Portugal, Ireland and Italy etc.) in particular, once more affirmed the fact that the international community has to work harder on improving the global economic system and its legal instruments.

Nowadays, although the age of globalisation is the main feature of the world it seems that regionalisation will challenge it as long as the trend in interpreting and applying the rules of international economic law is taken into consideration. The international community, on the one hand, has the EU, the Africa Union (AU), the NAFTA, and the MERCUSOR as regional organisations, and the WTO that may be seen as the equivalent of the United Nations for the world trading system on the other. However, the rules and

---

[205] One of the prominent definitions of economic sanction may be quoted as follows: "... measures of an economic –as contrasted with diplomatic or military- character taken by states to express disapproval of the acts of the target state or to induce that state to change some policy or practice or even its governmental structure." (Lowenfeld, p. 698).

[206] For a detailed examination of the USA practice, *see* Lowenfeld, pp. 731–64.

[207] Lowenfeld, p. 729.

their implementation within the same regional international organization may be different when similar situations occur at the international level. For instance, the EU law by the European Court of Justice is differently interpreted and applied when the case is only concerned with Member States as has been witnessed in the creation of the direct effect doctrine. By contrast, the same approach was not employed by the Court when the WTO agreements were in question. The basic reason for such a practice is to protect the interests of the EU in the first place. Similarly, the legal relationship between the NAFTA and the WTO is not clearly defined and it is ambiguous that whether NAFTA or WTO law will prevail in cases of inconsistency.[208] That is also true when the judicial organs of the WTO face with the ruling of a regional organisation which is conflicting with WTO agreements.[209] Based on these facts, the international community should create new rules and mechanisms governing the relations between international organisations, through which different international regional organizations and international/universal organizations can co-operate and operate side by side.[210] Thus should lastly note that the panels and the Appellate Body of the WTO in international trade law and the ICSID in international investment law by way of their interpretation and applications of the rules of international economic law provide the most convenient venue for the disputes which are either universal or regional in their nature.

---

[208] For a detailed paper on the legal relationship between the NAFTA and the WTO, *see* F. M. Abbott, "The North American Integration Regime and its Implications for the World Trading System", in J.H.H. Weiler (ed.), *The EU, The WTO and the NAFTA Towards a Common Law of International Trade*, Oxford: Oxford University Press, 2005, pp. 169–99.

[209] For an example, *see* the explanation made under the title of the doctrine of estoppel above with regard to the relationship between the MERCUSOR Tribunal and the dispute settlement bodies of the WTO in the *Argentina-Poultry Anti-Dumping Duties*, (para. 7.41).

[210] The Works on dispute prevention and dispute settlement between regional organisations, particularly the EU and the NAFTA have already taken its place in international economic law. For an excellent example, *see* E.-U. Petersmann and M. A. Pollack (eds.). *Transatlantic Economic Disputes, The EU, the US, and the WTO*, Oxford: Oxford University Press, 2003, reprinted in 2005.

CHAPTER TWO

# NEW CHALLENGES AND ISSUES IN INTERNATIONAL FINANCE LAW

Ilias Bantekas

## 2.1. *Introduction*

The purpose of this chapter is to thoroughly examine the current workings and operations of the World Bank Group – with a greater emphasis on the International Bank for Reconstruction and Development (IBRD) and the International Monetary Fund (IMF).[1] Through this examination we aim to analyse the problems and perspectives of international financial architecture and come to some concrete conclusions about the future role of these institutions and whether they require some sort of reform. Equally, we examine the role of other multilateral development banks (MDB), such as the African and Asian Development Banks with a view to ascertaining whether they are effective in achieving their stated goals. One of the key themes that permeate this chapter is the lack of coordination between regional MDBs themselves and with the World Bank. Prior to the 2008 global financial crisis, this lack of coordination did not have a significant impact because the West was well used to endemic poverty in Africa and parts of Asia. Following this crisis, however, and given the relatively frugal financial reserves of all MDBs, it became clear that centrality of coordination was of paramount importance in achieving developmental goals. Overall, the Bank has failed to halt poverty or achieve any of its other goals. This is a general criticism that is directed against Bank policy that has not favoured the poor.[2]

The primary purpose of this book is to explore the adequacy of the existing international financial architecture. What exactly is this? By this term we denote the multilateral system of currency and balance-of-payments that was agreed by the relatively developed countries of the world in the aftermath of the Second World War. This was achieved through a treaty and an Organisation, the World Bank, which is composed of various autonomous institutions. The Articles of Agreement (essentially the found treaties) of the various World Bank institutions are only binding upon the respective signatory States and

---

[1] *See* generally, I. Shihata, *The World Bank in a Changing World* Springer, 1991; K Marshall, *The World Bank: From Reconstruction to Development to Equity* Routledge, 2008.

[2] *See* H. Stein, *Beyond the World Bank Agenda: An Institutional Approach to Development* Chicago University Press, 2008.

besides loan and surveillance obligations, the Bank does not have the power to intervene in the financial affairs of States. So, why is it that the international financial system is said to be predicated on the World Bank? This is only partially true. Developing States would otherwise be unable to borrow money in order to finance infrastructure projects or support their budget, or more significantly to feed their starving populations when circumstances arise. Private banks would either find the collateral and guarantees of such governments inadequate to safeguard their money, or they would view the feeding of a starving population as lacking any investment by which they could secure any return on their loan. Thus, the World Bank and other MDBs play the role of financier. They not only loan their own funds at extremely preferential rates, they also borrow money from other financial institutions for their clients by putting forward their own good name. Under certain circumstances the World Bank provides concessional lending to needy countries. It is evident therefore that MDB play a significant part in financing low-income States, who in turn depend on them. In equal measure, the IMF, through the participation of the World's economically powerful nations, is responsible for ensuring international financial stability, among others. It is not the compulsion that makes this system work; rather, it is all predicated on the inter-connectedness of functions and institutions. The value of a currency is measured against other currencies and commodities and the willingness to loan under concessional terms is based on other benefits for the lending States. Moreover, the work of the World Trade Organisation (WTO) and that of private commerce is inextricably linked to the operations of the World Bank and other MDBs. In a larger sense, the maintenance of peace and security by the United Nations is also connected to international finance law. This is evident through the work of numerous UN bodies, such as the Food and Agriculture Organisation (FAO), the UN Development Program (UNDP), UN Habitat and many others.

Yet, financial liquidity is not wholly in the hands of States. Private banks and other private financial institutions hold much of the world's monetary resources, whether in the form of cash, valuable minerals or other commodities. This necessarily means that they have a significant role to play in the architecture of international finance. Their cash flows are required in order to finance projects approved by MDBs. As a result of their "power" they have been able to escape tight regulation, despite the fact that their operations were early on deemed to have a strong impact on national economies, employment and development. The 2008 financial crisis demonstrated that the lack of such regulation could in fact bring down national economies because globalisation had progressed far more than was originally conceived. The accumulation of bad debt in the banks of one country, or an investment firm, defined the level of bad debt in the banks of other countries. This chapter would have been very different had it been written in mid 2008. Currently, our interest is on identifying new roles for MDBs and whether or not we should alter our thinking about regulating the private sector at a global level with a view to avoid another crisis. It is hoped that the reader will make up his or her own mind at the end of this chapter.

### 2.2. *The International Bank for Reconstruction and Development*

When the IBRD was established in the aftermath of the Second World War its purpose was to secure the appropriate financial resources and subsequently fund the reconstruction of Europe – although in reality such reconstruction was available to all Bank members. This seems like a daunting task even for today's standards. As Europe's financial woes began to give way to a new phase of industrialisation, development and financial prosperity the Bank's development role was questioned. This eventually led the IBRD to re-examine its purpose and find new objectives. It was thus led to delve into poverty alleviation and poverty reduction and to tackle the problems of the developing world, particularly following the process of decolonisation. Aid, poverty and development are currently the backbone of the Bank's existence and together with research into these areas they occupy its policy makers and guide its banking activities.

Let us take things from the start, however, just to reflect on how the Bank has come this far. The IBRD was part of the founding institutions that made up the so-called World Bank Group. Although it does possess funds of its own, its status as a solid inter-governmental institution that has the financial backing of the world's strongest economies means that it can borrow money from private financial institutions and lend these on to qualifying member States or public sector institutions in respect of identified projects. Given the debtors' dire financial situation the loans were either medium-term (normally ten years), or relatively long-term (up to twenty years). Although the terms of the loan are such that the Bank itself ensures some profit from the transaction (the Bank charges an interest slightly above its own borrowing rate), the rates are substantially lower than the private sector. Nonetheless, these loans come with extensive conditions and monitoring, something which is new to the Bank's lending activities.

The World Bank Group is not composed solely of the IBRD and the IMF. Rather, its second component is the International Development Agency (IDA), established at a later date. IDA funding is not available to all World Bank member States, but only to those that have a very low GDP. Unlike normal IBRD loans, IDA loans involve a significant degree of concessional funding (i.e. their biggest component comes in the form of a grant that excludes any sort of repayment or interest) that is subject to long-term payment of up to forty years. As a result, the resources for IDA concessional lending cannot be derived from private sources, but from World Bank profits and grants from developed member States. Another component of the World Bank Group is the International Finance Corporation (IFC), which functions in more or less private banking terms and provides loans to private institutions and buys into equity shares thereof. In 1988 the Bank created through multilateral treaty the Multilateral Investment Guarantee Agency (MIGA), whose role is to minimise insurance premiums in the developing world (and thus render investment therein more attractive) by guaranteeing private sector investments against expropriation and other political risks. Finally, the World Bank Group was enhanced almost twenty years prior to MIGA with a facility that would place investors and host States on an equal par in respect of mutual disputes. This was achieved through the International Centre for the Settlement of Investment Disputes (ICSID). This chapter shall not be dealing with ICSID and MIGA to any serious degree. ICSID is examined in more detail in the chapter dealing with arbitration and dispute settlement.

As we have already noted the primary focus of the IBRD's attention in its first twenty-five years was on reconstruction. During this time the lack of capital in most countries outside North America meant that there were few funds for reconstruction projects. Thus, the Bank's development lending was geared towards projects that offered clearly quantifiable pecuniary returns and which would have otherwise been unattractive to private banks because the long horizon required for their implementation would have meant high interest rates. Eligible countries would either be unable to afford this type of funding from the private sector or the private sector itself would have found this unattractive for its own purposes.[3] By the early 1960s the so-called developed world was no longer in short demand for US dollars (the major trading currency of its time) and development projects (including infrastructure and industry) were booming. The picture, however, was not so bright in the developing world, which had just emerged from colonisation and lacked appropriate governance, fiscal and political organisation, internal stability and other factors conducive to good government. The inability of these newly emerged countries to raise sufficient capital rendered them ineligible for private financing, at least in respect of long-term infrastructure and development projects. It was at this juncture that the Bank repositioned itself from a development-related projects bank to a development agency. This involved funding of rural development, education and health, poverty alleviation and others. This role was necessarily assumed by the IDA through concessional funding, which was the only possible financing of projects in Africa and South Asia at the time.[4]

---

[3] M. Gavin, D. Rodrik, The World Bank in Historical Perspective, (1995) 85 *American Economic Review*, p. 329.

[4] C. L. Gilbert and D. Vines, "The World Bank: An Overview of Some Major Issues", in C. L. Gilbert and D. Vines (eds.), *The World Bank: Structure and Policies* Cambridge University Press, 2000, p. 15.

During the 1960s and 1970s the Bank's development policies had seemed to pay off and developing countries seemingly enjoyed foreign capital, whether by external investment or as a result of exports to the West. I purposely employ the word "seemingly" because the conditions for foreign direct investment (FDI) were often dictated by the World Bank and very rarely were in the best interests of the host State. Foreign investments, moreover, played along with the endemic corruption in the developing world, thus directly contributing to its financial annihilation and depletion of natural resources, which remained almost exclusively the principal target of FDI. Given that concession terms were very favourable to foreign investors, coupled with the imposition of few restrictions on repatriation of capital and the lack of labour-intensiveness in respect of natural resource extraction, little benefit accrued to the local populations. Thus, although developing countries suddenly found themselves with cash reserves as a result of the extractive and other natural resources/agriculture industry, they quickly fell prey to so-called Dutch disease. They were fooled into believing that cash was abundant and that it would flow their way indefinitely and so proceeded to expand both the public sector and their spending. When prices fell they had no savings to rely upon and soon their domestic and external debts spiralled out of control. The World Bank had certainly failed to put mechanisms in place to avert this predicament, believing that rampant FDI was the solution to all the problems facing developing countries. Cautious of its richest members' colonial past it refrained from warning or imposing conditions on developing countries out of fear of being branded a neo-imperialist institution.

By the early 1980s the debts accumulated by developing countries had become wholly unmanageable and it soon became clear that their governments had put no mechanisms in place to at least feed their people. The Ethiopian and other African famines made this abundantly clear. This period is thus dominated by the Bank's effort to minimise developing country debts and subsequently adjust their fiscal policies. By this time the debts of these countries to private banks risked bankrupting them, an event that would have had catastrophic consequences not only for the private banking industry itself but also for regional stability. The Bank ultimately devised a system of debt rescheduling that involved the imposition of fiscal policies as well as new loans in order to pay interest on existing debts. This can obviously be counted as disastrous because it meant a shift from developmental objectives.[5]

Obviously it is not sensible or even responsible to claim that an institution such as the IBRD is alone capable of preventing large-scale fiscal catastrophes

---

[5] The situation was saved as a result of the Brady Plan, named after US Treasury Secretary Nicholas Brady, who convinced private banks to accept lower value bonds guaranteed by the governments of developed States so that they could agree to lend fresh capital to developing countries. Ibid. p. 16.

around the globe, particularly since it lacks the authority to intervene. This is even more evident in the contemporary era in which we are witnesses to acute financial fluctuations from decade to decade. For example, the 1990s saw the rise of emerging markets, particularly in Asia, which later crashed spectacularly around 1997. This was gradually replaced by a global financial boom and an annual growth that that was unsustainable in the long run and which everyone described as a bubble waiting to burst. Yet, developed governments themselves consciously sustained this bubble, particularly in the real estate sector, giving little heed to environmental, job security and financial sustainability concerns. Although the Bank is unable to intervene in the financial affairs of States, its chief policy makers are derived from the States and as a result they bring their own policy perceptions to the Bank. The elusive "Washington Consensus" developed in the Bank in the 1990s did little to alleviate the bubble in the crumbling international financial architecture of the 2000s. Indeed, influenced by the world dominance of the only superpower, the USA, the Washington Consensus posited the neo-liberal mantra that the force of free markets and democratic governance is the only sure way of achieving growth and prosperity. The indicator of growth, which must necessarily reach a peak at some point, replaced well-being, which cannot be measured by any of the Bank's indicators. The World Bank, as indeed national governments and commercial banks themselves, closed their eyes to the inevitable bubble of toxic debts, unsustainable financial transactions that encompassed unmanageable risk that could only benefit the few. Inevitably, this brought about the collapse of financial markets in late 2008 that left millions jobless and caused a recession from which few see a light at the end of its tunnel. The 2008 crisis will be discussed in more detail at a later section of this chapter.

The Bank has been criticised manifold for its neo-liberal approach to trade and investment. This has had a tremendous impact on the lives of millions in the developing world and the Bank was forced in the past to adopt a rudimentary human rights policy to its development agenda.[6] Following the 2008 financial crisis not even the most ardent supporters of neo-liberalism are willing to adhere to the tenets of unrestricted capitalism. The IBRD's current program of action claims to be focused on two axes; the human dimension of poverty and development, albeit with greater emphasis on the former. This entails strengthening of universal education, increased health care (particularly in respect of infectious diseases such as HIV/AIDS), enhancement of local job markets and labour initiatives and others.[7] These initiatives do not necessarily translate into a total transformation of the IBRD or a radical

---

[6] *See* generally S. I. Skogly, *The Human Rights Obligations of the World Bank and the International Monetary Fund*, Cavendish Publishing, 2001.

[7] *See* Averting a Human Crisis During the Global Downturn: Policy Options from the World Bank's Human Development Network (2009), available at: <http://siteresources.worldbank.org/NEWS/Resources/AvertingTheHumanCrisis.pdf>.

change in policy. While the IBRD will seek from rich member States to dedicate a part of their GDP to fight global recession and poverty, there is no sign that it intends to change the way it lends money to developing nations. Perhaps there will be more IDA concessional lending and trust funds will be employed more and more in order to generate income for projects related to health, education, capacity-building and others,[8] but the IBRD will continue to provide preferential loans in respect of infrastructure development, as well as in other areas. It is expected, however, that the IBRD will seek to exert tighter control on its loans and grants and will demand greater civil society participation in order to enhance democracy building and avert corrupt practices. Despite the money that has been poured into Africa since the Bank began facilitating lending to African countries there has been little, or no improvement, to the continent as a whole. While much of this may be attributed to a proliferation of wars, the management of financial resources was very poor. Africa does not possess large infrastructure projects that will have lasting benefits (such as large highways linking different regions) but only project-specific infrastructure that is of no general use, such as oil pipelines that are useful only to the oil industry.

### 2.3. *The International Monetary Fund*

When the IMF's Articles of Agreement were first adopted the boundaries between itself and other intergovernmental financial institutions were clearly delineated. The IMF's role was focused on international monetary stability and balance-of-payments stability, but through the years it has undertaken sovereign debt restructuring in the developing world, regulation and supervision of banking and capital markets, as well as assuming the role of advisor to transition economies (particularly from communism to free market).[9] The objectives of the IMF are set out in Article I of its Articles of Agreement as follows:

i. To promote international monetary cooperation through a permanent institution which provides the machinery for consultation and collaboration on international monetary problems.
ii. To facilitate the expansion and balanced growth of international trade and to contribute thereby to the promotion and maintenance of high levels of employment and real income and to the development of productive resources of all members as primary objectives of economic policy.
iii. To promote exchange rate stability, to maintain orderly exchange arrangements among members and to avoid competitive exchange depreciation

[8] *See* I. Bantekas, *Trust Funds in International Law: Trustee Obligations of the UN and International Development Banks*, T M C Asser Press, 2009.

[9] *See* R. M. Lastra, *Legal Foundations of International Monetary Stability*, Oxford University Press, 2006, pp. 374–5.

iv. To assist in the establishment of a multilateral system of payments in respect of current transactions between members and in the elimination of foreign exchange restrictions which hamper the growth of world trade.
v. To give confidence to members by making the Fund's resources available to them under adequate safeguards, thus providing them with the opportunity to correct maladjustments in their balance of payments without resorting to measures destructive of national or international prosperity.
vi. In accordance with the above, to shorten the duration and lessen the degree of disequilibrium in the international balances of payments of members.

Typically, the IMF's contemporary resources are derived from four sources: a) member States generally provide assets in accordance with quotas prescribed by the IMF, on the basis of their economic size and financial characteristics. Quotas are denominated in Special Drawing Rights (SDRs), which is the IMF's unit of account.[10] The size of a member's quota is very important because it determines that member's voting rights in the Fund, as well as the maximum amount it can borrow from the Fund in the future; b) as a supplement to the Fund's quota-based resources, General Agreements to Borrow (GAB) were introduced, whereby eleven industrialised States, all members of the IMF, lent the Fund specified amounts of currencies with an interest consistent with prevailing market rates.[11] The IMF later adopted a decision giving itself power to call upon non-member States to make exceptional contributions where the inadequacy of the Fund's resources had the potential of "threatening the stability of the international monetary system".[12] However, the financial calamities that hit the global economy in successive waves from the late 1980s onwards necessitated the pooling of cash resources far in addition to the members' SDR and GAB contributions; c) as a result, and following the Mexican financial crisis of 1994, the IMF's Executive Board adopted a decision to establish the so-called New Arrangements to Borrow (NAB).[13] The NAB essentially creates a set of credit arrangements between the IMF and industrialised, predominantly, States with the purpose of doubling

[10] Quotas are divided into tranches, to which members have an automatic entitlement up to 25 percent of their initial contribution. The last three tranches are accessible following the negotiation of a stabilisation program and the adoption by the IMF of a stand-by arrangement under Art XXX(b) of its Articles of Agreement.

[11] IMF Executive Board Decision No 1289-(62/1) of 5 Jan 1962. *See* also J. Gold, "Symmetry as a Legal Objective of the International Monetary System," (1980) 12 *International Law & Politics*, p. 424. Lending to the IMF under the GAB is not perceived as contractual, but as a stand-by arrangement. This is reflected in the association agreement with Saudi Arabia. IMF Executive Board Decision No 7403-(83/73) of 20 May 1983.

[12] IMF Executive Board Decision No 7337-(83/37) of 24 Feb 1983, para. 21(b).

[13] IMF Executive Board Decision No 11428-(97/60) of 27 Jan 1997. Similar arrangements were not unknown prior to the NAB, however, since the IMF had in fact proceeded to create various facilities in the past to deal with particular economic woes of its members. Thus, the Compensatory Financing Facility (FCC) was aimed at addressing export instability in developing countries. For a survey of its operations, *see* G. Bird, *International Financial Policy and Economic Development: A Disaggregated Approach* Macmillan, 1987, pp. 43ff.

the amount of assets held by the IMF under the GAB.[14] Following the financial crisis of 2008 the IMF decided to enter into stand-by-arrangements with Iceland, Ukraine and Hungary in order to address short-term balance of payment shortages. These are not contracts,[15] however, but merely decisions of the IMF's executive board and are typically disbursed within a period of between twelve to twenty-four months. The repayment period is substantially longer and all such arrangements are subject to a range of conditionalities that are contingent on the design of comprehensive fiscal policies by the borrowing State. In the case of the three aforementioned borrowers this involved the adoption of a series of legislative measures, particularly with respect to the banking sector and fiscal management with an emphasis on addressing financial sector liquidity, and solvency, as well as the reduction of inflation.[16]

The fourth source of IMF financing is by means of special facilities that are organised in the form of trust funds and for which the Fund is acting as trustee, as is the case with the Poverty Reduction and Growth Facility (PRGF). The PRGF-ESF (Exogenous Shocks Facility) Trust borrows resources from central banks, governments, and official institutions generally at market-related interest rates and lends them on a pass-through basis to PRGF-eligible countries. The difference between the market-related interest rate paid to PRGF-ESF Trust lenders and the rate of interest of 0.5 percent per year paid by the borrowing members is financed by contributions from bilateral donors and the IMF's own resources.[17] The IMF has utilised trust funds in order to finance ongoing efforts to tackle poverty, underdevelopment and Third World debt by setting up a variety of trust vehicles and by combining its various initiatives therein. Examples include the Heavily Indebted Poor Countries (HIPC) Initiative, the Poverty Reduction and Growth Facility (PRGF) and the Exogenous Shocks Facility, all of which are inter-related. The IMF commenced a practice as early as 1976 of providing concessional financing to low-income countries through the establishment of a trust fund which loaned the profits generated from the sale of part of the IMF's holdings. The relative success of this trust vehicle was later followed by the establishment of a Structural

[14] *See* B. Rajagopal, *International Law from Below*, Cambridge University Press,2003, pp 127ff; World Bank Legal Memorandum (written by I. Shihata), Issues of Governance in Borrowing Members: The Extent of their Relevance under the Bank's Articles of Agreement (21 Dec 1990), SecM91-131, February 5, 1991.

[15] Under Art XXX(b) of the IMF Articles of Agreement, a stand-by-arrangement is defined as "a decision of the Fund by which a member is assured that it will be able to make purchases from the General Resources Account in accordance with the terms of the decision during a specified period and up to a specified amount". *See* J. Gold, *The Legal Character of the Fund's Stand-by-Arrangements and Why it Matters*, IMF Pamphlet Series No 35, 1980.

[16] IMF Set to Lend Ukraine 16.5 Billion, In Talks with Hungary, IMF Press Release (26 Oct 2008); IMF and Iceland Outline $2.1 Billion Plan, IMF Press Release (24 Oct 2008).

[17] *See* <http://www.imf.org/external/np/exr/facts/prgf.htm>.

Adjustment Facility (SAF) whose aim was to recycle resources loaned under the trust fund itself. A year later an Enhanced SAF came into being with the additional aim of putting in place stronger adjustment and reform measures.[18] In 1991 its name was changed even further and it became known as the Enhanced SAF to the Poverty Reduction Growth Facility and was later replaced by the Poverty Reduction Growth Facility.[19] The setting up of accounts (otherwise described as facilities) to achieve the purposes of trust funds were thus employed through the following instruments, among others: the Instrument to establish a Trust for Special PRGF Operations for the Heavily Indebted Poor Countries and Interim PRGF Subsidy Operations (Special PRGF Trust);[20] the Instrument to establish the Poverty Reduction and Growth Facility and Exogenous Shocks Facility Trust (PRGF-ESF Trust);[21] the Instrument to establish the Multilateral Debt Relief Initiative-I (MDRI-I Trust).[22]

Two issues in my opinion should provide a challenge for the IMF in the years to come. The first has to do with a more comprehensive and penetrative regime and enforcement of conditionalities on loans or grants offered to needy countries. The second has to do with global fiscal stabilisation and currency controls. Let us start with the latter. The public international law of currency exchanges has undergone dramatic changes in the course of the past one hundred years. The international gold standard was prevalent during the nineteenth century, whereby countries guaranteed the free convertibility of their currencies into gold at a fixed price. The gold standard was not predicated on any formal agreement and naturally crumbled in the wake of World War I.[23] During the inter-war years the world was witness to Germany's hyperinflation and the US stock market crash, all of which had an impact on global trading. It became readily evident that endogenous problems to national monetary and credit systems had a lasting effect on international trade and made foreign currency exchanges a volatile and risky enterprise. The Bretton Woods Conference imposed the so-called "par value" regime, also known as the gold-dollar standard. According to this system, the value of the currency of each member State was defined precisely in relation to gold or alternatively in terms

[18] IMF Executive Board Decision No 8757-(87/176) SAF/ESAF and Decision No 8759-(87/176) ESAF of 18 Dec 1987.

[19] The decision was endorsed by the IMF Interim Committee by Decision No EBS/99/193 of 14 Oct 1999. *See* P. Isard, "Globalisation and the International Financial System", Cambridge University Press, 2005, p. 90.

[20] IMF Decision 11436-(97/10) (4 Feb 1997), the most recent amendment to which was effected by Decisions 13588-(05/99) MDRI and 13590-(05/99) ESF (23 Nov 2005).

[21] IMF Decision 87-59-(87–176) ESAF (18 Dec 1987), the most recent amendment to which was effected by Decision 13689-(06/24) ESF (10 March 2006).

[22] IMF Decision 13588-(05/99) MDRI (23 Nov 2005).

[23] *See* P. de Grauwe, *International Money: Post-War Trends and Theories* Oxford University Press, 1990, pp. 11ff.

of the US dollar. Moreover, member States agreed to convert their currency into dollars at a fixed price.[24] It was only a matter of time before this system collapsed. For one thing, this agreement had no effect on private institutions that proceeded to trade in gold and currencies at market prices. Moreover, by the early 1960s gold reserves became insufficient in the wake of growing demand and by the end of that decade the gold-dollar ratio had declined to such a degree that the US was forced to suspend convertibility of dollars into gold.[25] The Second Amendment to the IMF's Articles of Agreement officially ended the par value regime and introduced floating exchange rates. This period was characterised by the rise of the dollar as the leading international currency and the vast majority of business transaction were predicated on the dollar (e.g. the price of oil). Increasingly, the currencies of other industrialised nations, such as the UK, Germany and Japan, were viewed by investors as solid, at least as compared to those of developing countries or nations prone to instability, but the lack of fixity rendered all currencies inherently risky because it is the nature of exchange rates to constantly fluctuate. Given that there exists no obligation on IMF member States to maintain exchange rate stability, some industrialised countries may find it expedient to devaluate their currencies in the era of globalisation with a view to lowering the costs of exports and thus to stimulate their labour markets and save jobs. This could otherwise be viewed as a form of market intervention or an indirect State aid, but is nonetheless permissible under the current international legal regime. The idea of a single international currency would have the effect of dissolving currency fluctuations and diminish all risks in that respect. It would also remove all direct and indirect market interventions. The introduction of the euro seems to have solved such problems – this is not to say that the euro did not cause many other problems particularly in relation to consumer spending - within the European Union, but it is true that the creation of a single international currency is no easy task and requires the constant agreement of all States and at all times. The organisation, logistics and politics for such a venture are absent at this time of human history.

The use of the US dollar as a commodity is, in my opinion, part of a wider problem which the IMF is unable and incompetent to solve. By making the US dollar the sole currency by which the price of crude oil is assessed, the USA has been able throughout the recent past to sell the dollar as a commodity. If the price of oil is measured against the dollar, then it makes psychological and financial sense to buy oil with dollars, particularly since the US is a superpower and thus this currency provides sound investment guarantees. This means, however, that the US assumes an unrivalled unilateral privilege to

[24] Lastra, *supra note* 9, pp. 356–9.
[25] Ibid. p. 360.

print dollars without any visible limitations when this currency is in short supply in the global markets. This is a privilege which the USA would not like to abandon or share with other nations. Anyone, thus, attempting to replace the dollar with another currency, in order to calculate the price of oil, runs undermining one of the most powerful financial tools of the US economy. This is exactly what the ex leader of Iraq, Saddam Hussein, tried to do, by assessing the price of oil by reference to the euro. He even tried to convince all Arab leaders to follow suit. Although not widely circulated for obvious reasons, it is believed that the single largest threat to the USA from the Hussein regime was not of course weapons of mass destruction or the need for Iraqi oil – the latter was certainly a bonus – but the financial threat emanating from the de-pegging of the dollar vis-a-vis the price of oil. This is an issue the IMF will have to face sooner or later, unless regional organisations or like-minded groupings undertake similar initiatives first, particularly the Arab League or the Organisation of the Islamic Conference (OIC).

The other issue that would strengthen international financial architecture and boost the finances of the Third World is that of conditionalities.[26] The IMF, as well as other international organisations, have employed economic conditionalities for some time in order to force recipient States to adhere to the terms of a loan or a grant. These vary considerably from contract to contract, but can penetrate the organisational and fiscal apparatus of the recipient State. The problem thus far is not so much the imposition of conditionalities between the Fund and developing countries, as is their diligent and uncompromising enforcement on the part of the Fund. In my opinion, the future of economic conditionalities depends on the means and methods of enforcement. Thus far they have been imposed by agreement but their implementation has been left to the recipient State and in extraordinary circumstances an external body has been charged with monitoring the country's adherence.[27]

---

[26] *See* generally, E. Denters, *Law and Policy of IMF Conditionality* Kluwer Law International 1996; the IMF adopted a new set of Guidelines on Conditionality in 2002. On 8 May 2003 the IMF adopted a note entitled "Operational Guidelines on the New Staff Conditionality Guidelines", as revised on 9 January 2006, available at: <http://www.imf.org/external/np/pp/eng/2006/010906g.pdf>.

[27] There is a long history behind this project. The Bank decided to lend Chad money in order to construct pipelines that would ship its meagre oil findings to the ocean through Cameroon. The Bank imposed a number of conditionalities, including the establishment of oversight committees and an obligation to distribute royalties to specific social programs. The government of Chad violated its obligations numerous times in the course of the project's life span. In late 2008 the World Bank formally announced its withdrawal from the project on account of improprieties perpetrated by the government of Chad. *See* Press Release No 2009/073/AFR. Available at: <http://web.worldbank.org/wbsite/external/countries/africaext/chadextn/0,,contentmdk:21894530~menuPK:349894~pagePK:2865066~piPK:2865079~theSitePK:349862,00.html>. The most significant accusation has been the violation of human rights by Chad, private firms and the indifference of the Bank. See Amnesty International, Contracting Out of Human Rights: The Chad-Cameroon Pipeline Project (September 2005),

This has proven ineffective, particularly as regards undemocratic regimes. The IMF should rethink its conditionalities policy, particularly as regards enforcement. To render the relevant process more efficient and legitimate, all the entities within the World Bank Group must strive to standardise this new conditionalities policy; this may well involve the involvement of the UN, if relevant consensus can be achieved. This policy reform should be premised on the following considerations. Where conditionalities do not work, or are ineffective, this is the result of mal-administration and enforcement by the recipient State. Equally, it is by now clear that external monitoring mechanisms do not possess binding powers and their role is only consultative. Moreover, while civil society is encouraged through various processes to participate in the projects financed its role is minimal and the respective governments are hostile as to their role. As a result, it is not difficult to see where the problem and the solution both lie. The World Bank must be able to co-manage the projects financed together with the recipient government. It must possess a deciding voice in both management and administration and should itself, through an agent, monitor the terms of the conditionalities. It must encourage and involve civil society in this process and must give the impression from the outset that grant or concessional loan agreements with the Bank constitute an erosion of sovereignty. This erosion, if at all possible, must be guided by a rights-based approach and should not have financial objectives as its primary targets.

### 2.4. *Regional Financial Institutions*

In this section we shall be discussing the role of international development banks as well as that of other regional financial institutions that although do not provide loans to developing countries, or other financial aid, they are, however, instrumental in the new international financial architecture. As to the latter, this includes informal international groupings whose role is to formulate common regulatory standards. Typical examples are the Basle Committee on Banking Supervision, the International Organisation for Securities Commissions (IOSCO) and others.

It was only following the Asian crisis that the Financial Stability Forum (FSF)[28] was established in 1999[29] as a result of a report that was commissioned by the G-7 with a view to devising a comprehensive framework to promote

---

available at: <http://www.amnesty.org/en/library/asset/POL34/012/2005/en/76f5b921-d4bf-11dd-8a23-d58a49c0d652/pol340122005en.pdf>.

[28] Available at: <http://www.fsforum.org>.

[29] *See* 'Communiqué of G-7 Finance Ministers and Central Bank Governors' February 20 1999, available at:,http://www.fsforum.org/attachments/g7pressrelease_on_establishment_ofFSF.pdf>.

international financial stability.[30] Its purported aims are to assess vulnerabilities affecting the international financial system, to identify and oversee actions needed to address these vulnerabilities, and to improve co-ordination and information exchange among the various authorities responsible for financial stability. Its composition includes G-7 central banks, supervisory authorities and treasury departments. Moreover, it is comprised of representatives from each of the international financial institutions (namely the IMF, IBRD, OECD and BIS), international supervisory agencies and from two BIS committees of central bank experts. One of the recurrent themes throughout this chapter is the lack of supervision and the catastrophic results in the wake of a financial crisis – in most cases it is these very activities that cause financial crises. In the case at hand, the inadequate supervision of banks in Asia resulted in the accumulation of large balance-sheet exposure and unhedged foreign currency exposure, which highlighted the vulnerability of these banks and the complete lack of prudence. The role of the FSF is one of standard-setting through the adoption of twelve global standards for the well-functioning of financial systems.[31] Much like other non-binding principles, no financial institution can afford to ignore them.[32]

Let us now turn to the role and function of regional development banks. Much like the World Bank Group their focus is naturally on development at the regional level, whether to complement the IBRD's efforts or to make new inroads. The Asian Development Bank (ADB) was set up in 1966 and is comprised of 66 member States, not all of which are derived from that continent.[33] Indeed, a good number of European States are members and are its most significant contributors. Following the worst of the Asian financial crisis in 1997 the Asian economy made a remarkable recovery and the pace of growth was unprecedented. Indeed, a record number of people rose above the US$ 1 a-day poverty line, but this did not last very long. Currently, half of Asia's population survives on less than US$ 2 a-day, while 15% of the population of its least developed countries lives in abject poverty. The Asian economy is good at distorting the image of its own poverty by masking it behind the figures of growth that only benefit a small portion of the population, the benefits of which never seem to trickle down to the masses. Thus, in the People's Republic of China

[30] *See* 'International Cooperation and Coordination in the Area of Financial Market Supervision and Surveillance' Report by Hans Tietmeyer, President of the Deutsche Bundesbank February 11, 1999. Available at: <http://www.fsforum.org/publications/publication_33_56.html>.

[31] Available at: <http://www.fsforum.org/compendium/key_standards_for_sound_financial_system.html>.

[32] *See* M. Giovanoli, "A New Architecture for the Global Financial System: Legal Aspect of International Financial Standard Setting" in M. Giovanoli (ed.), *International Monetary Law: Issues for the New Millennium* Oxford University Press, 2000.

[33] *See* generally, D. Knapman, *Reforms in the Pacific: An Assessment of the Asian Development Bank's Assistance for Reform Programs in the* Pacific, ADB Press, 1999.

those living on less than US$ 2 a-day is 452 million, while in India this figure is 868 million.[34] Growth figures are essentially irrelevant when read against these grim statistics. In its 2020 Strategy, therefore, the ADB placed its emphasis on three inter-related areas: inclusive growth, environmentally sustainable growth and regional integration. Inclusive growth requires sustainable growth and the creation of economic opportunities. This is particularly crucial given that the population of Asia is set to increase by almost half a billion by 2020. It is imperative that access to these economic opportunities be universal through strategic planning. This can only come about by improving overall governance, removing market-resistant obstacles and especially by expanding human capacities. This is something that countries like India have failed to invest in. The expansion of human capacities requires access to universal and free education, especially for the disadvantaged, access to health and basic social protections. These States must also improve the poor's access to markets and basic productive assets, as well as strengthen social safety nets. It is also imperative that social equality be strengthened so that women and girls are not excluded from the aforementioned.[35] There is clear danger in Asia, particularly as a result of widespread poverty, uncontrolled growth and population expansion, that the strain on its natural environment will be destructive in the years to come. It is no secret that there is little concern among relevant States about the long-term effects of environmental degradation.[36] As a result, the ADB commits itself in the context of its 2020 Strategy to fund projects that conform to environmental standards and promote sustainable development.[37] The ADB attempts to tackle the endemic problems of Asia, poverty and under-development, by focusing on the systemic failures behind them. Its drivers of change are predicated on the following axes: private sector development and private sector operations; good governance and capacity development; gender equity; knowledge solutions; partnerships.[38]

The African Development Bank (AfDB) follows in the footsteps of its Asian counterpart.[39] The situation in Africa may be somewhat differentiated by the fact that overall growth is not as high as in Asia, given that the Asian economy is far more industrialised, and that climatic conditions in Africa, particularly desertification, are exacerbating the continent's fragile ecosystem and are contributing towards the first generation of environmental refugees.

---

[34] ADB, *Strategy 2020: The Long-Term Strategic Framework of the Asian Development Bank 2008–2020* (ADB, 2008) [*ADB Report*], p. 6.

[35] Ibid. pp. 11–2.

[36] J. A. Boyd, From Rio to Johannesburg: A Review of Asian Development Bank Environmental Practice and Policy, (2002) 6 *Singapore Journal of International and Comparative Law*, p. 723.

[37] *ADB Report, supra note* 34, p. 12.

[38] Ibid. pp. 14–6.

[39] *See* E. P. English, The *African Development Bank* Rienner Publishers, 1996.

Certainly there are other parameters at play, such as the plethora of internal armed conflicts that are not encountered to such a degree in Asia. Equally, population growth in Africa is no way near the figures discussed for Asia. Finally, Africa has suffered from deadly famines far more than Asia and this is something that all relevant actors working for Africa are acutely aware of in their development agendas.[40] Nonetheless, the problems are similar. Poverty is endemic as is environmental degradation and investment in human capacities is poor as a result of bad governance, corruption, lack of market opportunities, inadequate infrastructure etc. The African Development Bank's Strategy for 2012 is aimed at poverty reduction (particularly through equitable growth, opportunity and economic integration); focus on infrastructure, governance, private sector operations, higher education and technology and vocational training; support for regional integration and support to fragile States; mainstream gender, climate change and knowledge management more fully in all its operations; contribute to broader human development in least developed countries, especially through the water[41] and sanitation sector; build new partnerships, particularly with the private sector; and finally to provide competitive services to its clients.[42]

One of the issues that emerged from the AfDB latest policy report is that the Bank must focus far more tightly on selected projects and themes, rather than be a general provider of aid.[43] This is crucial and a lesson for aid harmonisation generally. The AfDB is only the seventh largest development aid organisation in Africa, accounting for only 3–4% of development funds in the continent. If it is to have any impact in its operations it is required to focus its operations on exclusive themes.[44] This necessitates a great degree of responsible governance, prioritisation and collaboration with other development institutions, development banks and private financial institutions. Moreover, it is

[40] On 24 July 2008, the AfDB Boards of Directors, through Resolution B/BD/2008/14 Rev.1–F/BD/2008/09/Rev. 1, approved the Africa Food Crisis Response (AFCR). The AFCR provides a framework for accelerated support to regional member countries affected by increased food prices. Its interventions are to contribute to these countries' efforts to reduce the risk for African populations of increased poverty in the short term and to ensure sustainable food security in the medium to long term.

[41] This is a particularly acute problem for Africa, for which a number of extensive initiatives have been undertaken. *See* AfDB Fund, Policy for Integrated Water Resources Management (April 2000), available at: <http://www.afdb.org/fileadmin/uploads/afdb/Documents/Policy-Documents/IWRMP-EN-E%26P.V02-APL.25.2001TW.pdf>.

[42] *AFDB Group, Medium-Term Strategy 2008–2012 (AFDB, 2008)*, p. 18.

[43] Ibid. p. 11.

[44] This is all the more important in the current financial climate because prior to the G20 London Summit in early 2009, a Statement by African nations pointed out that the AfDB does not have the necessary capital to finance important projects in the continent. By way of example, seven large infrastructure projects that had been approved were frozen by the Bank. *See* Report from the Committee of African Finance Ministers and Central Bank Governors, Impact of the Crisis on African Economies: Sustaining Growth and Poverty Reduction, 17 March 2009 (on file with author).

significant that all interested actors working in the field of international development and poverty reduction join forces. The only visible agenda towards this aim concerns the Millennium Development Goals and the Paris Declaration on Aid Effectiveness.[45] These, along with the Monterey Consensus and the Doha Declaration on Financing for Development[46] urge interested parties to coordinate their efforts but unless development aid (whether loans or concessional funding) is synchronised and compartmentalised, much of this effort will not reach its full potential. One of the problems in this respect is the institutional obligation of development banks towards their clients (i.e. the sponsoring States) to which they must demonstrate results. Thus, a project partly financed by a multiplicity of banks does not verily reflect the role of bank A as opposed to bank B. Furthermore, a donor may ask himself what is the purpose of lending to a smaller development bank when projects are undertaken by a group thereof. These are issues that have to be resolved internally and to which this chapter does not offer any solutions or recommendations.

### 2.5. *The 2008 Global Financial Crisis*

The September 2008 global financial crisis is not exceptional in the recent history of capital markets. We have already alluded to the 1997 Asian financial crisis. One would have thought that given previous experiences the 2008 meltdown should have been avoided. Although it is not the place of this chapter to explain in detail the financial and policy causes behind the 2008 events, it suffices to argue that the reasons behind the global effect of the crisis are the following: a) national economies do not function in isolation, but are dependent on each other for their operation and survival; b) international monetary institutions do not yield sufficient control over national financial institutions; c) private banks are able to function with relatively little control in respect of how they handle their assets and the mode of their transactions with their customers; d) private banking is ultimately beyond of the realm of international law and possesses a sovereignty of its own; e) we have relatively little, or no, knowledge as to how the financial operations of one institution can affect the finances of other institutions and thereafter bring about a domino effect.

What is of interest in this chapter in relation to the 2008 crisis is the response of the international community and the role of international law and regulation. If the IMF were to undertake a lead role in respect of regulating

[45] Paris Declaration on Aid Effectiveness, Ownership, Harmonisation, Alignment, Results and Mutual Accountability (28 Feb – 3 March 2005).

[46] Adopted on 2 December 2008 as a follow-up on the Monterey Consensus, available at: <http://www.un.org/esa/ffd/doha/documents/Doha_Declaration_FFD.pdf>.

international banking it would either have to amend its Articles of Agreement or come to some sort of *ad hoc* understanding. In practice, the recent experience of the IMF demonstrates that it will rely on a combination of both; i.e. reliance on its own institutional law, applicable under *sui generis* circumstances. Thus, following the near-bankruptcy of three European nations following the 2008 crisis the IMF decided to enter into stand-by-arrangements with them, namely Iceland, Ukraine and Hungary in order to address short-term balance of payment shortages. These are not contractual arrangements but simply decisions of the IMF's executive board they typically disbursed within a period of between twelve to twenty-four months. The repayment period is substantially longer and all such arrangements are subject to a range of conditionalities that are contingent on the design of comprehensive fiscal policies by the borrowing State. In the case of the three aforementioned borrowers this involved the adoption of a series of legislative measures, particularly with respect to the banking sector and fiscal management with an emphasis on addressing financial sector liquidity, and solvency, as well as the reduction of inflation.[47] This is just an indicative measure of the IMF, which was thereafter followed by more concrete measures following the London G20 summit that will be analysed in more detail later on in this section. However, apart from the fiscal obligations of IMF member States, it is clear that financial crises are not borne solely from governmental policies, but from the actions of private actors.[48] As a result, the IMF can only play a limited role in respect of international financial stability because it is unable to control or play any substantial part in the operations of the private banking sector, albeit this can be accomplished through measures imposed on borrowing States.[49] In practice,

[47] IMF Set to Lend Ukraine 16.5 Billion, In Talks with Hungary, IMF Press Release (26 Oct 2008); IMF and Iceland Outline $2.1 Billion Plan, IMF Press Release (24 Oct 2008).

[48] *See* G20, Working Group 1: Enhancing Sound Regulation and Strengthening Transparency, Final Report, 25 March 2009, pp iii-iv, which cites as the underlying reasons for the 2008 financial crisis the trading of innovative over-the-counter financial products, particularly those aimed at transferring credit risk, notably credit default swaps and collateralized debt obligations. No one predicted their popularity and financial institutions generally failed to properly manage and monitor risks to liquidity in the event that these markets froze. These unregulated pools of capital were injected with more cash by establishing off-balance sheets and structured investment vehicles. These lacked minimum capital buffers or adequate liquidity plans. In addition, the risks they were exposed to, including maturity mismatches, were often misunderstood. Risk management during this time failed to keep track of these innovations. Eventually the increase in asset prices could not be sustained. Delinquencies translated into price decreases on U.S. sub-prime mortgage-backed securities, which in turn produced losses for investors and led to margin calls for leveraged sub-prime asset holders. As the market turmoil spread across a wide range of markets for structured and securitized products, increased risk aversion, reduced liquidity, and concerns about the soundness of major financial institutions fed on each other. Many institutions experienced significant balance sheet pressures, which led to a tightening of lending standards with adverse effects on real economic growth.

[49] The best that government reports expect from the IMF is immediate crisis control, particularly through balance of payments lending to developing countries and increased

this has never amounted to any degree of control by the IMF. The IMF itself has not made any concrete radical proposals as to how it can partake in global policy making beyond unilateral measures by afflicted States. Although it is apt to identify the reasons for the financial meltdown and predict its reversal, it leaves the availability of responses to each country.[50] That is exactly why the London G20 Summit in early 2009 identified measures, which do not implicate the existing international financial architecture, that involve better and tighter regulation of the private financial sector.

One may debate for ever as to the anticipated policy of international financial institutions, but it is only in real life situations that fiction may be distinguished from fact. Following the 2008 financial crisis it soon became evident that besides powerful regional economic blocks, such as the EU, countries were not willing to take strong collective action, particularly where this concerned their finances and the regulation of their private finance sectors. This was even true in the EU, wherein although it was agreed that the European Central Bank was to take some measures to alleviate the economic strain and decrease its interest rates, all other measures were of a unilateral character.[51] There is a lesson to be drawn from this and it is something which should permeate this chapter. Despite the inter-connectedness of the global economy and our global village created by globalisation, no country is ready to abandon its finances to the world or the community of nations. The loss of business, the loss of investment and the ensuing loss of trust in that system, as well as of jobs are enough to bring down the country's structures, whether these are of a social, security or other nature. Each country decides during a global crisis how best to turn its fortunes around. The UK government, for example, focused on reviving the crippled bank sector and injected huge amounts of cash and partly-privatised the ailing banks.[52] The USA, *inter alia*, introduced a series of tax cuts for lower earning populations so that consumer spending can be stimulated and struggling families can better cope through the crisis.[53] There is no reason why the EU or other European countries would create a pool of money to augment British efforts, since countries do not necessarily suffer in the same way and the efforts of the UK government, for example, did not aim to alleviate in any way the financial woes of other nations, other than its own. In this sense, we are not as globalised as we would like to think. This is further attested by the fact that in the aftermath of the global crisis the EU has

---

surveillance. *See* CRS Report for Congress, The Global Financial Crisis: The Role of the IMF (30 Oct 2008), available at: <http://assets.opencrs.com/rpts/RS22976_20081030.pdf>.

[50] IMF, World Economic Outlook October 2000: Financial Stress, Downturns and Recoveries, available at: <http://www.imf.org/external/pubs/ft/weo/2008/02/pdf/text.pdf>.

[51] EU Council, Presidency Conclusions, Doc CONLC 4 (14368/08) 16 Oct 2008.

[52] *See* <http://www.londonsummit.gov.uk/en/summit-aims/economic-crisis/UK-response/>.

[53] American Recovery and Reinvestment Tax Act of 2009.

taken more concrete steps to avert the flow of illegal migrants to Europe who are in search of employment.

Eventually, however, the strong of the world cannot view their own financial woes in isolation from the global community, because of the interconnectedness of markets, for which a relatively global health is of the utmost importance. What was needed was restoration of trust and sufficient liquidity to stimulate trade. Thus, when the G20 met in London in early 2009 they were forced to create stimuli to invigorate global markets and increase spending. This required significant funds of its own. It was thus agreed to make available $850 billion to the IMF and multilateral development banks in order to support growth in vulnerable countries, particularly so that they can meet their counter-cyclical spending, bank recapitalisation, balance of payments, debt payments and others. In particular, it was agreed that the IMF make available bilateral financing from members up to $250 billion; it incorporates the immediate financing from members into an expanded and more flexible New Arrangements to Borrow, which will include other G20 countries, and be increased by up to $500 billion; asked the IMF to consider market borrowing; doubling of the IMF's concessional lending capacity for low income countries and a doubling of access limits; in addition, the G20 agreed to support a general allocation of SDRs equivalent to $250 billion to increase global liquidity, $100 billion of which will go directly to emerging market and developing countries. In respect of other multilateral development banks (MDB) they agreed a substantial increase in lending of $100 billion including to low income countries, to a total of around $300 billion over the next three years; full and exceptional use of MDB balance sheets, to create further capacity for lending to meet crisis needs; a 200 per cent general capital increase at the Asian Development Bank and reviews of the need for capital increases at the Inter-American Development Bank, the African Development Bank and the European Bank for Reconstruction and Development; actions by the MDBs to leverage private capital more effectively, including through the use of guarantees, bond insurance and bridging finance; and the new IFC Global Trade Liquidity Pool which should provide up to $50 billion of trade liquidity support over the next three years, with significant co-financing from the private sector (as part of the global effort to ensure the availability of at least $250 billion of trade finance until 2011).[54]

What is of greater significance is the regulation of the private sector by the international community. Toxic debt was accumulated by greedy banks and the same is true of hedge funds, pyramidal schemes and other investment portfolios that wiped out the life's savings of pensioners and vulnerable populations.

[54] *See* G20, Declaration on Delivering Resources through the International Financial Institutions, London Summit, 2 April 2009, available at: <http://www.londonsummit.gov.uk/resources/en/PDF/annex-ifi>.

To acknowledge the failure of the free market in this respect is slightly short of a revolution for capitalism. Yet, it is absolutely true. It is therefore of no surprise that the G20 focused the majority of their action and the reshaping of the international financial architecture not on the basis of existing multilateral institutions but with a view to reforming and regulating private financing. This does not mean that new institutions were not made available. Thus, following the Washington Action Plan the leaders of the G20 Summit in London agreed to "re-invent" the Financial Stability Forum (FSF)" they had earlier created and replace it with a new and more powerful institution, the Financial Stability Board (FSB). Its role is to act as an early warning mechanism in respect of international financial crises, so as to assess vulnerabilities before they arise. In this respect, it is mandated to undertake joint strategic reviews of the policy development work of the international Standard Setting Bodies to ensure their work is timely, coordinated, focused on priorities and addressing gaps. This is to be achieved through collaboration and co-ordination with the IMF and central banks.[55] This collaboration, however, remains hortatory, as is suggested by the language of the Declaration and is dependent on agreement between the two institutions.

The G20 further committed to tightening their controls on private entities in respect of risky transactions. Whereas it was agreed that the capital buffers of States should be allowed to decline in order to stimulate spending, private buffers above regulatory minima should be increased and the quality of the capital enhanced. Moreover, it was agreed that risk-based capital requirements should be supplemented with a simple, transparent, non-risk based measure which is internationally comparable, properly takes into account off-balance sheet exposures and can help contain the build-up of leverage in the banking system. The G20 agreed that prudential regulatory standards should be re-designed and that all countries gradually adopt the Basel II capital framework.[56] In particular, the G20 countries committed to realising this regulation as follows:

- we will amend our regulatory systems to ensure authorities are able to identify and take account of macro-prudential risks across the financial system including in the case of regulated banks, shadow banks, and private pools of capital to limit the build up of systemic risk.
- we will ensure that our national regulators possess the powers for gathering relevant information on all material financial institutions, markets, and instruments in order to assess the potential for their failure or severe stress to contribute to systemic risk. This will be done in close

[55] Declaration on Strengthening the Financial System, London Summit, 2 April 2009, available at: <http://www.londonsummit.gov.uk/resources/en/PDF/annex-strengthening-fin-sysm>.
[56] Ibid.

coordination at international level in order to achieve as much consistency as possible across jurisdictions;

- hedge funds or their managers will be registered and will be required to disclose appropriate information on an ongoing basis to supervisors or regulators, including on their leverage, necessary for assessment of the systemic risks that they pose individually or collectively. Where appropriate, registration should be subject to a minimum size. They will be subject to oversight to ensure that they have adequate risk management. We ask the FSB to develop mechanisms for cooperation and information sharing between relevant authorities in order to
- ensure that effective oversight is maintained where a fund is located in a different jurisdiction from the manager. We will, cooperating through the FSB, develop measures that implement these principles by the end of 2009.
- supervisors should require that institutions which have hedge funds as their counterparties have effective risk management. This should include mechanisms to monitor the funds' leverage and set limits for single counterparty exposures.
- we will promote the standardisation and resilience of credit derivatives markets, in particular through the establishment of central clearing counterparties subject to effective regulation and supervision. We call on the industry to develop an action plan on standardisation by autumn 2009.[57]

The Declaration further imposed limits on private firms' compensation packages to their directors and called for the standardisation of accounting practices. Finally, it called for the removal of tax havens and bank secrecy. It is not at all certain how the last two issues are to be addressed. The Financial Action Task Force (FATF) of the OECD has for some time highlighted the problem posed by tax havens and loose banking regulation, particularly in small-island States in the Caribbean and elsewhere and has for this purpose drawn up a black list with such jurisdictions, which it has termed as non-coopeative (NCCT).[58] The dangers posed by these countries are manifold, although not always visible. For one thing, loose banking regulation and complete bank secrecy, particularly under the circumstances operated by the banking authorities of these uncooperative States, gives rise to money

---

[57] Ibid..

[58] *See* the latest report by the FATF, entitled Annual Review of Non-Cooperative Countries and Territories, 2006–07: Eighth NCCT Review (12 October 2007), available at: <http://www.fatf-gafi.org/dataoecd/14/11/39552632.pdf>. It should be noted that the FATF stressed in its latest report that all former NCCT countries had made significant efforts towards eliminating money laundering and terrorist financing loopholes in their legislation and were no longer classified as NCCT.

laundering,[59] terrorist financing activities[60] and tax evasion. They, therefore, provide a safe venue for disguising illicit proceeds from crimes committed across the globe. These countries have been the target of very mild unilateral sanctions from directly affected States, but the assets received as a result of their banking practices has not permitted these sanctions to have any lasting impact upon their national economies. Another issue that came up in the aftermath of the 2008 financial crisis is that it is hard enough to monitor the transactions of highly regulated financial institutions in the developed world, let alone those for which there exist no available data. Hence, if international authorities and States are to monitor the global economy with a view to averting a new financial crisis it is important that all countries play along with the same rules. In the current financial climate it is therefore imperative that even a single exception may turn out to be catastrophic. On the other hand, I am not oblivious to the fact that one of the reasons the G20 block has been arguing for the elimination of tax havens concerns the loss of vast amounts of tax revenues which these countries would have otherwise collected from their taxpayers. If this aggressive G20 policy is maintained with the same vigour in the foreseeable future it is not unlikely for more severe measures to be imposed against tax havens and a State's own nationals, such that would render trading therein redundant.

These developments clearly demonstrate that change is certainly in the horizon and that the impact of these decisions will impact on both the private and the public sector. Certainly, many of these measures need to be translated into legislative action by the countries concerned and in most circumstances this will require an overhaul of corporate governance and company laws. On the other hand, central banks and multilateral financial institutions, if they are to play any overarching part in this affair, must coordinate their efforts in line with the G20 Declarations. The next and final section of this chapter will provide a framework of things to come in respect of the future of the Bretton Woods system. The reader will have by now, however, gleaned a pretty good picture of my assessment of the Bretton Woods institutions.

### 2.6. *The Greek Public Deficit and the Eurozone Crisis of 2010*

By late 2009 it became known that Greece's public deficit had spiralled to almost 30 billion euros. This was the result of increased and unnecessary public spending, years of poor fiscal management and corruption. The unveiling

[59] *See* FATF Forty Recommendations (as amended 22 October 2004), available at: <http://www.fatf-gafi.org/dataoecd/7/40/34849567.PDF>.

[60] I. Bantekas, "The International Law of Terrorist Financing", (2003) 97 *American Journal of International Law*, p. 315.

of the crisis coincided with the assumption of power by a new government in the end of 2009. Although the deficit was projected as being much lower than the aforementioned number it turned out that the outgoing government had grossly manipulated its figures and the data submitted to the Commission and the European Central Bank. This was a particularly difficult situation not only for Greece but more importantly for the Eurozone. As far as Greece was concerned its preoccupation was to pay public salaries and pensions and service its debt to creditors. In both cases the currency of payment is the euro over which it has no control; thereby being forced to borrow from foreign lenders. However, because of the poor state of its economy its borrowing status was severely downgraded to junk status and hence it was either unable to borrow or was alternatively offered excessively high interest rates. The only viable and credible solution was for the member States of the EU to offer EU funds at non-commercial market rates and back the Greek economy through solid guarantees. Such a development did not occur straight away, principally because of political consternation spearheaded by Germany. Chancellor Merkel's position was that since Greece got itself into a dire financial situation through its own fault it would have to come out of it on its own. Perhaps a different approach may have been adopted had the whole affair not coincided with German regional elections, in respect of which the Chancellor was forced to abide with local opinion – bolstered no doubt by the local press – that Germany should not bail out Greece at the expense of the German tax-payer. Thus, while all powerful Eurozone countries rallied around Greece with a view to finding an acceptable formula, Germany procrastinated in the hope that any outcome would be achieved after its elections and with a financial gain for itself.

As events began to unfold it became obvious that Greece's failure had a domino effect on the euro as well as other economies in the Eurozone. By late May 2010 France, Italy and Spain had declared huge public deficits – although unlike Greece these nations possess a strong industrial sector and significant export capacity – and the threat of contagion was looming. Not only had the euro weakened – which is not altogether a negative development as far as the EU's export capacity was concerned – but there was now a real danger that 300 billion euros worth of Greek government bonds would become useless for their purchasers. It was at this point that fundamental questions were asked about the solidarity of the Union, particularly in times of crises, such as the one at hand. The imminent risk of contagion signalled two possible outcomes: either assist Greece or remove her from the Eurozone, although the latter would not have immediately solved the EU's woes because former Greek government bonds were guaranteed by the European Central Bank.

Given that things were at breaking point Germany belatedly realised that providing financial relief to Greece was crucial for avoiding contagion and upsetting the markets and so a deal was hurriedly agreed. This involved distinct bilateral agreements between Greece and the wealthier members of the European Union, including Germany which provided the biggest loan,[61] as well as an additional agreement with the IMF, which carried with it an obligation to undertaken deep structural adjustments upon the Greek public sectors and its economy in general.[62] At the very least this deal rendered it certain that the Greek economy would not collapse and the risk of insolvency was eliminated. Yet, it should not be thought that the terms of the arrangement were wholly favourable for Greece. On the one hand, it turned out that the interest for borrowing was significantly higher than that with which other EU member States borrowed – although obviously less than commercial rates – which seems to indicate that despite the crisis the lending countries intended to make some inevitable profit from their lending of Greece. Secondly, the European institutions did not even discuss their own share of responsibility for the state of the Greek economy. After all, supposedly all the financial data procured by Greece to the Commission was checked, validated and rubber stamped by the EU institutions and hence the Union should have been well aware of the situation even if Greece had fabricated much of the relevant data. Finally, the austerity measures agreed to be adopted by the government – which in my opinion were to a large degree necessary, particularly the decrease in public spending – did little to cater for the weaker classes and pensioners, whose income was slashed by about 30%, despite the IMF-EU agreement's stipulation that the more vulnerable classes would not suffer any adverse consequences.

This is by no means a straightforward arrangement and one has to wait and see if it will be emulated in the case of other faltering Eurozone economies. One would have expected that the group of the wealthiest countries in the world would have been able to concoct a plan for saving one of their own without the need of the IMF and yet this has proven not to be the case. In fact, their procrastination led to the infiltration of speculators – guised as investors – whose aim was to downgrade the Greek economy to such a degree that it could no longer received any viable guarantees from the EU that it would have to resort to borrowing from commercial lenders at extortionate rates. Following the debacle the EU announced that it will be examining how to avert similar situations in the future and exclude speculators from crises of this nature.

---

[61] The total combined loan amounted to 110 billion euros. See Joint Statement on Greece by EU Commissioner Olli Rehn and IMF Managing Director Dominique Strauss-Kahn, Press Release 10/177 (2 May 2010).

[62] The IMF in fact contributed 30 billion euros by means of a stand-by-arrangement, 5,5 billion of which through a fast track procedure. See <http://www.imf.org/external/pubs/ft/survey/so/2010/new050910a.htm>

### 2.7. *Reform of the Bretton Woods Institutions*

The reform, if any, of the Bretton Woods institutions is wholly dependent on a visible deficiency in its operation. The World Bank Group has certainly demonstrated numerous deficiencies over the years, but these have been exacerbated as a result of the recent financial crisis. Is this, however, enough for a complete overhaul of these institutions? If our knowledge of reform of international institutions is anything to go about, two major reforms have taken place in the last seventy years; the creation of the United Nations (UN) through the replacement of the League of Nations and the transformation of the GATT into the World Trade Organisation (WTO). As regards the UN, its creation was necessitated by the absolute failure of the League of Nations in fulfilling its primary task, which was the maintenance of international peace and security. The rise of the WTO, on the other hand, was a direct result of the inadequate and antiquated system brought about by a system that predated the fall of communism and globalisation. Are any of the two reasons associated with the new institutions (i.e. the UN and the WTO) relevant to the deficiencies associated with the World Bank? There seems to be no pressing reason for a total overhaul of the World Bank, despite the plethora of issues that arose in connection to the 2008 global financial crisis. Moreover, even if the Bretton Woods institutions were to give way to something new, this new institution would have to be able to deliver something completely new in a way that definitively addresses the current global financial situation and which the existing international financial architecture is unable to do. I do not believe that anything new is feasible or on the horizon. Moreover, given that an overhaul to an existing system presupposes a change of power politics as a result of other political transformations, no such transformations have taken place that would necessitate an overhaul.

Nonetheless, this does not mean that the World Bank Group does not require some change in order to adapt to the new global financial environment.[63] The question is what type of change and how much? One should remember that significant inter-governmental institutions such as the UN, NATO, the WTO and the World Bank Group are predicated on the element of control which powerful nations want to retain and perhaps increase. Power politics thus constitute a significant component of these organisations. As a result, when we discuss the World Bank's institutional change we must primarily take into consideration the prospect of power imbalances and the desire of the powerful members to give up, if any, their prerogatives within the organisation. This is the basis of the ensuing discussion.

---

[63] When commentators discuss the issue of World Bank reform they focus on policy, rather than institutional reform. See A. Paloni, M. Zanardi, The IMF, World Bank and Policy Reform Routledge, 2007.

The G20 recently put forward their propositions for a so-called "reform" of the IMF and the World Bank more generally. This is a powerfully emotive word, but it must not be thought that its use conveys all those meanings typically associated with it. More specifically, the plans for the reform of the IMF centre around the expansion of its financial capacity and the increase in its members' quotas and SDR rights, as well as the more meaningful inclusion in its decision-making centres of less developed States.[64] This is hardly an overhaul of the IMF, as compared to its initial Articles of Agreement, albeit it does constitute a reform agenda that should not be overlooked. Let us examine these one at a time. Following the 2008 financial crisis the lack of cash liquidity became clear not only at national but international level. If an international financial institution possessed enough financial resources it could spread these to its members and thus help stave the flow of recession. The IMF clearly proved inadequate in this respect and although willing was unable to provide liquidity to its members. More embarrassingly, by failing to do it lost much of its credibility and legitimacy in the international sphere. The adequacy of the financial resources of the IMF was linked to the adequacy of resources of other international development banks.[65] The G20 thus decided in favour of an increase in the Fund's resources, particularly through the doubling of said resources. This is to be achieved through temporary borrowing, including additional bilateral or multilateral borrowing from members.[66] The G20 also supported the commencement of the processes for an expansion and increase in the New Arrangements to Borrow (NAB), on the basis of fair burden sharing, recognising that an increase in the NAB will require legislative changes for a number of Fund members.[67] In order to increase its capital, the G20 also agreed for a review of existing IMF quotas. This review will allow an assessment to be made as to whether the permanent resources of the Fund need to be increased taking account of the magnitude of the crisis, the significant change in international economic conditions, changes to the Fund's financing instruments and the unanticipated increase in financing demands on the Fund since the Thirteenth Review of Quotas was completed in January 2008. Most G-20 members indicated that this review should be concluded by January 2011. This is to be achieved by ratification of the Fourth Amendment to the Fund's Articles of Agreement, which would have the effect of doubling SDR allocations and enabling all Fund members to participate in the SDR system in proportion to their quotas.[68] These are not intended as long-term measures,

---

[64] G20 Working Group 3, Reform of the IMF: Final Report (4 March 2009).

[65] Ibid. p. 3.

[66] Ibid. Japan was the first IMF member to sign a bilateral agreement with the IMF worth $100 billion. *See* <http://www.imf.org/external/pubs/ft/survey/so/2009/NEW021309A.htm>.

[67] Ibid..

[68] Ibid. Working Group 3 Report, p. 4.

but are instead crucial to the current state of the global economy, given that the IMF itself has pointed out that global recession is continuing to put stress on States without a definite end in sight.[69]

The G20 further stressed the need for the IMF to review its lending instrument with a view to adapting them to the current financial crisis, particularly as regards developing and low-income countries. In particular, it became evident that many low-income countries do not have the capacity to even benefit from the least demanding instruments available by the IMF, such as the PRGF and the Exogenous Shocks Facility (ESF). Equally, such countries must have access to concessional funding that is not otherwise available to them through other lending facilities. Obviously, in order to counter the effects of this type of "looser" lending, the G20 prompted the IMF to tighten its conditionalities requirements to borrowing States, as well as improve the effectiveness of its surveillance mechanisms. Throughout this chapter we have highlighted the need for public international financial institutions to offset generous lending schemes through enhanced and rigid conditionalities.[70] In this respect, the relevant G20 proposals constitute a move towards the right direction, but there is no element of democracy-building in these proposals. One of the stated objectives of enhanced surveillance is to prevent similar crises to international financial architecture.

Finally, the G20 called for greater participation in the management of the IMF by developing countries, with a view to enhancing the Fund's common ownership and by giving voice to all in order to achieve universal membership. To this end, the G20 called for a realignment of quota shares that is expected to result in increases in the quota shares of dynamic economies, and hence in the share of emerging market and developing countries as a whole. Equally, it called for a review of the structure of representation on the Executive Board and IMFC and the decision making rules, consistent with the comprehensive reform of the IMF, so as to more adequately reflect changing weights in the world economy and to ensure that emerging markets and developing countries have greater voice and representation. Such a review should include deepening the participation of low-income countries, lifting the burden on constituencies that have a large number of members, and the consideration of a third chair for Sub-Saharan Africa.[71] The executive structure of the IMF was also put under the G20 microscope given the accusations that it acts as a gentlemen's club, catering for the interests of powerful members and dominated by a handful of nationalities and their cronies. As a result, some G-20 members supported the activation of a Council of Ministers as a

---

[69] *See* IMF, Global Financial Stability Report: Market Update (28 January 2009), available at: <http://www.imf.org/External/Pubs/FT/fmu/eng/2009/01/pdf/0109.pdf>.

[70] Working Group 3 Report, *supra note* 62, pp. 4–6.

[71] Ibid. p. 7.

mechanism to elevate the level of policy dialogue in the Fund. Many others were of the view that such a Council of Ministers can only be established after meaningful quota, voice and representation reform is achieved for emerging markets and developing countries. Some stressed the need to safeguard the role of the Executive Board. There was broad support from G-20 members for open, merit-based selection processes, irrespective of nationality and geographical preferences, for the appointment of the next Managing Director and Deputy Managing Directors of the IMF. While beyond the scope of the Working Group, it must be linked to a similar mechanism which should apply to the selection of senior management in the World Bank and other MDBs.[72] These are bold moves that are aimed at enhancing the Fund's legitimacy, albeit I cannot be fully certain of other implications to poorer members and the politics of appointments. Whatever the outcome, there is an obvious effort to link together all MDBs into a single, coherent and viable mechanism. This has been discussed in previous sections and permeates much of the discussion in this chapter.[73]

### 2.8. *Conclusion*

It is not always straightforward to draw sound conclusions in the aftermath of a financial crisis, particularly where this is of a global nature. For this reason, it should not wholly surprise the reader the fact that central banks and other financial authorities failed to identify the dangers looming behind the accumulation of toxic debt by private banks or the unchecked and largely unregulated investment transactions. To a very large degree this lack of foresight is associated with an insatiable human greed and which for the purposes of government translates into numbers that somehow never reveal the real story. The number I have in mind is that which reflects growth. As long as bad transactions translated into cash, which made the growth indicators rise to increasingly higher levels, we were led to believe that all was fine and the economy was booming. No one stopped to think whether we were in fact depleting our natural resources, whether growth was sustainable, or whether most of the accumulated wealth was based on thin air. It certainly seems that regulation of all types, including financial regulation, is not at all predicated

[72] Ibid. p. 8.

[73] In fact, the G20's discussion of the reform of the IBRD and MDB's generally focussed on exactly the same issues, with the addition of sustainable development. The need for capital mobilisation in respect of all MDBs, as well as their immediate cooperation was also stressed. *See* G20 Working Group 4, The World Bank and Other Multilateral Development Banks: Final Report (March 2009). *See* also, Brookings Institution, The G20 London Summit 2009: Recommendations for Global Policy Coordination (26 March 2009), available at: <http://www.brookings.edu/~/media/Files/rc/reports/2009/0326_g20_summit/0326_g20_summit.pdf>.

on predictive and investigative methodologies, but on knee-jerk reactions. Does this mean that we should not trust government assurances? My answer to this question is affirmative!

It should not all be bad news, however. We should ask ourselves where we can go from here. Throughout this chapter it has become evident that the work of MDBs, including the World Bank, has failed the developing world and has done little to alleviate the financial woes of the developed world in the aftermath of the 2008 crisis. This does not mean that these institutions require a complete overhaul. International institutions are only as effective as the effort and resources put in by their members. Thus, once cannot expect the African Development Bank to engage and solve all African problems, nor finance every infrastructure project in the continent. This is hardly feasible for the World Bank Group, let alone a weak regional MDB. It is no secret that World Bank policies tended to favour investment generally over the specific benefits to the host nation. Investment is not panacea to all matters associated with under-development. In the case of Africa, for example, the World Bank focused on natural resources investment, which produced very few local jobs and did not raise the general level of welfare, while at the same time created a wave of corruption. The future of international financial architecture lies primarily in the restructuring and reshaping of institutions. The IBRD and the IMF require significant financial resources in order to meet the needs of developing countries. Lending to these countries must become less cumbersome, but checks and balances must be put in place. More specifically, the Bank must demand political and social reforms. This can only be achieved through a vigorous campaign of conditionalities, imposed in equal manner across all borrowing countries. There must be no more room for undemocratic governance, which is the principal reason for corruption. Equally, the World Bank and the G20 must make sure that authoritarian regimes are unable to borrow from private financial institutions by mortgaging their natural wealth under onerous conditions that are detrimental to the present and future of their people. Lending must not only seek to build necessary infrastructures but should lead to the creation of meaningful employment and sustainable development, something that is currently escaping the impoverished parts of our planet. It is true that affirmations to this end were not highlighted in the recent G20 declarations, but at least they were given some prominence.

Governments should tackle the root causes of under-development and at the same time mitigate the effects of unregulated business. From a robust and uncompromising neo-liberalism we have now moved to State ownership in banks, automobile industries and others. Perhaps this is the shape of things to come for the next 10–20 years, until the global economy stabilises and we forget the lessons of the past. This is after all part of human nature. If the large powers of this world do not convincingly engage with realism with the problems of our planet, very soon financial crises will not seem like problems.

If we run out of oil, gas and water and are plagued with the full effects of global warming, money will not be able to buy us out of the catastrophic effects that follow. It is therefore imperative that world leaders of this generation set aside their differences and offer concrete solutions to these problems and forget their internal politics for the sake of humankind.

CHAPTER THREE

# DISPUTE SETTLEMENT IN INTERNATIONAL TRADE LAW

Pınar Karacan Baklaci

## 3.1. *Introduction*
## *The Role of WTO Dispute Settlement System for International Trade Law*

The dispute settlement of the World Trade Organization (WTO) is a central element in providing security and predictability to the multilateral trading system.[1] It is very important to have a binding and enforceable dispute system. The dispute settlement of the WTO is effective, reliable and has been widely used by most Members.[2] The WTO-Dispute Settlement Body's (DSB) compulsory jurisdiction also explains the wide usage of the system. Unlike some other international courts, WTO panels do not require the consent of the defendant in order to have jurisdiction.

For the first 13 years until January 2008, there were 369 complaints and for less than half of them panels were established.[3] The settlement at the consultation level shows the strength of the system. There have been 115 adopted panel decisions and 84 appellate body reports.[4]

The system is also effective in terms of compliance as will be discussed. Besides, members' willingness to use and comply with the system shows the confidence and faith they have in it.[5]

The prime purpose of WTO dispute settlement system is to enforce WTO rules and to facilitate and expedite the resolution of disputes among Member States.[6] A prompt settlement of disputes is also important for maintaining the

---

[1] Dispute Settlement Understanding (DSU), Art. 3(2). *Japan-Alcoholic Beverages*, para. 31, United States-Section 301 Trade Act, para. 7.75.

[2] K. Leitner and S. Lester, "WTO Dispute Settlement 1995–2008-A Statistical Analysis", (2009) 12/1 *Journal of International Economic* Law, pp. 195–208. For countries involvements, *see* V. Hughes, "The WTO Dispute Settlement System-from Initiating Proceedings to Ensuring Implementation: What Need Improvement?, in Y. Taniguchi, A. Yanovich and J. Bohanes (eds.), *The Twenty-first Century Dispute Settlement, Negotiations, and the Regionalism in Asia*, Cambridge: Cambridge University Press, 2007, pp. 208–10.

[3] For the statistical analysis *see* S. Lester, B. Mercurio, A. Davies and K. Leitner, *World Trade Law Text, Materials and Commentary*, Hart Publishing, 2008, p. 153.

[4] J. H. Jackson, "The Case of the World Trade Organization, (2008) 84/3 *International Affairs*, p. 439.

[5] Leitner and Lester, pp. 195–208; Lester, Mercurio, Davies and Leitner, p. 153.

[6] P. V. Bossche, *The Law and Policy of the World Trade Organization*, Cambridge: Cambridge University Press, 2007, pp. 182–3.

balance between the rights and obligations of Members.[7] The goal of the dispute settlement procedure is to secure a solution and the withdrawal of the inconsistent measures concerned.[8] A satisfactory settlement, especially a mutually acceptable solution, is preferred.[9]

The dispute settlement system also clarifies the provisions of the covered agreements in accordance with customary rules of interpretation of public international law.[10] The dispute settlement system preserves the rights and obligations of the Members under the covered agreements.[11] The solutions have to be consistent with the covered agreements and cannot nullify or impair benefits accruing to any Member under those agreements.[12]

DSB's mandate is to interpret the law of the covered agreements and to rule whether a measure is inconsistent or not. What happens afterwards is mostly up to the parties.[13]

The dispute settlement of the WTO and the Dispute Settlement Understanding (DSU) have been considered as the greatest achievement of the international trade community since the Bretton Woods.[14] Furthermore, the dispute settlement of the WTO has been referred as the "jewel in the crown."[15]

## 3.2. *The Dispute Settlement System of the WTO*

### 3.2.1. *Origins: GATT 1947 Dispute Settlement*

Article XXII (consultation) and Article XXIII (nullification or impairment) were the foundation of dispute settlement provisions of the General Agreement on Tariffs and Trade (GATT) in 1947.[16]

There were only a few paragraphs devoted to dispute settlement in the GATT 47.[17] Within time there was a shift from ambiguous ideas about

---

7 DSU, Art. 3(3).

8 DSU, Art. 3(7).; Hughes, p. 195.

9 DSU, Art. 3(7).

10 DSU, Art. 3(2).

11 DSU, Art. 3(2).

12 DSU, Art. 3(5).

13 A. Jara, "WTO Dispute Settlement: A Brief Reality Check", in G. Sacerdoti, A. Yanovich and J. Bohanes (eds.), *The WTO at Ten The Contribution of the Dispute Settlement System*, Cambridge: Cambridge University Press, 2006, p. 83.

14 By Former DG of GATT Peter Sutherland: Lester, Mercurio, Davies and Leitner, p. 153.

15 Director General Mike Moore, < http://www.wto.org/english/news_e/pres02_e/pr307_e.htm>, (accessed on 10.03.2010).

16 For comprehensive historical development *see* J. H. Jackson, *The Jurisprudence of GATT and the WTO Insights on Treaty Law and Economic Relations*, Cambridge: Cambridge University Press, 2000, pp. 118–132, 169–179. (hereinafter Jackson, *The Jurisprudence of GATT.*). Also for statistical information on GATT Dispute Settlement *see* R. Hudec, L. M. D. Kennedy and M. Sgarbossa, "A Statistical Profile of GATT Dispute Settlement Cases: 1948–1989", (1993) 2 *Minnesota Journal of Global Trade,* pp. 1–216.; Jackson, pp. 437–54.

17 GATT 47 was left without detailed dispute settlement provisions, because International Trade Organization (ITO) that would have the detailed provisions on dispute settlement failed. Lester, Mercurio, Davies and Leitner, p. 154.

nullification or impairment to more analytical or legalistic approaches to interpreting rules of treaty obligations.[18]

The first two decades of GATT it was not clear how the committee would work, whether it would function like an arbitral tribunal or a committee of conciliators.[19] Later there was a shift from conciliatory model of dispute settlement to an adjudicatory model.[20]

There were also no clear procedural rules under GATT 47. The procedures were developed within time and were codified in an understanding in 1979 during the Tokyo Round.[21]

The system was slow and causing long delays and there were transparency problem.[22] Decision-making process was also problematic. The system required positive consensus for establishing panels and adopting panel decisions. In other words, the defendant had veto power over decisions.

### 3.2.2. *The Structure of the WTO Dispute Settlement*

The dispute settlement under the WTO consists of phases. First there is the consultation phase, if there is no agreement or if the consultation phase is not successful, complaining party can request the establishment of panels. If the panel is established, then there is the panel process, the adoption of the panel decision by the DSB. There is also the appeal procedure in the WTO system unlike the GATT 47. If the parties to the dispute appeal the panel decision, there will be an appeal process, and later the adoption of the Appellate Body report by the DSB and the compliance and implementation of the panel decision or the appeal report if there has been an appeal. If there is no prompt compliance, there is the possibility of compensation or lastly retaliation. The phases will be discussed in greater detail in the following sections.

Compared to GATT 47, the WTO system is more rule based, more legalistic, and less diplomacy oriented. Furthermore the decision-making procedure changed with the WTO. The DSB required consensus not to adopt a panel decision (negative consensus) unlike the consensus required to adopt a decision under GATT 47. Besides, the appeal process was a major contribution to the WTO dispute settlement system. The DSU sets the rules and procedures for the settlement of disputes. The new more rule based system contributed to participation by developing countries.[23]

---

[18] Jackson, p. 444.

[19] A. Lowenfeld, *International Economic Law,* Oxford: Oxford University Press, 2002, p. 139.

[20] Lester, Mercurio, Davies and Leitner, p. 159.

[21] A. Yanovich, "The Evolving WTO Dispute Settlement System, in The WTO in the Twenty-first Century Dispute Settlement, Negotiations, and the Regionalism in Asia", in Taniguchi, Yanovich and Bohanes (eds.), p. 249.

[22] Lester, Mercurio, Davies and Leitner, p. 157.

[23] V. Hughes, "Accomplishments of the WTO Dispute Settlement Mechanism", in Y. Taniguchi, A. Yanovich and J. Bohanes (eds.), *The WTO in the Twenty-first Century Dispute Settlement, Negotiations, and the Regionalism in Asia,* Cambridge: Cambridge University Press, 2007, p. 188.(hereinafter Hughes, "Accomplishments of the WTO ...").

3.2.2.1. *Legal Text*

3.2.2.1.1. *GATT*

GATT Article XXIII is the Article that sets the circumstances where complaints be brought. Trade-Related Aspects of Intellectual Property Rights (TRIPS) and General Agreement in Trade on Services (GATS) have similar provisions but they will be covered in the next section. According to Article XXIII nullification or impairment:[24]

> *1. If any contracting party should consider that any benefit accruing to it directly or indirectly under this Agreement is being nullified or impaired or that the attainment of any objective of the Agreement is being impeded as the result of*
>
> *(a) the failure of another contracting party to carry out its obligations under this Agreement, or*
>
> *(b) the application by another contracting party of any measure, whether or not it conflicts with the provisions of this Agreement, or*
>
> *(c) the existence of any other situation,*
>
> *the contracting party may, with a view to the satisfactory adjustment of the matter, make written representations or proposals to the other contracting party or parties which it considers to be concerned. Any contracting party thus approached shall give sympathetic consideration to the representations or proposals made to it.*
>
> *2. If no satisfactory adjustment is effected between the contracting parties concerned within a reasonable time, or if the difficulty is of the type described in paragraph 1 (c) of this Article, the matter may be referred to the CONTRACTING PARTIES. The CONTRACTING PARTIES shall promptly investigate any matter so referred to them and shall make appropriate recommendations to the contracting parties which they consider to be concerned, or give a ruling on the matter, as appropriate. ... If the CONTRACTING PARTIES consider that the circumstances are serious enough to justify such action, they may authorize a contracting party or parties to suspend the application to any other contracting party or parties of such concessions or other obligations under this Agreement as they determine to be appropriate in the circumstances. If the application to any contracting party of any concession or other obligation is in fact suspended, that contracting party shall then be free, not later than sixty days after such action is taken, to give written notice to the Executive Secretary[25] to the Contracting Parties of its intention to withdraw from this Agreement and such withdrawal shall take effect upon the sixtieth day following the day on which such notice is received by him.*[26]

Under Article XXIII the complaints can be brought if a benefit accruing to it directly or indirectly under the Agreement is being nullified or impaired or if the attainment of any objective of the Agreement is being impeded. In application usually the nullification and impairment of benefits are discussed.[27]

---

[24] GATS and TRIPS have similar provisions.

[25] Changed to Director General in March 23, 1965.

[26] For practice of GATT, art. XXIII.2 look at DSU, Art. 4, 6, 11 and 22.

[27] Lester, Mercurio, Davies and Leitner, p. 183.

The causes of action for the above two complaints are: the failure of another contracting party to carry out its obligations under this Agreement which is the violation complaints,[28] the application by another contracting party of any measure, whether or not it conflicts with the provisions of this Agreement which is the non-violation complaints,[29] and lastly the existence of any other situation.[30]

For non-violation and situation complaints the complainant must demonstrate that there is nullification or impairment of a benefit or that the achievement of an objective is impeded. For the violation complaints, there is a presumption of nullification or impairment as will be discussed.

3.2.2.1.1.1. *Violation Complaints*

In violation complaints, the complainant alleges that a measure is inconsistent with the WTO rules, breaches an obligation under the agreements, and as a result there is direct or indirect nullification and impairment of benefits.[31] Member is alleged to have failed to carry out obligations and acted inconsistently with a provision of the WTO rules.[32]

There is a rebuttable presumption that if there is a violation there is a breach that causes nullification or impairment.[33] In other words, a violation of a norm amounts to nullification and impairment of benefits.[34]

What is challenged?

A government measure is challenged. According to the Appellate Body government measures are "*acts setting forth rules or norms that are intended to have general and prospective application are challengeable measures*".[35]

There is the distinction of mandatory and discretionary measures under the WTO. Legislation that mandates action that is inconsistent with WTO rules will result in violation, whereas legislation that merely contains the discretion to act inconsistently will not result in violation.[36]

3.2.2.1.1.2. *Non-Violation Complaints*

In this situation there is no violation of the covered agreements but the benefits have been nullified or impaired as a result of application of a measure of

28 GATT, Art. XXIII.1(a).
29 GATT, Art. XXIII.1(b).
30 GATT, Art. XXIII.1(c).
31 Lester, Mercurio, Davies and Leitner, pp. 183–91, Bossche, pp. 192–3.
32 AB when discussing the relationship of Art XXIII (a) and XXIII (b) in *EC-Asbestos*.
33 DSU, Art 3(8), *Argentina-Ceramic Tiles*, para. 6.103–5.
34 T. Cottier and M. Oesch, *International Trade Regulation Law and Policy in the WTO, The European Union and Switzerland, Cases, Materials and Comments*, Staempfli Publishers Ltd., 2005, pp. 126–42, p. 127.
35 AB Report *United States-OCTG Sunset Reviews*, para. 187, Lester, Mercurio, Davies and Leitner, p. 189.
36 *United States -Exports Restraints*, Lester, Mercurio, Davies and Leitner, p. 189.

another Member. It is related to principle of good faith and legitimate exceptions.[37] The first WTO non-violation complaint was *Japan-Film*[38] and the first Appellate Body report on non-violation complaint was *EC-Asbestos*[39].

As discussed in the *EC-Asbestos Case*:

> *The idea underlying the provisions of Article XXIII:1(b) is that the improved competitive opportunities that can legitimately be expected from a tariff concession can be frustrated not only by measures proscribed by the General Agreement but also by measures consistent with that Agreement. In order to encourage contracting parties to make tariff concessions they must therefore be given a right of redress when a reciprocal concession is impaired by another contracting party as a result of the application of any measure, whether or not it conflicts with the General Agreement.*[40]

Also in *Japan-Film*:

> *The purpose of Article XXIII.1(b) is to protect the balance of concessions under GATT by providing a means to redress government actions not otherwise regulated by GATT rules that nonetheless nullify or impair a Member's legitimate expectations of benefits from tariff negotiations.*[41]

The *Japan-Film* summarized the elements of non-violation[42]: there has to be an application of a measure by a Member, benefit has to occur under agreement, and there has to be nullification or impairment of benefit due to the application of the measure. The measure does not have to be binding can also be non-binding. As the Panel stated non-binding actions "can potentially have adverse effects on competitive conditions of market access."[43]

The burden of proof will be on the complaining party.[44] In addition, the remedy for non-violation complaints is to make a mutually satisfactory adjustment. The remedies in these situations are not effective as in violation cases.[45]

#### 3.2.2.1.1.3. *Situation Complaints*

There has not been a panel decision on situation complaints that causes nullification or impairment. It was designed for emergencies such as when a state is

---

[37] Expectations, reasonable expectations discussed in: *Japan-Film*, (Panel Report, *Japan-Measures Affecting Consumer Photographic Film and Paper*, WT/DS44/R, adopted 22 April 1999), (hereinafter *Japan-Film*), *EC-Asbestos*, Cottier and Oesch, p. 127.

[38] *Japan-Photographic Film and Paper (Japan-Film)*, para. 10.50, WT/DS44/R, Cottier ans Oesch, p. 127.

[39] *EC-Asbestos*, para. 185, WT/DS135/AB/R.

[40] *EC-Asbestos*, para. 185.

[41] *Japan-Film*, para. 10.50.

[42] *Japan-Film*, para. 10.41, also *Korea-Measures Affecting Government Procurement*, para. 7.85, WT/DS163/R.

[43] *Japan-Film*, para. 10.49.

[44] Ibid. para. 10.32.

[45] For discussion *see* Lester, Mercurio, Davies and Leitner, p. 187.

overwhelmed by massive unemployment or depression[46] or having balance of payment difficulties.[47]

3.2.2.1.2. *Articles in Other WTO Agreements Regarding Dispute Settlement*

Agreements covered under the DSU are stated under Appendix 1.[48] There are also provisions on dispute settlement on other WTO agreements. Appendix 2 of the DSU is stating the Special or Additional Rules and Procedures Contained in the Covered Agreements.[49]

In the case of a conflict between the rules and procedures of the DSU and the special or additional rules and procedures set forth in Appendix 2, the special or additional rules and procedures will prevail.[50]

If the disputes involve rules and procedures under more than one covered agreement, and if there is a conflict between special or additional rules and procedures of such agreements under review, and where the parties to the dispute cannot agree on rules and procedures within twenty days of the establishment of the panel, the Chairman of the Dispute Settlement Body in consultation with the parties to the dispute, shall determine the rules and procedures to be followed within ten days after a request by either Member.[51] The Chairman will use special or additional rules and procedures where possible, and will use the DSU rules and procedures to the extent necessary to avoid conflict.[52]

3.2.2.1.3. *Dispute Settlement Understanding*

Understanding on Rules and Procedures Governing the Settlement of Disputes (Dispute Settlement Understanding-DSU) are the rules for the dispute settlement under the WTO. The rules and procedures of the DSU apply to

---

[46] Lovenfeld, p. 176.

[47] Lester, Mercurio, Davies and Leitner, pp. 187–8.

[48] Agreement Establishing the World Trade Organization, Multilateral Trade Agreements: Multilateral Agreements on Trade in Goods, General Agreement on Trade in Services, Agreement on Trade-Related Aspects of Intellectual Property Rights, Understanding on Rules and Procedures Governing the Settlement of Disputes, Plurilateral Trade Agreements: Agreement on Trade in Civil Aircraft, Agreement on Government Procurement, International Dairy Agreement (terminated 1997), International Bovine Meat Agreement (terminated 1997). (The applicability of this Understanding to the Plurilateral Trade Agreements shall be subject to the adoption of a decision by the parties to each agreement setting out the terms for the application of the Understanding to the individual agreement).

[49] Art. 11(2) of theAgreement on the Application of Sanitary and Phytosanitary Measures, Art. 8(1)-8(12), 2(14), 2(21), 4(4), 5(2), 5(4), 6(9), 6(10), 6(11) on the expired Agreement on Textiles and Clothing, Art. 14(2)-14(4), annex 2 on Agreement on Technical Barriers to Trade, Art. 17(4)-17(7) of Agreement on Implementation of Art. VI GATTT 94, Art. 19(3)-19(5), annex II.2 f, 3, 9, 21 of Agreement on Implementation Art. VII GATT 94, Art. 4(2)-4(12), 6(6), 7(2)-7(10), 8(5), fn 35, 24(4), 27(7), annex V 30 on Agreement on Subsidies and Countervailing Measures, Art. XXII.3, XXIII.3 of GATS. For case discussion, *see Guatamala-Cement I*, para. 65. *Australia- Automative Leather II* (Article 21.5-US) para. 6.41.

[50] DSU, Art. 1(2).

[51] DSU, Art. 1(2).

[52] DSU, Art. 1(2).

disputes brought pursuant to the consultation and dispute settlement provisions of the agreements listed in Appendix 1.[53] The DSU also apply to consultations and the settlement of disputes between Members concerning their rights and obligations under the provisions of the Agreement Establishing the World Trade Organization (WTO Agreement) and disputes brought under the DSU.[54] DSU is annex 2 of the WTO Agreement and is an important contribution of the WTO.

3.2.2.2. *The Dispute Settlement Body*

The Dispute Settlement Body (DSB) administers the WTO dispute settlement. The General Council shall convene as appropriate to discharge the responsibilities of the DSB provided for in the Dispute Settlement Understanding.[55] When the General Council administers the WTO dispute settlement system it convenes and acts like the DSB. The General Council is composed of ambassador level diplomats of all WTO Members. The DSB administers the rules and procedures for the consultation and dispute settlement provisions of the covered agreements. The DSB is in charge of establishing panels and appointment of the Appellate Body members, adopting panel decisions and the Appellate Body reports, maintain the surveillance of implementation of rulings and recommendations, and lastly authorizing the suspension of concessions and other obligations under the covered agreements.[56]

The DSB informs the relevant WTO Councils and Committees of any developments in disputes related to provisions of the respective covered agreements.[57]

The DSB meets as often as necessary to carry out its functions within the time frames provided in the DSU.[58] The DSB may elect its own chairman[59] and can establish rules of procedure as it deems necessary for the fulfillment of responsibilities.[60] All consultations are notified to the DSB.[61] There are Rules of Procedure for meetings of the DSB.

3.2.2.3. *Panels*

If the consultation process fails, the complaining party can request the establishment of a panel.[62] The DSB decides to establish the panel unless it decides by consensus not to establish a panel. Panels are composed of well-qualified

[53] DSU, Art. 1(1).
[54] DSU, Art. 1(1).
[55] Treaty Establishing the WTO, IV (3).
[56] DSU, Art. 2(1).
[57] DSU, Art. 2(2).
[58] DSU, Art. 2(3).
[59] The Dispute Settlement Body shall apply the relevant guidelines contained in the "Guidelines for Appointment of Officers to WTO Bodies" (WT/L/31).
[60] Treaty Establishing the WTO, IV (3)
[61] DSU, Art. 4(4).
[62] DSU, Articles 6, 7, 8, 11, 12 and 16.

governmental and/or non-governmental individuals. Within the specified time and the terms of reference procedure the panel makes its assessments. The panels assist the DSB in discharging its responsibilities. The panel makes an objective assessment of the matter before it and make other findings decides on a recommendation. Panels consult regularly with the parties in order to develop a mutually satisfactory solution. Later the panel report is adopted by the DSB unless it decides by consensus not to adopt it.

3.2.2.4. *The Appellate Body*

The Appellate Body is established by the DSB. It is composed of seven members with recognized authority and expertise in law, international trade, and the subject matter of the covered agreements.[63] The Appellate Body hears appeals from panel cases. Appeal is limited to issues of law covered in the panel report and legal interpretations developed by the panel. The Appellate Body reviews the case within the specified time and procedure. The Appellate Body may uphold, modify or reverse the legal findings and conclusions of the panel. The Appellate Body report has to be adopted by the DSB unless it decides by consensus not to adopt it.

3.2.2.5. *Secretariat*

The Secretariat has responsibility of assisting panels, especially on the legal, historical, and procedural aspects of the matters dealt with, and of providing secretarial and technical support.[64]

### 3.2.3. *Overview of the Dispute Settlement Procedure in the WTO*

3.2.3.1. *Complaint-Consultation*

One of the other purposes of the dispute settlement mechanism is to secure a positive solution to a dispute. A mutually acceptable solution by the parties that is consistent with the covered agreements is the preferred outcome.[65] There is a high percentage of settlement at this level and this high percentage suggests that the consultation process is working effectively.[66] During the consultation process the measure at issue can be withdrawn, or a favorable change or clarification can be made.[67] Consultation is very important in the dispute settlement procedure under the WTO.[68]

---

[63] DSU, Art. 17.

[64] DSU, Art. 27.

[65] DSU, Art 3 (7).

[66] J. W. Davey, "Evaluating WTO Dispute Settlement: What Results Have Been Achieved Through Consultation and Implementation of Panel Reports?", in Y. Taniguchi, A. Yanovich and J. Bohanes (eds.), *The WTO in the Twenty-first Century Dispute Settlement, Negotiations, and the Regionalism in Asia*, Cambridge: Cambridge University Press, 2007, pp. 102–7.

[67] Davey, pp. 104–5.

[68] *Brazil-Desiccated Coconut*, (Appellate Body Report, *Brazil-Measures Affecting Desiccated Coconut*, WT/DS22/AB/R, adopted 20 March 1997), para. 287, *Mexico- Corn Syrup, (Panel*

According to Article XXII of GATT contracting parties should afford adequate opportunity for consultations.

The DSU do not have an explicit provision requiring a Member to have a "legal interest" in order to have recourse to the WTO dispute settlement.[69] The Appellate Body also confirmed that there is no requirement to have a legal interest; it is sufficient if the action will be fruitful.[70]

There is also no guidance in the DSU on how the consultations will be done. The method of consultation is up to the parties. However it is stated that the consultation has to be done in good faith and the consultation is confidential.[71]

If a request for consultations is made pursuant to a covered agreement, the Member, within ten days from the date of its receipt shall reply to the request and within a period of no more than thirty days after the date of receipt of the request shall enter into consultations in good faith.[72] The goal of consultation is to reach a mutually satisfactory solution. If the Member does not reply or enter into consultation within the specified time then the Member that requested consultations may proceed directly to request the establishment of a panel.[73]

If the consultations start but fail to settle the dispute within sixty days after the date of receipt of the request for consultations, the complaining party may again request the establishment of a panel.[74] If the parties jointly consider that consultations have failed to settle the dispute the complaining party may request a panel during the sixty-day period.[75]

In cases of urgency, such as in the case of perishable goods, Members shall enter into consultations within a period of no more than ten days after the date of receipt of the request.[76] And if the consultations fail to settle the

---

Report, *Mexico-Anti-Dumping Investigation of High Fructose Corn Syrup (HFCS) from the United States,* WT/DS132/R and Corr. 1, adopted 24 February 2000). (hereinafter *Mexico Corn Syrup),* paras. 54–6.

[69] Bossche, p. 193.

[70] *EC-Bananas III,* (Appellate Body Report, *European Communities-Report for the Importation, Sale and Distribution of Bananas,* WT/DS27/AB/R, adopted 25 September 1997), (hereinafter *EC-Bananas III*), para. 135–8, Mexico-Corn Syrup, para. 74, Lester, Mercurio, Davies and Leitner, p. 192.

[71] DSU, Art. 4(6), *Korea-Alcoholic Beverages,* (Award of the Arbitrator, *Korea-Taxes on Alcoholic Beverages-Arbitration under Article 21.3 (c) of the DSU,* WT/DS75/16, WT/DS84/14, adopted 4 June 1999), para. 10.23.

[72] DSU, Art. 4(3), they can also mutually agree on different time periods.

[73] DSU, Art. 4(3), "…In such a case, the responding party, by its own conduct, relinquishes the potential benefits that could be derived from those consultations.": *Appellate Body Report on Mexico-Corn Syrup (Article 21.5 -US), (Mexico-Anti-Dumping Investigation of High Fructose Corn Syrup (HFCS), from the United States, Recourse to Article 21.5 of the DSU by the United States,* WT/DS132/AB/RW, adopted 21 November 2001), paras. 58–9.

[74] DSU, Art. 4(7).

[75] DSU, Art. 4(7).

[76] DSU, Art. 4(8).

dispute within a period of twenty days after the date of receipt of the request, the complaining party may request the establishment of a panel.[77] In cases of urgency, the parties to the dispute, panels, and the Appellate Body shall make every effort to accelerate the proceedings to the greatest extent possible.[78]

Multiple complaints are possible under the DSU.[79] More than one Member may request the establishment of a panel related to the same matter. Also a single panel may be established to examine these complaints taking into account the rights of all Members concerned whenever feasible.[80] But the rights of the parties will not be impaired and they will enjoy the rights as if there are separate panels.[81]

When more than one panel is established on similar issues, if possible, the same persons will serve as panelists, and harmonized timetables will apply. For example, joint meetings were held with scientific experts in the *EC -Hormones Case.*[82]

If a Member other than the consulting Member has "substantial trade interest" in consultations may notify the consulting Members and the DSB of its desire to be joined in the consultations within ten days after the date of the circulation of the request.[83] If the Member to whom the request for consultation is addressed agrees that the claim of "substantial trade interest" is well founded such Member may join the consultations.[84] If the request to be joined in the consultations is not accepted, the applicant Member shall be free to request consultations.

3.2.3.2. *Request for a Panel and Panel Establishment*

If the consultation process fails the complaining party can request the establishment of a panel in writing. The request should indicate whether consultations were held. Also it should identify the specific measures at issue and provide a brief summary of the legal basis of the complaint sufficient to present the problem clearly.[85]

The panel should be established at the latest at the DSB meeting following that at which the request first appears as an item on the DSB's agenda.

---

[77] DSU, Art. 4(8).

[78] DSU, Art. 4(9), *Canada-Patent Term.*

[79] *EC-Bananas III.*

[80] DSU, Art. 9 (1), *India-Patents*, (Panel Report, *India-Patent Protection for Pharmaceutical and Agricultural Chemical Products*, WT/DS50/R, 5 September 1997), (hereinafter *India-Patents)*, paras. 7.13–7.16, requesting separate reports: *EC-Bananas III*, paras. 7.55–7.57.

[81] DSU, Art. 9(2).

[82] *EC-Hormones*, (Appellate Body Report, *EC Measures Concerning Meat and Meat Products (Hormones)*, WT/DS26/AB/R, WT/DS48/AB/R, adopted 13 February 1998). (hereinafter *EC-Hormones*), Lester, Mercurio, Davies and Leitner, pp. 193–4.

[83] DSU, Art. 4(11).

[84] DSU, Art. 4(11).

[85] DSU, Art. 6.

The panel will be established unless DSB decides by consensus not to establish a panel.

3.2.3.2.1. *Composition of Panels*

Panels are composed of well-qualified governmental or non-governmental individuals.[86] There is a list of panelists to choose from and the Members can also suggest other names.[87] The panel selection is done to ensure the independence of the members.[88] Unless parties to the dispute agree otherwise the panelists cannot be citizens of the dispute parties or third parties.[89] Panelists serve in their individual capacities and not as government representatives, nor as representatives of any organization.[90]

Panels are composed on an ad hoc basis and include three panelists, unless the parties agree for five panelists.[91] After the establishment of the panel the members are informed promptly of the composition of the panel.

If the parties cannot agree on panelists within ten days after the date of the establishment of a panel, at the request of either party, the Director-General, in consultation with the Chairman of the DSB and the Chairman of the relevant Council or Committee, shall determine the composition of the panel no later than ten days after the date the Chairman receives such a request.[92] When appointing panelists, the Director-General consults the parties to the dispute and considers the most appropriate in accordance with any relevant special or additional rules or procedures of the covered agreement or agreements, which are at issue in the dispute. The Chairman of the DSB informs the Members of the composition of the panel formed.[93]

3.2.3.2.2. *Function of Panels*

3.2.3.2.2.1. *Working Procedures*

The panels assist the DSB in discharging its responsibilities under the DSU and the covered agreements.[94] The panels make an objective assessment of the matter before them. Panels try to develop a mutually satisfactory solution by consulting with the parties to the dispute regularly and giving them adequate opportunity to be involved.[95] If the parties fail to develop a mutually satisfactory solution, the panel submits its written findings to the DSB. The report of a

86 DSU, Art. 8 (1).
87 DSU, Art. 8 (4).
88 DSU, Art. 8 (2).
89 DSU, Art. 8 (3).
90 DSU, Art. 8 (9).
91 DSU, Art. 8 (5).
92 DSU, Art. 8 (7).
93 DSU, Art. 8 (7).
94 DSU, Art. 11.
95 DSU, Art. 11.

panel will include the findings of fact, the applicability of relevant provisions, and the basic rationale behind any findings and recommendations that it makes.[96] If the parties reach a settlement, the panel report will include a brief description of the case and a note that a solution has been reached.[97]

The panel meets in closed session.[98] The parties to the dispute and interested parties are present at the meetings only when the panel invites them.[99] Each party to the dispute shall deposit its written submissions.[100] The complainant and the defendant can also use legal counsel.

According to the Panel Working Procedures,[101] first the parties present their written submissions to the panel before the substantive meeting.[102] At the first substantive meeting with the parties, the complainant presents its case and the defendant will be asked to present its point of view.[103] All third parties who have notified their interest in the dispute will also be invited in writing to present their views during this session.[104] Formal rebuttals will be made at the second substantive meeting of the panel.[105] Later the interim report will be issued. The interim review procedure is discussed separately. After the interim review the final report will be circulated to the Members and for adoption by the DSB.

3.2.3.2.2.1.1. *Terms of Reference*

Unless the parties agree otherwise within the specified time the panels shall have the following terms of reference:

> *To examine, in the light of the relevant provisions in (name of the covered agreement(s) cited by the parties to the dispute), the matter referred to the DSB by (name of party) in document ... and to make such findings as will assist the DSB in making the recommendations or in giving the rulings provided for in that/those agreement(s).*[106]

The importance of the terms of reference is that it gives parties information on claims at issue in order to give them opportunity to respond. In addition, the term of reference establishes the jurisdiction of the panel.[107] The panel can only consider the claims that it has authority under its terms of reference.[108]

---

96 DSU, Art. 12(7).
97 DSU, Art. 12(7).
98 DSU Appendix 3, Panel Working Procedures, 2.
99 Panel Working procedure, 2.
100 DSU, Art. 12 (6).
101 Appendix 3 of the DSU.
102 Panel Working procedure, 4.
103 Panel Working procedure, 5.
104 Panel Working procedure, 6.
105 Panel Working procedure, 7.
106 DSU, Art. 7, Terms of Reference of Panels.
107 *The AB stated in Brazil-Desiccated Coconut*, para. 186.; Bossche, p. 237.
108 *US-Carbon Steel*, (Appellate Body Report, *United States –Countervailing Duties on Certain Corrosion-Resistant Carbon Steel Flat Products from Germany*, WT/DS213/AB/R and Corr. 1, adopted 19 December 2002), para. 126: "....terms of reference define the scope of the

3.2.3.2.2.1.2. *Standard of Review*

Panel will review the challenged measure with the WTO law.[109] The standard is "objective assessment":

> *...a panel should make an objective assessment of the matter before it, including an objective assessment of the facts of the case and the applicability of and conformity with the relevant covered agreements...*[110]

The question of whether "objective assessment" was made was addressed in Appellate Body reports.[111]

Panels do not need to rule on every single claim made by complaining parties, but only on those required to settle the dispute in question.[112] A panel can abstain from making multiple findings on a claim presented by complaining party on the ground that another finding of inconsistency already resolves the dispute at hand.[113] This is the "judicial economy" argument.[114]

3.2.3.2.2.2. *Interim Review*

After the rebuttal submissions and oral arguments, the panel issues a descriptive (factual and argument) draft report to the parties to the dispute. Within the time period set by the panel, the parties can submit their comments in writing.[115] When the time period expires the panel issues an interim report to the parties, the report includes descriptive sections and the panel's findings and conclusions.[116] Before the circulation of the final report to the Members,

dispute..."; *India-Patents,* paras. 92–93: "A panel may consider only those claims that it has the authority to consider under its terms of reference. A panel cannot assume jurisdiction that it does not have. The panel is bound by its terms of reference.".

[109] Bossche, pp. 238–40.; Lester, Mercurio, Davies and Leitner, pp. 206–16.; Jackson, pp. 133–61.

[110] DSU, Art. 11, this is the standard of review however there might be special standard of review as in the Antidumping Agreement Article 17.6. For detailed discussion *see* T. A. Guzman, "Determining the Appropriate Standard of Review in WTO Disputes", 42/1 *Cornell International Law Journal,* pp. 45–76.

[111] *EC-Hormones.*; *EC-Poultry,* (Panel Report, *European Communities-Measures Affecting the Importation of Certain Poultry Products,* WT/DS69/R, modified by the Appellate Body Report, WT/DS69/AB/R, adopted 23 July 1998).; *Chile-Price Band System,* (Panel Report, *Chile-Price Band System and Safeguard Measures Relating to Certain Agricultural Products,* WT/DS207/R, modified by the Appellate Body Report WTO Doc. WT/DS207/AB/R, adopted 23 October 2002); Bossche, pp. 238–9.

[112] Also *see* A. Alvarez-Jimenez, "The WTO Appellate Body's Exercise of Judicial Economy", (2009) 12/2 *Journal of International Economic Law,* pp. 393–415.

[113] *Canada-Wheat Exports and Grain Imports* para. 133; J. Bohanes and A. Sennekamp, "Reflections on the Concept of 'Judicial Economy', in G. Sacerdoti, A. Yanovich and J. Bohanes (eds.), *WTO Dispute Settlement, in The WTO at Ten The Contribution of the Dispute Settlement System,* Cambridge: Cambridge University Press, 2006, p. 424.; Bohanes and Sennekamp, p. 424.

[114] Lester, Mercurio, Davies and Leitner, pp. 216–218.; Bossche, pp. 240–1. The Appellate Body in US-Wool Shirts and Blouses stated that a panel need only address those claims, which must be addressed in order to resolve the matter in issue in the dispute, US-Wool Shirts and Blouses, para. 19. For further discussion of judicial economy *see* Bohanes and Sennekamp, pp. 424–49.

[115] DSU, Art. 15(1).

[116] DSU, Art. 15(2).

a party within the specified time period can submit written request for the panel to review precise aspects of the interim report.[117] If the party requests it, the panel holds a further meeting with the parties on the issues identified in the written comments. This is a review for precise aspects of the interim report and not the whole report.[118] The parties cannot introduce new evidence at this stage.[119] If no comment is received from any party within the time period, the interim report is considered as the final panel report and is circulated promptly to the Members. The final report should include the arguments made at the interim review stage.[120]

In sum, interim review provides a last opportunity to settle the dispute amicably and reach a mutually agreed solution before the issuance of the final report.[121]

Interim review was introduced in the Uruguay Round negotiations in order to avoid errors, misrepresentation based on arguments, which the parties did not have opportunity to comment. On the other hand it is worth discussion whether it is still necessary and serves its purpose after the introduction of the Appellate Body.[122]

3.2.3.2.2.3. *Time Period*

The period that a panel should conclude its examination, from the composition of the panel until the final report is issued, should not exceed six months.[123] In cases of urgency, such as when perishable goods are concerned, the panel shall aim to issue its report within three months.[124]

If the panel cannot conclude its examination in time, it shall inform the DSB in writing with the reasons for the delay together with an estimate of the period within which it will issue its report.[125] However, the period from the establishment of the panel to the circulation of the report to the Members exceed nine months.[126]

The panel may also suspend its examination at any time at the request of the complaining party for a period not to exceed 12 months.[127] If the work of the

---

[117] DSU, Art. 15(2).

[118] *Australia-Salmon*, (Panel Report, *Australia-Measures Affecting Importation of Salmon*, WT/DS18/R, modified by the Appellate Body, WTO Doc. WT/DS18/AB/R, adopted 6 November 1998), para. 7.3.

[119] *EC-Sardines*, (Appellate Body Report, *European Communities-Trade Description of Sardines*, WTO Doc. WT/DS231/AB/R, adopted 23 October 2002) (hereinafter *EC-Sardines)*, para. 302.

[120] DSU, Art. 15(3).

[121] A. Steinbach, "The DSU Interim Review-Need for Its Elimination or Extension to the Appellate Body Stage?",(2009) 12/2 *Journal of International Economic Law* pp. 417–34.

[122] Cottier and Oesch, (from T. Cottier, "Dispute Settlement in the World Trade organization: Characteristics and Structure for the European Union", (1998) 35 *Common Market Law Review*, pp. 325–50), p. 155.

[123] DSU, Art. 12(8).

[124] DSU, Art. 12(8).

[125] DSU, Art. 12(9).

[126] DSU, Art. 12(9).

[127] DSU, Art. 12(12).

panel has been suspended for more than 12 months, the authority of the panel will fall.

For a summary of the proposed timetable for panel work there is a guideline in the Panel Working Procedures:[128]

(a) Receipt of first written submissions of the parties: complaining Party: 3–6 weeks, party complained against 2–3 weeks. (b) Date, time and place of first substantive meeting with the parties; third party session 1–2 weeks, (c) Receipt of written rebuttals of the parties: 2–3 weeks, (d) Date, time and place of second substantive meeting with the parties 1–2 weeks, (e) issuance of descriptive part of the report to the parties 2–4 weeks, (f) receipt of comments by the parties on the descriptive part of the report 2 weeks, (g) Issuance of the interim report, including the findings and conclusions, to the parties: 2–4 weeks, (h) deadline for party to request review of part(s) of report: 1 week, (i) Period of review by panel, including possible additional meeting with parties:2 weeks, (j) issuance of final report to parties to dispute: 2 weeks, (k) Circulation of the final report to the Members:3 weeks. The calendar may be changed in the light of unforeseen developments. Additional meetings with the parties shall be scheduled if required.

3.2.3.2.2.4. *Burden of Proof*

There is no provision in the WTO Agreement or in the DSU regarding the burden of proof in a dispute settlement proceeding. The issue was discussed in panels and Appellate Body.[129] The Appellate Body has progressively developed principles of burden of proof to guide panels in their resolution of disputes.[130]

The burden of proof rests upon the party, whether complaining or defending, who asserts the affirmative of a particular claim or defense.[131]

Complaining party should prove first.[132] And the party invoking an exception or defense should prove that the conditions are met.[133] Defendant party cannot come up with inconsistencies directed at complaining party,

---

[128] Appendix 3, Working Procedures, 12.

[129] The first dispute in which the issue of burden of proof arose United States- Measure Affecting Imports of Woven Wool Shirts and Blouses from India, (*US-Wool Shirts and Blouses*, Appellate Body Report, *United States-Measures Affecting Imports of Woven Wool Shirts and Blouses from India*, WT/DS33/AB/R and Corr. 1, adopted 23 May 1997), (hereinafter *US-Wool Shirts and Blouses)*, para. 14.

[130] P. D. Steger, "The Appellate Body and Its Contribution to WTO Dispute Settlement, in M. L. D. Kennedy and D. J. Southwick (eds.), *The Political Economy of International Trade Law Essays in Honor of Robert E. Hudec*, Cambridge: Cambridge University Press 2002, pp. 487–8.

[131] Steger, pp. 487–8.; Bossche, pp. 210–12.

[132] In *Japan-Alcohol, India-Patent*, J. Pauwelyn, "Evidence, Proof and Persuasion in the WTO Dispute Settlement Who Bears the Burden", (2008) 11/1 *Journal of International Economic Law*, pp. 227–58.

[133] *US-Wool Shirts and Blouses*, also *US-Gasoline*, (Panel Report, *United States-Standards for Reformulated and Conventional Gasoline*, WT/DS2/R, modified by the Appellate Body Report, WT/DS2/AB/R, adopted 20 May 1996), Pauwelyn, pp. 227–58.

only the complaining party can claim violations of GATT on the other party's actions.[134]

But in cases where there is an infringement of the obligations assumed under a covered agreement, the action is considered "prima facie" to constitute a case of nullification or impairment.[135] There is a presumption that a breach of the rules has an adverse impact on other Members parties to that covered agreement, and in such cases, it is up to the Member against whom the complaint has been brought to rebut the charge.[136] The case law also contributed to the development of concept of "prima facie" case of WTO inconsistency.[137]

Complaining party will establish a prima facie evidence of nullification and impairment of benefits.[138] After establishment of proof the burden shifts to the defendant; if party invokes an exception or affirmative defense has to prove that the conditions are met, it is for the party asserting a fact to prove it.[139]

#### 3.2.3.2.3. *Third Party Participation*

There is possibility of third party participation at the panels. Any Member having a "substantial interest" in a matter before a panel can notify the DSB of its interest and may have the opportunity to be heard by the panel and to make written submissions to the panel.[140] These third parties are again Member states and they are not non-state actors.

At the panel level "substantial interest" is required for third party participation however at consultation level "substantial trade interest" is required.[141]

Third party submissions are also given to the parties to the dispute. Third parties shall also receive the submissions of the parties to the dispute at the first meeting of the panel.[142]

---

134 Pauwelyn, pp. 227–58.

135 DSU, Art. 3(8), *EC-Bananas III*, paras. 251–253.

136 DSU, Art. 3(8).

137 Cottier and Oesch, p. 161. In J. J. Barcel'o III, "Burden of Proof, Prima Facie Case and Presumption in WTO Dispute Settlement", (2009) 42/1 *Cornell International Law Journal*, pp. 23–42, the author argues that the Appellate Body should abandon the concepts of prima facie case, presumption, and a shifting burden. They need clarification; they have different meanings in common law and civil law countries and it is more the burden of persuasion. It is better if the Appellate Body simply state that a complaining member bears the burden of proof on its basic claim and that the responding member, in good faith, should submit rebutting evidence to assist the panel and support its version of the disputed facts. Also for burden of proof and whether the panel is activist discussion *see* A. D. Gantz and A. B. S. Schropp, "Rice Age: Comments on the Panel Report in Turkey- Measures Affecting the Importation of Rice", (2009) 8/1 *World Trade Review*, pp. 145–77. Also look at N. Meagher, "Turkey - Measures Affecting the Importation of Rice (DS334), Prepared for the ALI Project on the Case Law of the WTO", (2009) 8/1 *World Trade Review*, pp. 79–186.

138 Turkey-Textiles summarized the burden of proof rules, Lester, Mercurio, Davies and Leitner, pp. 191–3.

139 Cottier ans Oesch, p. 161, *US-Wool Shirts and Blouses*.

140 DSU, Art. 10(2), *United States -1916 Act*, paras. 139–50.

141 DSU, Art. 4(11), Hughes, p. 203.

142 DSU, Art. 10(3).

3.2.3.2.4. *Amicus Curiae Briefs*

*Amicus curiae* briefs are unsolicited documents, which are submitted by a source other than the parties and the third parties to the dispute without having been requested by a panel or the Appellate Body.[143] It can be defined as a written legal argument submitted by a private individual, an interested group such as an industry association or non-governmental organization to panels or the Appellate Body.[144] They set out views how the case should be resolved. *Amicus curiae* literally means "friend of the court" and is used in the common law system. The DSU is silent on the issue and there is no express authority. It was argued in the *US- Shrimp Case* and the Appellate Body concluded, on the basis of Articles 11, 12 and 13 of the DSU, that panels have authority to accept amicus briefs.[145] Also it was argued whether the application could fit under Article 17(9) of the DSU and the Working Procedures Article 16(1) when the authority of the Appellate Body to accept amicus briefs was considered.[146]

The Appellate Body discussed this issue in some of the disputes. The Appellate Body asserted powers on the handling of *amicus curiae* briefs. At first the Appellate Body only admitted amicus briefs attached to party's submission, later the Appellate Body provided legal justification supporting broader authority to consider briefs independent of party submission.[147]

The Appellate Body made distinction between parties and third parties to a dispute that has legal right to participate and others.[148] The admissibility of *amicus curiae* briefs was a major issue when the Appellate Body was addressing the *EC-Asbestos Case*.[149] The Appellate Body adopted additional procedures to deal with amicus briefs.[150] Because of the strong opposition

---

[143] Cottier and Oesch, p. 170.

[144] Hughes, pp. 211–214, for a list of cases look at fn. 78–80.

[145] *US-Shrimp*, (Appellate Body Report, United States-Import Prohibition of Certain Shrimp and Shrimp Products, WTO Doc. WT/DS58/AB/R, adopted on 6 November 1998) (hereinafter *US-Shrimp Case)*, paras. 101, 104–6.

[146] Mentioned in a footnote in the Appellate Body *US-Lead and Bismuth II*, (Appellate Body Report, *United States – Imposition of Countervailing Duties on Certain Hot Rolled Lead and Bismuth Carbon Steel Products Originating in the United Kingdom*, WT/DS138/AB/R, adopted 7 June 2000), (hereinafter *US-Lead and Bismuth II*), also paras. 40– 2.; B. Stern, "The Emergence of Non-State Actors in International Commercial Disputes Through WTO Appellate Body Case-Law", in G. Sacerdoti, A. Yanovich and J. Bohanes (eds.), *The WTO at Ten The Contribution of the Dispute Settlement System*, Cambridge: Cambridge University Press, 2006, pp. 376–7.

[147] *US-Shrimp Case*, paras. 04–106; Stern, pp. 372–85.; F. Weiss, "The Limits of the WTO: Facing Non-Trade Issues in the Twenty-First Century Dispute Settlement, Negotiations, and the Regionalism in Asia", in Taniguchi, Yanovich and Bohanes (eds.), pp. 164–5.; Bossche, pp. 197–8.

[148] *US-Lead and Bismuth II*, Appellate Body considered that it had discretionary authority to accept them directly sent to it.

[149] Appellate Body Report, *European Communities-Measures Affecting Asbestos and Asbestos-Containing Products*, WT/DS135/AB/R (Mar. 12, 2001).

[150] *EC-Asbestos*, paras. 51–2. the additional procedures were adopted according to Working procedures for Appellate Review art 16 (1): Bossche, pp. 198–9.

from the membership, the Appellate Body denied all the applications in the case.[151]

There is no legal duty of the Appellate Body to accept and consider unsolicited amicus briefs.[152] The Appellate Body settled the issue finding that panels have discretionary power to accept or reject them.[153]

The dispute settlement process under the WTO is for Member States. However, *amicus curiae* briefs make it possible for non-State actors to be involved in the process to some extend.

But the discussion got more complicated when a Member State, Morocco, submitted *amicus curiae* brief.[154] Although the Member State could have participated as a third party, it preferred to submit *amicus curiae* brief.[155]

There is the danger of overloading the system, therefore there should be clear and reasonable rules on *amicus curiae* briefs as will be discussed in the last section. It would be helpful to have rules on who can file them and regulate the format and the length of applications.[156]

#### 3.2.3.2.5. *Experts*

The panels can seek information and technical advice from any individual or body, which it deems appropriate.[157] If individual or body is within the jurisdiction of a Member, the panel has to inform the Member and the Member should respond promptly and fully to any request by a panel.[158] The confidentiality principles will apply.

The panels can also consult experts on certain matters. With respect to a factual issue concerning a scientific or other technical matter raised by a party to a dispute, a panel may request an advisory report in writing from an expert review group.[159] Rules for the establishment of such a group and its procedures are set forth in DSU Appendix 4. The panel shall decide their terms of reference and detailed working procedures. Finally, the final report of the expert review group is advisory in nature.

#### 3.2.3.2.6. *Applying Non-WTO Law*

Dispute settlement proceedings are based on WTO agreements. Besides, the WTO is part of general international law. Nevertheless, can non-WTO rules

---

[151] Y. Taniguch, "The WTO Dispute Settlement as Seen by a Proceduralist", (2009) 42 *Cornell International Law Journal*, pp. 1–21.

[152] *US-Lead and Bismuth II*, Hughes, p. 214.

[153] In *US-Shrimp Case.*

[154] *EC-Sardines.*

[155] Bossche, pp. 196–202.; Lester, Mercurio, Davies and Leitner, pp. 200–1.

[156] Hughes, p. 213.

[157] DSU, Art. 13(1), *EC-Hormones*, para. 148, *US-Shrimp*, paras. 104–6.

[158] DSU, Art. 13(1).

[159] DSU, Art. 13(2). *Argentina-Textiles and Apparel,* (Panel Report, Argentina-Measures Affecting Imports of Footwear, Textiles, Apparel and Other Items, WT/DS56/R,

of international law (such as human rights, environment, and labor law) be used for interpreting WTO dispute settlement procedures and can they be directly applicable in the WTO dispute settlement procedure?[160] Moreover can a defendant fence off a WTO complaint based on other treaties or rulings from other courts or tribunals?[161]

The basis for use of non-WTO law can be the DSU Art. 3(2):

> *...The Members recognize that it (dispute settlement system of the WTO) serves to preserve the rights and obligations of Members under the covered agreements, and to clarify the existing provisions of those agreements in accordance with customary rules of interpretation of public international law...*

And according to the DSU, Art. 7(2):

> *...Panels shall address the relevant provisions in any covered agreement or agreements cited by the parties to the dispute...*

According to one study, it was argued that it has become standard practice for WTO panels and the Appellate Body to use non-WTO law when interpreting the meaning in the WTO agreements.[162] The use of non-WTO law in interpretation leads to broad application of exceptions. For example, in interpreting exhaustible natural resources with reference to some environmental agreements broad exceptions were applied.[163] The author argued that non-WTO law can be used for filling procedural gaps such as burden of proof, standing, and retroactive application.[164]

The DSU states that agreements should be clarified in accordance with customary rules of interpretation of public international law.[165] And resorting to general principles of national or international law will solve some shortcomings.[166]

But how far can the argument go? There will also be "lex specialis" arguments. For example, there are special Articles under the DSU for example

---

modified by the Appellate Body Report, WT/DS56/AB/R and Corr. 1, adopted 22 April 1998), paras. 82–6.

160 E.- U. Petersmann, "WTO Dispute Settlement Practice 1995–2005: Lessons from the Past and Future Challenges in The WTO", in Y. Taniguchi, A. Yanovich and J. Bohanes (eds.), *The Twenty-First Century Dispute Settlement, Negotiations, and the Regionalism in Asia*, Cambridge: Cambridge University Press, 2007, p. 61.

161 J. Pauwelyn, "How to Win a World Trade Organization Dispute Based on Non-World Trade Organization Law? Questions of Jurisdiction and Merits", (2003) 37/6 *Journal of World Trade*, pp. 997–1030. (hereinafter Pauwelyn, "How to Win a World Trade Organization Dispute ...").

162 Pauwelyn, "How to Win a World Trade Organization Dispute ...", pp. 997–1030.

163 *US-Shrimp Case.*

164 Pauwelyn, "How to Win a World Trade Organization Dispute ...", pp. 997–1030.

165 DSU, Art. 7, Art. 3(2) and Art. 11.

166 Petersmann, pp. 40–1, discussed the development of WTO rules through WTO jurisprudence like zeroing methodology for calculating antidumping margins.

Articles 21 and 22[167] providing special norms and they would trump customary international law due to "lex specialis".[168]

### 3.2.3.2.7. *Interpretation*

With respect to treaty interpretation and interpretation of the relevant agreements Articles 31, 32 and 33[169] of the Vienna Convention on the Law of Treaties (the "Vienna Convention") will apply.[170] The Appellate Body also confirmed that the rules of treaty interpretation in Articles 31 and 32 the "Vienna Convention" apply in interpreting the WTO Agreement.[171]

The treaty interpretation has contributed to the development of international trade.[172]

### 3.2.3.2.8. *Confidentiality*

Panel deliberations are confidential.[173] Opinions expressed in the panel report by individual panelists are anonymous.[174] Report becomes public after they are circulated to all WTO Members. Also the information asked by the panel from individual or body is also confidential and are not revealed unless there is formal authorization from the individual or body that the information is

---

[167] Surveilance of implementation, compenstation and suspension of concessions provisions.

[168] *The Future of the WTO, Addressing Institutional Challenges in the new millennium Report* by the Consultative Board to the DG Panitchpakdi, 2004 (hereinafter The Future of WTO Report), para. 234.

[169] Vienna Convention Art. 33 for interpretation of treaties, due to different languages and translation there might be discrepancy between texts. Might lead to problems also in application at national level. Differences should be resolved according to Vienna Convention Art 33. For an Article on this issue that is arguing for systematic use of Vienna Convention Art 33 and considering alternative mechanisms *see* J. B. Condon, "Lost in Translation: Plurilingual Interpretation of WTO Law", (2010) 1/1 *Journal of International Dispute Settlement*, pp. 191–216.

[170] Petersmann, pp. 47–60.; Condon, pp. 200–6.; Bossche, pp. 206–9.

[171] *US-Gasoline, Japan-Alcoholic Beverages II*, United States -Section 301 Trade Act, *India-Patents (US)*, (Appellate Body Report, *India-Patent Protection for Pharmaceutical and Agricultural Chemical Products*, WT/DS50/AB/R, adopted 16 January 1998), in accordance with Article 3.2 of the DSU, Steger, p. 487.; P. V. Bossche, "From Afterthought to Centerpiece: The WTO Appellate Body and Its Rise to Prominence in the World Trading System in WTO Dispute Settlement", in G. Sacerdoti, A. Yanovich and J. Bohanes (eds.), *The WTO at Ten The Contribution of the Dispute Settlement System*, Cambridge: Cambridge University Press, 2006, pp. 306–10. (hereinafter Bossche, "From Afterthought to Centerpiece …").

[172] D. Mcrae, "Treaty Interpretation and the Development of International Trade Law by the WTO Appellate Body", in G. Sacerdoti, A. Yanovich and J. Bohanes (eds.), *The WTO at Ten The Contribution of the Dispute Settlement System*, Cambridge: Cambridge University Press, 2006, pp. 360–71.

[173] DSU, Art. 14 (1), *Brazil-Aircraft (Article 21.5 Canada)*,(Panel Report, *Brazil-Export Financing Programme for Aircraft, Recourse by Canada to Article 21.5 of the DSU*, WT/DS46/RW, modified by the Appellate Body Report,WT/DS46/AB/RW, adopted 4 August 2000), Annex 1.; Bossche, pp. 213–5.

[174] DSU, Art. 14(3).

asked from.[175] Similarly the proceedings at the appeal level are also confidential and opinions are anonymous.[176]

There is still limited openness although submissions of parties to panel are confidential the parties can make their submissions public. For example, the US national legislation makes it mandatory to have the submissions available to the public. Also as discussed in cases, nothing in the rules prohibits parties from agreeing to open the hearings to observers.[177] This was the case in the *EC -Hormones*, in which the Appellate Body, in agreeing to open up its hearing to the public in the case had to de-emphasize the meaning of confidentiality in the DSU, reading it as not applying to every aspect of the appellate process since the DSU appeared to require confidential proceedings.[178]

#### 3.2.3.2.9. *Adoption of Panel Decision*

The panel decision can be in favor of respondent or the complainant. It is possible to decide by majority, and dissenting or concurring opinions are also included if there are any.[179] However, dissenting opinions are not very common.[180]

Panel decisions are only recommendations and they are not binding judgments. The panel reports need to be adopted by the DSB to be binding.

First, the panel report is circulated to Members. Members having objections to the panel report give their written reasons in order to explain their objections.[181] Unless the party to the dispute formally notifies the DSB its decision to appeal the report shall be adopted at the DSB within sixty days after the date of circulation of the panel report to the Members.[182] The DSB can only decide by consensus not to adopt the panel report. The adoption procedure is without prejudice to the right of Members to express their views on a panel report.[183]

#### 3.2.3.3. *Appeal*

As discussed before, the panel report is adopted by the DSB by consensus. The party to the dispute can formally inform the DSB its decision to appeal.

---

175 DSU, Art 13(1).

176 DSU, Art. 18(2).

177 *EC-Hormones* dispute. B. Mercurio and R. Laforgia, "Expanding Democracy: Why Austalia Should Negotiate For Open and Transparent Dispute Settlement in Its Free trade Agreements", (2005) 6 *Melbourne Journal of International Law,* pp. 485, 495–9, in Lester, Mercurio, Davies and Leitner (eds.), pp. 195–7.

178 R. Howse, "Moving the WTO Forward- One Case at a Time", (2009) 42/1 *Cornell International Law Journal,* p. 227.

179 DSU, Art. 7.

180 Discusses the usage of dissent in panel and appeal decisions and also evaluates the importance of dissent opinion: K. M. Lewis, "The Lack of Dissent in WTO Dispute Settlement", (2006) 9/4 *Journal of International Economic Law* pp. 895–931.

181 DSU, Art. 16(2).

182 DSU, Art. 16.

183 DSU, Art. 16.

The DSB will not decide on the panel report if there is an appeal and will wait until the completion of the appeal.[184] In the appeal process there is the appellant, appellee, and participants.[185]

Also a party to the dispute other than the original appellant may join in that appeal, or appeal on the basis of other alleged errors in the issues of law covered in the panel report and legal interpretations developed by the panel.[186]

The overall average of panel reports that have been appealed from 1995 to 2009 is 68 percent.[187] As evaluated in one study, functioning of the Appellate Body is virtually perfect, it has produced many reports dealing with controversial trade and non-trade issues with results that are simply astonishing and has met the deadlines.[188]

The scope of the appeal is limited with the issues covered in the panel report and legal interpretations developed by the panel.[189]

3.2.3.3.1. *Composition of the Appellate Body*

The Appellate Body is composed of seven members that serve for four years. They can be reappointed once.[190] Three of them serve on one case but before finalizing their report they exchange views with the other four Appellate Body Members and this procedure is called "exchange of views".[191] Due to the "exchange of views" procedure it was argued that effective decision-making was possible with lower cost of reflections compared with *en banc* decisions.[192] Also, exchange of views have allowed the Appellate Body to ensure consistency and coherence in its case law.[193]

---

184 DSU, Art. 16.

185 For further information, *see* J. Lochart, "Assessing the 'Success' of the Appellate Body over the First Ten Years, in G. Sacerdoti, A. Yanovich and J. Bohanes (eds.), *The WTO at Ten The Contribution of the Dispute Settlement System*, Cambridge: Cambridge University Press, 2006, pp. 285–325.

186 Rule 23(1) Working Procedures for Appellate Review.,

187 WT/AB/13, 17.02.2010, Appellate Body Annual Report for 2009. < http://www.wto.org/english/tratop_e/dispu_e/ab_annual_report09_e.doc> (date of access 18.03.2010), p.15, for the activity in 2008 *see* The WTO Appellate Body's Activities in 2008, *Journal of International Economic Law* 12(1), 209–25, (2009).

188 A. Alvarez-Jimenez, "The WTO Appellate Body's Decision Making Process: A Perfect Model for International Adjudication?", (2009) 12/2 *Journal of International Economic Law*, pp. 289–331. (hereinafter Alvarez-Jimenez, "The Appellate Body's Decision Making Process …"). The Appellate Body has the unity of its case law except in few cases, EC-Asbestos and United States - Upland Cotton, the Appellate Body has managed to avoid separate opinions: Alvarez-Jimenez, "The Appellate Body's Decision Making Process …", pp. 289–331.

189 DSU, Art. 17.

190 DSU, Art. 17.

191 Rule 4(3) Working Procedure. This normally lasts for two or three days (Rule (4)(3). Working Procedures for Appellate Review.

192 Alvarez-Jimenez, pp. 289–331.

193 Bossche, "From Afterthought to Centerpiece …", p. 304.

In sum the Appellate Body does not hear appeals *en banc* and three members take the decisions. The Appellate Body members are people with recognized authority, with demonstrated expertise in law, international trade, and the subject matter of the covered agreements. Besides, the nationalities of the Appellate Body members are irrelevant and they can sit in cases in their country of origin.[194]

3.2.3.3.2. *Functions of the Appellate Body*

3.2.3.3.2.1. *Working Procedures*

Establishing the Appellate Body and introducing the appeal process is among the most important contributions of the Uruguay Round. Appeal review is limited to issues of law covered in the panel report and legal interpretations developed by the panel.[195]

There is a Working Procedures for Appellate review.[196] The Working Procedures set out the duties and responsibilities of the Appellate Body, the due process, and appellate review process. The Working Procedures also give authority to the Appellate Body to adopt additional rules for the purposes of appeal in the interests of fairness and orderly procedure in the conduct of appeal.[197] The Appellate Body also adopted the Rules of Conduct for the Understanding on Rules and Procedures Governing the Settlement of Disputes.[198]

There are three official languages in the dispute settlement: English, French, and Spanish. But in practice English is the working language and most cases are written in English and later translated into French and Spanish.[199]

Judicial economy discussion, where a panel can abstain from making multiple findings on a claim presented by complaining party on the ground that another finding of inconsistency already resolves the dispute at hand, is discussed whether it is possible at the appeal level.[200]

The Appellate Body can uphold, modify, or reverse legal findings and conclusions of the panel decision.[201]

---

[194] Bossche, p. 247.

[195] DSU, Art. 17(6).

[196] 04.01.2005, WT/AB/WP/5. V. Donaldson and A. Yanovich, "The Appellate Body's Working Procedures for Appellate Review, in in G. Sacerdoti, A. Yanovich and J. Bohanes (eds.), *The WTO at Ten The Contribution of the Dispute Settlement System*, Cambridge: Cambridge University Press, 2006, pp. 386–423. Has a detailed analysis of the 5 amendments.

[197] Bossche, "From Afterthought to Centerpiece …", p. 306- argued that it might be the basis of dealing with amicus curiae briefs.

[198] (Rules of Conduct)-WT/DSB/RC/1, 11.12.1996.

[199] On 12th September 2006 for the first time a panel hearing was held in Spanish: *Mexico-Antidumping Duties on Steel Pipes and Tubes from Guatemala*, DS 331, *EC-Asbestos* case was in French.

[200] Term not used for the Appellate Body, Appellate Body moved away from a strict reading of the provision, *United States- Subsidies on Upland Cotton*, *See* Alvarez-Jimenez.

[201] DSU, Art. 17(13).

*Precedent*

There is no binding precedent for Appellate Body reports. The reports are binding for the parties after the adoption by the DSB.[202] However, the Appellate Body attempts to follow its own decisions to achieve consistency and coherence, and this has been an important stabilizer.[203] The reports are normally binding only on parties, but in some cases it was discussed that they might create legitimate expectations and they should be taken into account where relevant.[204] In the *United States-Zeroing* (Japan) *Case*, the panel openly rejected the earlier approach and adopted a different one baseing its argument on making an objective assessment of the matter before it. The panel decision was appealed on substance but this issue was not raised.[205]

3.2.3.3.2.2. *Time Period*

Once appeal is filed, the appellant has seven days to file written submission.[206] The parties wishing to respond to allegations as well as the third parties can write submissions within twenty five days of filing.

The appellate proceedings shall not exceed sixty days from the date a party notifies its decision to appeal to the date the Appellate Body report is circulated.[207]

If the Appellate Body considers that it cannot provide its report in time, it shall inform the DSB in writing with the reasons for the delay together with an estimate of the period within which it will issue its report.[208] However, the proceedings cannot exceed ninety days.

Unless agreed by the parties, the period from the date of establishment of the panel until the date the DSB considers the panel or appellate report for adoption shall, as a general rule, not exceed nine months where the panel report is not appealed or twelve months where the report is appealed. If the time period is extended according to relevant Articles, additional time will be added to the above periods.[209]

---

202 For a discussion on the difference of precedent and *stare decisis* and the use of precedent in WTO Dispute Settlement *see* J. H. Jackson, "Process and Procedure in WTO Dispute Settlement", (2009) 42/1 *Cornell International Law Journal*, pp. 233–40. (hereinafter Jackson, "Process and Procedure …").

203 R. Howse and S. Esserman, "The Appellate Body, the WTO Dispute Settlement System, and the Politics of Multilateralism, in in G. Sacerdoti, A. Yanovich and J. Bohanes (eds.), *The WTO at Ten The Contribution of the Dispute Settlement System*, Cambridge: Cambridge University Press, 2006, p. 65.

204 Lester, Mercurio, Davies and Leitner, pp. 204–6.

205 Lester, Mercurio, Davies and Leitner, p. 205.

206 Working procedure Rule 21(1).

207 DSU 17(5). *EC-Hormones, US-Lead Bismuth II, EC-Asbestos,; Thailand-H-Beams*, (Panel Report, *Thailand-Anti-Dumping Duties on Angles, Shapes and Sections of Iron or Non-Alloy Steel and H-Beams from Poland*, WT/DS122/R, modified by the Appellate Body Report, adopted 5 April 2001).

208 DSU 17(5).

209 DSU, Art. 20.

3.2.3.3.3. *Third Party Participation*

The parties to the dispute may appeal a panel report; third parties do not have the right to appeal. However, third parties which have notified the DSB of a "substantial interest" in the matter may make written submissions to, and will be given an opportunity to be heard by, the Appellate Body.[210] Third parties can attend oral hearings as passive observer. Public observation of oral hearings was authorized for the first time in the *US-Continued Suspension* and *Canada-Continued Suspension* cases at appeal.[211]

In the *China-Publications Case,*[212] the European Union was very influential as a third party participant in the appeal.

3.2.3.3.4. *Adoption of the Appellate Body Report*

Appellate Body report is adopted by the DSB within thirty days following its circulation to the Members unless the DSB decides by consensus not to adopt the Appellate Body report.[213] As discussed before, the General Council, which is composed of representatives of all the Members, convenes and acts like the DSB when administering the WTO dispute settlement system.

Panels and the Appellate Body can only issue advisory reports with recommendations addressed to Members and they are not legally binding judgments.[214] They have to be adopted by the DSB. The parties to the dispute accept the adopted report unconditionally. In addition, the adoption procedure is without prejudice to the right of Members to express their views on an Appellate Body report.[215]

3.2.3.4. *Implementation*

When the panel or the Appellate Body finds a measure inconsistent with a covered agreement, it shall recommend the Member concerned to bring its measure into conformity with the agreement.[216] The panel or the Appellate Body can make suggestions for the implementation of recommendations.[217]

---

[210] DSU, Art. 17(4).

[211] The WTO Appellate Body's Activities in 2008, *Journal of International Economic Law* 12(1), 218, 2009.

[212] *China-Publications,* (Appellate Body Report, *China-Measures Affecting Trading Rights and Distribution Services for Certain Publications and Audiovisual Entertainment Products,* WT/DS363/AB/R, adopted 21 December 2009). <http://worldtradelaw.typepad.com/ielpblog/2010/01/the-china-publications-ab-report-and-the-role-of-third-participants.html>, (date of acces 18.03.2010).

[213] DSU, Art. 17(14).

[214] Petersmann, p. 87.

[215] DSU, Art. 17(14).

[216] DSU, Art. 19.

[217] *US-Stainless Steel,* (Panel Report, *United States – Anti-Dumping Measures on Stainless Steel Plate in Coils and Stainless Steel and Strip from Korea,* WT/DS179/R, adopted 1 February 2001).; *US-Underwear,* (Panel Report, *United States -Cotton and Underwear, (United States-Restrictions on Imports of Cotton and Man-made Fibre Underwear,* WT/DS24/R, modified by the Appellate Body Report, WT/DS24/AB/R, adopted 25 February 1997).; *EC-Bananas III (Ecuador),* (Panel Report, *European Communities- Regime for the Importation, Sale and Distribution of Bananas,*

But the panel and the Appellate Body cannot add to or diminish the rights and obligations provided in the covered agreements in their findings and recommendations.[218]

Members will determine how to implement. They can withdraw or modify the measure. However, adopting a new measure can be problematic due to consistency problems.

The Member shall inform the DSB of its intentions in respect of implementation of the recommendations and rulings of the DSB.[219] The implementation is also monitored.[220]

When there is a disagreement on whether the implementation is satisfactory, the DSU provisions do not work harmoniously and this is referred as the sequencing issue. According to Article 21(5) of the DSU on the Surveillance of Implementation of Recommendations and Rulings:

> *...Where there is disagreement as to the existence or consistency with a covered agreement of measures taken to comply with the recommendations and rulings such dispute shall be decided through recourse to these dispute settlement procedures, including wherever possible resort to the original panel. The panel shall circulate its report within 90 days after the date of referral of the matter to it.*

Article 22(6) of the DSU, the Compensation and the Suspension of Concessions provision states that:

> *...the DSB, upon request, shall grant authorization to suspend concessions or other obligations within 30 days of the expiry of the reasonable period of time unless the DSB decides by consensus to reject the request...*

The timelines do not work together. The relationship between these two procedures is referred as the sequencing issue. This was the case in the *EC – Banana* dispute.

3.2.3.5. *Compliance*

Prompt compliance by the Member State is required.[221] If it is impracticable to comply with the recommendations and rulings immediately, the Member will have a reasonable period of time.[222]

---

*Complaint by Ecuador*, WT/DS27/R/ECU, modified by the Appellate Body Report, WT/DS27/AB/R, adopted 25 September 1997).

[218] DSU, Art. 19(2).

[219] DSU, Art. 21(3).

[220] DSU, Art. 19(1), *Brazil-Aircraft*, (Panel Report, *Brazil-Export Financing for Aircraft*, WT/DS46/R, modified by the Appellate Body Report, WT/DS46/AB/R, adopted 20 August 1999).

[221] DSU, Art. 21.1. For evaluation of the compliance records and the quality and timeliness of compliance, *see* J. W. Davey, "Compliance Problems in WTO Dispute Settlement", (2009) 42/1 *Cornell International Law Journal*, pp. 119–28. (hereinafter Davey, "Compliance Problems ...").

[222] The reasonable time is discussed under DSU, Art. 21.3, Compliance was discussed in the Award of Arbitrator: Argentina-Hides and Leather (21.3), Prompt compliance in: DSU, Art. 21(3), *US-Hot Rolled Steel*, (Award of the Arbitrator, *United States – Anti-Dumping Measures on Certain Hot-Rolled Steel Products from Japan- Arbitration under Article 21.3 (c) of the DSU*,

The reasonable period of time shall not exceed fifteen months from the date of establishment of the panel by the DSB unless the panel or the Appellate Body extends the time or the parties to the dispute agree otherwise.[223] If the panel or the Appellate Body extends the time, the total time cannot exceed eighteen months unless the parties to the dispute agree that there are exceptional circumstances.[224]

If there is no agreement on reasonable time, the complainant can refer the matter to arbitration under Article 21(3) c of the DSU. The arbitrator's mandate is defined as: "*... not to suggest ways or means to implement the recommendations and rulings of the Appellate Body Report and Panel Reports but to determine the reasonable period of time within which implementation must be completed*".[225] It is for the implementing Member, and not for the arbitrator, to determine the proper scope and content of anticipated legislation.[226] The arbitrator focuses on the time for implementation.

Also according to Article 21(5) of the DSU on the Surveillance of Implementation of Recommendations and Rulings:

> *...Where there is disagreement as to the existence or consistency with a covered agreement of measures taken to comply with the recommendations and rulings such dispute shall be decided through recourse to these dispute settlement procedures, including wherever possible resort to the original panel. The panel shall circulate its report within 90 days after the date of referral of the matter to it.*

3.2.3.6. *Compensation*

The Member State that fails to bring the inconsistent measure into compliance and does not implement the recommendations and rulings within the determined time, if requested should enter into negotiations with any party having that invoked the dispute settlement procedures, to agree on mutually acceptable compensation.[227]

Compensation is a temporary measure and it is voluntary and, if granted, shall be consistent with the covered agreements.[228] Because it is voluntary there might be a problem for its enforcement. Compensation is not always money, it can be trade benefits or more market access.[229] For enforcement

---

WT/DS184/13, 19 February 2002), paras. 84–5. Also for evaluation of the cases and the implementation timing, *see* Davey, pp. 112–3.

223 DSU, Art. 21(4).

224 DSU, Art. 21(4).

225 Arbitration Award: *EC-Hormones* (Article 21.3), para. 38. Also *see Colombia-Ports of Entry (21.3),* (Award of the Arbitrator, *Colombia – Indicative Prices and Restrictions on Ports of Entry* – ARB 2009-1/25 – Arbitration under Article 21.3(c) of the DSU, WT/DS366/13, 2 October 2009).

226 Arbitration Award: *US-Hot Rolled Steel* (Article 21.3), para. 30.

227 DSU, Art. 22(2).

228 DSU, Art. 22(1).

229 *The Future of WTO Report*, para. 238.

problems there have been proposals for mandatory trade compensation.[230] And applying more monetary compensation[231]

One interesting discussion on the application of compensation is if a strict interpretation is done any agreement need to be in conformity with all WTO obligations, and there is the "Most Favored Nation" (MFN) treatment. If compensation is a benefit or an advantage would the others also demand and benefit from it?[232]

Compensation remedy has been used rarely, in the *Turkey-Textiles Case*, compensation was in form of tariff reductions but there was the discussion of MFN application.[233] Therefore compensation is not preferred.

3.2.3.7. *Suspension of Concession—Retaliation*

If it is not possible to agree on a satisfactory compensation within twenty days after the expiration of the reasonable time, any party that invoked the dispute settlement procedures may request authorization from the DSB to suspend the application to the Member concerned of concessions or other obligations under the covered agreements.[234] Retaliation is not often used; it was authorized and used in only four cases.[235]

The DSB, upon request, shall grant authorization to suspend concessions or other obligations within thirty days of the expiration of the reasonable period of time unless the DSB decides by consensus to reject the request.[236]

However, the Member concerned can object to the level of suspension proposed, or if it claims that the principles and procedures set forth in the Article have not been followed, the matter shall be referred to arbitration. The original panel will carry out the arbitration if the members are available or an arbitrator (individual or group) appointed by the Director-General.[237] The procedures should be completed within sixty days after the date of expiry of the reasonable period of time. In addition, the concessions or other obligations shall not be suspended during the course of the arbitration.

The party first seeks to suspend concessions or other obligations with respect to the same sector.[238] If it is not practicable or effective to suspend

[230] Mercurio and Hughes, p. 232.

[231] *The Future of WTO Report*, para. 243.

[232] Lester, Mercurio, Davies and Leitner (eds.), p. 165.

[233] A. Davies, "Reviewing Dispute Settlement at the World Trade Organization: a Time to Reconsider the Role/s of Compensation", (2006) 5/1 *World Trade Review*, p. 31 in Lester, Mercurio, Davies and Leitner (eds.), p. 165.

[234] DSU, Art. 22(2).

[235] Davey, p. 128, also Davey, "Compliance Problems …", p. 124.; *EC-Bananas, EC-Hormones*, United States- Foreign Sales Corporation (FSC) and United States Byrd Amendment.

[236] DSU, Art. 22(6).

[237] DSU, Art. 22(6). *EC-Bananas* III (Ecuador) (Article 22.6 -EC), *EC-Hormones (US)* (Article 22.6 – EC).

[238] DSU, Art. 22(3) f defines sector.

concessions or other obligations with respect to the same sectors, it may seek to suspend concessions or other obligations in other sectors under the same agreement.[239] If it is not practicable or effective to suspend concessions or other obligations under the same agreement and if the circumstances are serious enough, it may seek to suspend concessions or other obligations under another covered agreement.[240] For the last two cases, the party should state the reasons in its request. The request is forwarded to the DSB, the relevant Councils, and the relevant sectoral bodies.[241]

For example, in the *EC-Banana* dispute, although the dispute was related to bananas, the US retaliated in meat products, cheese, bed linen, handbags, and so on in order to target the powerful interest groups.[242]

If retaliatory measure is in different agreement, it is called cross retaliation. Cross retaliation is especially important for developing countries. Due to asymmetrical relationship particular sector or agreement might not be large enough, developing countries rely on certain imports from certain countries and raising barriers would decrease supply or increase price of domestic producers and consumers.[243]

In the *EC -Bananas (Ecuador) Case*, suspension was on TRIPS Agreement, Ecuador's banana trade sector and economy on the whole was serious enough to justify suspension in another agreement.[244]

The party shall take into account: -the trade in the sector or under the agreement under which the panel or Appellate Body has found a violation or other nullification or impairment, the importance of such trade to that party; -the broader economic elements related to the nullification or impairment and the broader economic consequences of the suspension of concessions or other obligations.[245]

The level of the suspension of concessions or other obligations authorized by the DSB shall be equivalent to the level of nullification or impairment.[246]

The suspension of concessions or other obligations are temporary.[247] They should be applied until the inconsistent measure is removed or the Member provides a solution to the nullification or impairment of benefits, or when a mutually satisfactory solution is reached.[248]

---

[239] DSU, Art. 22(3) g defines agreement.

[240] DSU, Art. 22(3).

[241] DSU, Art. 22(3)e.

[242] Lester, Mercurio, Davies and Leitner (eds.), p. 167. The target groups will lobby for compliance and induce Members to comply with obligations.

[243] Lester, Mercurio, Davies and Leitner (eds.), pp. 168–9.

[244] Lester, Mercurio, Davies and Leitner (eds.), pp. 168–9. European Communities argued Ecuador did not demonstrate why not practicable and effective. The Arbitration Decision: WT/DS27/ARB/ECU, excerpt in the book, pp. 168–72.

[245] DSU, Art. 22 (3)d.

[246] DSU, Art. 22(4).

[247] DSU, Art. 22(8).

[248] DSU, Art. 22(8).

Possibility of retaliation under the dispute settlement process has been criticized. Some argued that imposition of retaliatory trade measures is economically inefficient for both the country imposing the retaliatory measures as well as the target nation.[249] The consumers in the nation imposing retaliation may end up paying more for imported goods.[250]

Also, it was argued that retaliation is contradicting with the goals of the WTO because retaliation will lead to reduction of trade and will limit trade.[251]And by allowing some Members to buy out of their obligations would create major asymmetries in the system.[252]

There has been a discussion on the goal of retaliation as well.[253] Is retaliation for rebalancing concessions, inducing a Member to comply with the obligations, or bringing its measures in conformity? In many cases, the threat of retaliation was enough to coerce a Member.[254] The goal of the WTO dispute settlement is not to punish but to settle.[255]

There is also a separate argument on developing countries' positions and the likelihood of developing countries using retaliatory measures. There is an imbalance between developed and developing countries. Suspension of concessions might not be practical for developing countries since there is little incentive for developed countries to bring measures in conformity.[256] Developing countries' retaliatory measures might be counterproductive since there might not be any alternative supplier or additional costs may make goods inaccessible to local market.[257] Also, developing countries might not

---

249 B. Mercurio, "Why Compensation Cannot Replace Trade Retaliation in the WTO Dispute Settlement Understanding", (2009) 8/2 *World Trade Review*, p. 318.

250 Mercurio, p. 318 etc., also *see* C. P. Bown and B. M. Hoekman, "WTO Dispute Settlement and the Missing Developing Country Cases: Engaging the Private Sector", (2005) 8 *Journal of International Economic Law*, pp. 861–90.

251 Mercurio, p. 319.; K. Anderson, "Peculiarities of Retaliation in WTO Dispute Settlement", CIES Discussion Paper No. 0207/CEPR Discussion Paper No. 3578, available at http://papers.ssrn.com/sol3/papers.cfm?abstract_id=348582, (date of access 18.03.2010). Also *The Future of WTO Report*, para. 240.

252 *The Future of WTO Report*, para. 242.

253 *See* J. Bello, "The WTO Dispute Settlement Understanding: Less is More", (1996) 90 *American Journal of International Law*, p. 416.; J. H. Jackson, "The WTO Dispute Settlement Understanding-Misunderstandings on the Nature of Legal Obligation", (1997) 91*American Journal of International Law*, p. 60. (hereinafter Jackson, "The WTO Dispute Settlement Understanding …").; J. H. Jackson, "International Law Status of WTO Dispute Settlement Reports: Obligation to Comply or Option to "Buy Out"?", (2004) 98 *American Journal of International Law*, p. 109. (hereinafter Jackson, "International Law Status of WTO …"). Also Lester, Mercurio, Davies and Leitner (eds.), p. 167.

254 F. Breuss, (2005), Economic Integration, EU–US Trade Conflicts and WTO Dispute Settlement, European Integration Online Papers, 9(12): 1–24, available at <http://eiop.or.at/eiop/pdf/2005-012.pdf.>, (Date of access 18.03.2010).

255 Y. Fukunaga, "Securing Compliance through the WTO Dispute Settlement System: Implementation of DSB Recommendations", (2006) 9/2 *Journal of International Economic Law*, p. 386.

256 Hughes, p. 231 and fn 162.

257 Mercurio, p. 318 etc., also *see* C. P. Bown and B. M. Hoekman, pp. 861–90.

want to retaliate due to the negative effect retaliation may have on the retaliating country's own economy, the insignificant impact it will have on the economy of the offending State, especially if it is a developed country Member, and lastly the possibility of trade wars.[258] For a solution for these arguments, the idea of collective suspension of concessions by all WTO Members against the Member that fail to comply in a case against a developing country was raised.[259] Also, possibility of trading "the right to suspend concessions" to another Member at a better position was discussed.[260] The developing countries will be discussed later under a separate heading.

Retaliation is the last resort in the dispute settlement process.[261] However, retaliation procedure is problematic because it is prospective and not applied retroactively.[262]

#### 3.2.3.8. *Surveillance*

Surveillance of implementation of the recommendations is very important. The DSB keeps the implementation of adopted recommendations and rulings under surveillance.[263] If there is discussion on the implementation of rulings or recommendations by the DSB or any Member after the adoption, the issue of implementation shall be placed on the agenda of the DSB meeting after six months following the date of establishment of the reasonable period of time and shall remain on the DSB's agenda until the issue is resolved unless the DSB decides otherwise.[264] Before the DSB meetings, the Member concerned should provide the DSB a status report in writing of its progress in the implementation of the recommendations or rulings.

The implementation of the recommendations and rulings of adopted decisions are also reviewed under the Trade Policy Review Mechanism.[265]

### 3.3. *Alternative Ways*

If the parties to the dispute agree voluntarily, they can use procedures such as good offices, conciliation, and mediation.[266] However, since the strong party

---

[258] M. Shahin, "WTO Dispute Settlement for a Middle Income Developing Country: A Case Study of Egypt", Online Proceedings, Working Paper No. 09/08, Inaugural Conference Geneva July 5–17, 2008.
[259] Hughes, p. 232, fn 163.
[260] Hughes, p. 232, fn 164.
[261] DSU, Art 3(7).
[262] Davey, p. 129, Mercurio, p. 320.
[263] DSU, Art. 21(6).
[264] DSU, Art. 21(6).
[265] J. Chaisse and D. Chakraborty, "Implementing WTO Rules through Negotiations and Sanctions: The Role of Trade Policy Review Mechanism and Dispute Settlement System", (2007) 28 *University of Pennsylvania Journal of International Economic Law*, pp. 158–61.
[266] DSU, Art. 5.

does not want to put the other party to an equal footing, these procedures are not that effective.[267]

There is also the arbitration procedure under the DSU.[268] Arbitration is also an alternative means of dispute settlement under the DSU.[269] Except otherwise provided, the DSU mutual agreement of the parties is required.[270] If the parties agree, other members may become party to arbitration. The arbitration award is binding on the parties.[271] The award cannot be appealed and is enforceable through the DSU.

There is also the arbitration procedure under Article 22.6 of the DSU on surveillance of implementation of recommendations and rulings. As discussed in the suspension of the concessions part, the Member concerned can object to the level of suspension proposed, or it can claim that the principles and procedures set forth in the Article have not been followed. In such a case the matter will be referred to arbitration.[272] For example this was the case in the *Banana Arbitration*.[273] There is also a working procedure for the application of this Article.[274]

### 3.4. *The WTO Dispute Settlement and Developing Countries*

The WTO dispute settlement is mostly used by the United States and the European Union.[275] The developing countries also use the system moderately.[276]

---

[267] H. Nordstorm and G. Shaffer, "Access to Justice in the World Trade Organization: A Case for a Small Claims Procedure?", (2008) 7/4 *World Trade Review*, p. 606.

[268] Arbitration Award: United States -Section 110(5)Copyright Act (Art 25.3).

[269] DSU, Art. 25(1).

[270] DSU, Art. 25(2).

[271] DSU, Art. 25(3).

[272] DSU, Art. 22(6).

[273] H. Nottage and J. Bohanes, "Arbitration as an Alternative Litigation in the WTO: Observations in the Light of the 2005 Banana Tariff Arbitrations, in Y. Taniguchi, A. Yanovich and J. Bohanes (eds.), *The Twenty-First Century Dispute Settlement, Negotiations, and the Regionalism in Asia*, Cambridge: Cambridge University Press, 2007, pp. 212–47.

[274] Working Procedure for the application of DSU, Art. 22(6). Also DSU, Art. 21(3) arbitration for determinining reasonable period of time for implementation was mentioned in the implementation part.

[275] C. Bown and R. Mcculloch, "Developing Countries, Dispute Settlement, and the Advisory Center on WTO Law", (2010) 19/1 *The Journal of International Trade & Economic Development*, pp. 33–63.

[276] For the the ratio of developed country Members to developing country Members in terms of appearances made as appellant, other appellant, appellee, and third participant in appellate proceedings from 1996 through 2009, *see* WT/AB/13, 17.02.2010, Appellate Body Annual Report for 2009, Figure 4. For a case study of developing countries, Egypt example *see* M. Shahin. For the assessment of the developing countries participation in GATT and the Rounds, *see* R. Wilkinson and J. Scott, "Developing Country Participation in the GATT: a Reassessment", (2008) 7/3 *World Trade Review*, pp. 473–510. Bossche, pp. 226–8.

For example, Antigua filed complaint against the United States and won.[277] Peru has also won against the European Communities.[278] However, the position of developing countries and the usage of the dispute settlement system by developing countries have been discussed widely. It was argued that it is hard for developing countries to find expertise and resources for dispute settlement. Developing countries have unequal access to resources.[279] Small trading nations are constrained from being able to use the legal system.[280] The procedure is very expensive, may cost more than half million dollars (including the cost of legal counsel, government employees, government resources, and personnel[281]) and the process is very complex and may take up to three years.[282] Due to long time period, developing countries can lose their market niches. Minor claims are unlikely to be pursued unless there is an important principle at stake.[283]

Developing countries lack retaliatory capacity of the large and rich countries. Also poor countries are dependant on developed countries for development assistance or preferential market access.

The dispute settlement period can be very expensive. Some countries proposed to form permanent funds and pool of experts.[284] Attorney fees in trade litigation cases at a billable rate of $350 per hour, the average cost of legal service runs from $89,950 for a 'low' complexity case to $247,100 for a 'high' complexity case.[285] There are also other expenses such as data collection, expert witnesses, overhead costs such as travel, accommodation, communication, etc.[286]

In order to overcome this disadvantage the WTO established an "Advisory Center for WTO Law" (ACWL) to provide legal advice to developing countries.[287] Has the ACWL been successful? According to some, the ACWL has not been effective in encouraging new countries to participate in the WTO dispute settlement but provided current developing countries resources to pursue cases differently and ability to file sole complainant cases.[288]

---

[277] *United States-Measures Affecting the Cross- Border Supply of Gambling and Betting Services*, Appellate Body Report, WT/DS285/AB/R, 7 April 2005), from: Taniguch, pp. 1–21.

[278] *EC-Sardines*, from: Taniguch, pp. 1–21.

[279] A. J. Conti, "The Good Case: Decisions to Litigate at the World Trade Organization", (2008) 42/1 *Law & Society Review*, pp. 145–82.

[280] Nordstorm and Shaffer, pp. 587–640.

[281] For estimated legal costs look at p. 601. *See* <http://www.acwl.ch/e/index.html >, (date of access 18.03.2010).

[282] Nordstorm and Shaffer, pp. 587–640.

[283] Ibid.

[284] Hughes, p. 233, fn 173.

[285] Bown and Hoekman, pp. 861–90. 2005 update at Advisory Centre on WTO Law, Billing Policy and Revised Time Budget, <http://www.acwl.ch/e/pdf/time_budget_e.pdf>.

[286] Bown and Hoekman, pp. 861–90.

[287] S. Laird, "The WTO Agenda and the Developing Countries" in C. Milner and R. Read (eds.), *Trade Liberalization, Competition and the WTO*, Edward Elgar Publishing, 2002, pp. 227–31.

[288] Bown and Mcculloch, pp. 33–63.

The developing countries most likely bring cases when the cause of lost market access is obvious to the exporting firms or government. But it was argued that developing countries lack information required to identify potential cases for the WTO dispute settlement when the market access loss is not obvious.[289] The developing countries need additional monitoring resources, such as public provision of information on potential WTO cases, to help them identify less observable causes of lost market access.[290]

For a solution some authors argued for the use of a public prosecutor and legal aid other than ACWL. It was argued that the ACWL, which provides legal advice on discounted rates, is not free –albeit subsidized-, has limited staff, and the process still requires a lot of internal work.[291] Others argued NGOs, development organizations, economists, consumer groups, and even law schools can be involved in this process to improve poor country access and to lower the costs of legal assistance and provide guidance to developing countries for WTO cases.[292]

One way to circumvent the problem of high costs is that similar interest countries can join and put sources together to reduce individual costs.[293] For example, at the African level, an inter-African legal consultancy team that could work closely to examine the rules and procedures of the DSU was formed.[294] Relatively similar States can share their experience and cut down on financial burdens, as the cost of operation would be dispersed among all members of the group.[295]

There are also advantageous procedures for developing countries in the WTO system. For example, developing countries are given more time for consultation, to present their case, and for implementation.[296] Special attention is given to interests of developing countries during consultations[297] and there is possibility of extending the time periods during consultation.[298] When the dispute is between a developing and a developed country, if the developing country requests it, the panel will include at least one panelist from a developing country Member.[299] Where there is a developing country involved, the panel's

---

[289] Ibid.

[290] Ibid.

[291] Nordstorm and Shaffer, p. 600.

[292] Bown and Hoekman, pp. 861–90.

[293] L. C. Davis, "Do WTO Rules Create a Level Playing Field? Lessons from the Experience of Peru and Vietnam", in S. J. Odell (ed.), *Negotiating Trade Developing Countries in the WTO and NAFTA*, Cambridge: Cambridge University Press 2006, pp. 219–55.

[294] *See* Shahin.

[295] Ibid.

[296] DSU, Art. 12(10), 21(2).

[297] DSU, Art. 4(10).

[298] DSU, Art. 12(10), *India-Quantitative Restrictions*, (Panel Report, *India-Quantitative Restrictions on Imports of Agricultural, Textile and Industrial Products*, WT/DS90/R, upheld by the Appellate Body Report, WT/DS90/AB/R, adopted 22 September 1999).

[299] DSU, Art. 8(10).

report shall explicitly indicate the form in which account has been taken of relevant provisions on differential and more-favorable treatment for developing country Members that form part of the covered agreements which have been raised by the developing country Member in the course of the dispute settlement procedures.[300] Particular attention should be paid to matters affecting the interests of developing country Members with respect to measures, which have been subject to dispute settlement.[301] If the matter is one, which has been raised by a developing country Member, the DSB shall consider what further action it might take which would be appropriate to the circumstances.[302] If the case is one brought by a developing country Member, in considering what appropriate action might be taken, the DSB shall take into account not only the trade coverage of measures complained of, but also their impact on the economy of developing country Members concerned.[303]

### 3.5. *Proposal for Change*

The dispute settlement procedure is evaluated in each round and proposals for change are discussed at rounds to make the system better. Discussions regarding dispute settlement are done at the current DOHA Round and mentioned in the Doha Development Agenda (DDA).[304]

In this part issues that needs to be raised will be covered, some topics have been raised in current negotiations.

The first proposal is that the system needs more transparency.[305] There has been some positive change in this area. The United States and the European Communities agreed in their dispute to make their panel proceedings open to the public. The oral hearing before the Appellate Body was open to public observation as well.[306] The Appellate Body decided to hold an open hearing in the appeal with a closed circuit television system; the Appellate Body preserved the right to confidentiality for third party participants who did not

---

300 DSU, Art. 12(11).

301 DSU, Art. 21(2), *Indonesia-Autos (Article 21.3),* (Award of the Arbitrator, *Indonesia-Certain Measures Affecting the Automobile Industry – Arbitration under Article 21.3 (c) of the DSU,* WT/DS54/15, WTDS55/14, WT/DS59/13, WT/DS64/12, 7 December 1998).; *Chile-Alcoholic Beverages* (Article 21.3), (Award of the Arbitrator, *Chile-Taxes on Alcoholic Beverages-Arbitration under Article 21.3 (c) of the DSU,* WT/DS87/15, WT/DS110/14, 23 May 2000).

302 DSU, Art. 21(7).

303 DSU, Art. 21(8).

304 Bossche, pp. 289–99.

305 Davey, pp. 116–33, Bossche, pp. 292–7.

306 United States-Continued Suspension of Obligations in the *EC-Hormones Dispute, Canada-Continued Suspension of Obligations in the EC-Hormones Dispute,* WT/DS320/8, WT/DS321/8 (Aug. 2, 2005), Y. Taniguch, "The WTO Dispute Settlement as Seen by a Proceduralist", 42 *Cornell International Law Journal,* (2009), pp. 1–21. L. Ehring, "Public Access to Dispute Settlement Hearings in the World Trade Organization", *Journal of International Economic Law* 11(4), 2008, pp. 1021–1034. Also The WTO Appellate Body's Activities in 2008, *Journal of International Economic Law* 12(1), p. 218, 2009.

agree to the opening of the hearing.[307] Because in case of the Appellate Body, the DSU appeared to require confidential proceedings, the Appellate Body, in agreeing to open up its hearing to the public in *EC-Hormones*, had to de-emphasize the meaning of confidentiality in the DSU, reading it as not applying to every aspect of the appellate process.[308]

The second proposal is the establishment of permanent panels and permanent panelists from qualified individuals.[309] Having permanent panels would make it possible to deliver decisions on timely manner.[310] The idea of permanent panel body and the experience of the panelists will make procedural amendments more workable.[311] It is also possible to establish a pool of permanent chairs as an alternative to permanent panels.[312] A further suggestion was that panel and Appellate Body members could become full-time judges of the proposed World Trade Court, where the Court will become independent from the WTO in form.[313]

The third suggestion is to eliminate the interim review. Interim review idea was introduced when there was no appeal body. With the establishment of appeal procedure in the dispute settlement process interim review might not be necessary. The removal of the interim review process will also shorten the time period for decision-making.

The fourth suggestion is the introduction of the remand authority to the Appellate Body; remand the case back to panel. The European Union also proposed for amendment and adding remand procedure.[314] Currently there is lack of remand at appeal level.[315] If the Appellate Body finds that the panel erred in the application of law in the covered agreements, the parties should be given opportunity to present arguments and evidence under the applicable law that the Appellate Body will apply.[316]

The fifth suggestion is solving the sequencing problem. As discussed above in case of where complaining party claims that defending country has not implemented the ruling there is a problem with the timing in Article 21(5) and 22(6) of the DSU and they are not compatible.[317] This has caused a problem in

---

307 Taniguch, pp. 1–21.

308 R. Howse, "Moving the WTO Forward- One Case at a Time", (2009) 42/1 *Cornell International Law Journal*, p. 227.

309 Bossche, pp. 291–2.

310 L. M. Busch and J. K. Pelc, "Does the WTO Need a Permanent Body of Panelists?", (2009) 12/3 *Journal of International Economic Law* pp. 579–94. Also look at Hughes, for the discussion, pp. 206–9.; Lowenfeld, p. 166.; Cottier and Oesch, p. 178.

311 J. W. Davey, The WTO: Looking Forwards, *Journal of International Economic Law*, 9(1), 2006, pp. 3–29.(hereinafter Davey, "The WTO: Looking Forwards…").

312 Busch and Pelc, pp. 579–94.

313 Taniguch, pp. 1–21.

314 Lester, Mercurio, Davies and Leitner, p. 219. For similar discussion look at Hughes, pp. 223–4, Hong Kong WTO Ministerial 2005, *The Future of WTO Report*, para. 256.

315 Cottier and Oesch, p. 178.

316 Taniguch, pp. 1–21.

317 Bossche, p. 280, Lester, Mercurio, Davies and Leitner, pp. 172–4.

the *EC -Banana Case*. Currently there are two approaches: suspending Article 22 proceedings until Article 21(5) procedure is complete or voluntarily waiving Article 22 timetable. This issue is discussed in DOHA yet has not been resolved.

Sixth, there is discussion on third party rights[318] and more debate on *amicus curiae* briefs. There is demand for guidelines and clearance on *amicus curiae* briefs. Guidelines on rules and timetables will bring legal certainty.[319] The United States especially made proposals on this issue.

Seventh, there are suggestions for prompt implementation. Lack of retroactive remedies and lack of interim relief has been criticized.[320] Responsibilities of a WTO member that violated WTO obligation are limited compared to responsibilities under international law.[321] It is also disputed whether retaliation is effective. In the *Hormones Case* the European Union changed its policy after nine years.[322] Having retroactive application, issuing fines or damages can be a solution for prompt implementation. Other remedies for non-implementation can be having some adjustment mechanism to increase the level of sanctions over time, so as to preclude non-compliance from becoming an acceptable *status quo* position.[323] Also in the same Article it was argued that in order to prevent buyouts it would be possible to tie the amount of fines to the size of the member's economy or otherwise providing for a sliding scale that would minimize "discrimination" against poor Members.[324]

Lastly, as discussed above there are proposals for developing countries to be involved in the process more often.

### 3.6. *Conclusion*

The WTO and its agreements set the major rules for international trade law for the current 153 member countries.[325] Without enforcement the rules would not be effective. The Members have to know that they have to bring their measures and actions in conformity with the rules otherwise there will be consequences such as compensation and retaliation.

---

318 Hong Kong WTO Ministerial 2005.

319 Cottier and Oesch, (excerpt: G. Marceau and M. Stilwell, "Practical Suggestions for Amicus Curiae Briefs Before WTO Adjudicating Bodies", (2001) 4 *Journal of International Economic Law* 4, pp. 185–7), pp. 174–5.

320 F. Roessler, "The Responsibilities of a WTO Member Found to have Violated WTO Law", in Y. Taniguchi, A. Yanovich and J. Bohanes (eds.), *The WTO in the Twenty-First Century Dispute Settlement, Negotiations, and the Regionalism in Asia*, Cambridge: Cambridge University Press, 2007, p. 143.

321 Roessler, p. 145.

322 Davey, "Compliance Problems …", p. 125.

323 Davey, "Compliance Problems …", pp. 124–5.

324 Davey, "Compliance Problems …", p. 126.

325 Members as of 18.03.2010.

Dispute settlement of the WTO is a vital contribution to international trade law. Dispute settlement is the central element in providing security and predictability to the multilateral trading system. The WTO dispute settlement has compulsory jurisdiction and it is widely used. The wide usage also supports the credibility of the system.

If any contracting party considers that any benefit accruing to it directly or indirectly under the Agreement is being nullified or impaired or that the attainment of any objective of the Agreement is being impeded, it can initiate consultations. The aim of the system is to settle the disputes through consultation. However, if there is no agreement and if the consultation phase is not successful, complaining party can request the establishment of a panel. After the panel review the panel decision is adopted by the DSB. The DSB administers the WTO dispute settlement. The parties involved in the dispute can appeal to the panel decision. The Appellate Body reviews the panel decision and the Appellate Body report is also adopted by the DSB. If the panel or the Appellate Body finds a measure inconsistent with a covered agreement, the Member concerned has to bring its measure in conformity with the agreement. If there is no implementation or compliance by the Member there is the possibility of requesting compensation or retaliation. The rule-oriented DSU sets the working procedures.

As is well-known, the aim of the dispute settlement mechanism is to secure a solution to the dispute. It is preferred to agree on a mutually acceptable solution that is consistent with the covered agreements.

The dispute settlement system has evolved with the establishment of the WTO. The decision-making procedure was revised to make the decision making easier, workable procedures in the DSU were adopted and most importantly the appeal review was added to the dispute settlement procedure.

The dispute settlement system is still open for improvement and there are ongoing debates for changes on the shortcomings of the system. However, considering the works of the dispute settlement system, the contribution of the dispute settlement system to the development of international trade law, the WTO dispute settlement system is a very effective and important mechanism.

CHAPTER FOUR

# DISPUTE SETTLEMENT IN INTERNATIONAL INVESTMENT LAW

Yusuf Caliskan

## 4.1. *Introduction*

The proliferation of Bilateral Investment Treaties (BITs) which include Investor-State dispute settlement provisions has a vital role in the development of international investment arbitration. Indeed in recent years, international arbitration has become an essential dispute settlement mechanism for foreign investors' interests to resolve disputes with host States and to recover losses caused by States' action.[1] Even though there are various forums and dispute settlement procedures for investment disputes, in this study, we are dealing with ICSID arbitration only.

As noted above, the explosion of BITs is one of the reasons for recent development of international arbitration in international investment disputes. Thus, this chapter first explains BITs in brief and then analyzes the main aspects of ICSID arbitration proceedings. In particular, amendments of the ICSID rules will be explained so as to demonstrate the previous ICSID tribunals' decisions impact on the new rules. Furthermore, the issues of transparency and third party participation in ICSID arbitration will be discussed through studying some cases for accepting amicus curiae submissions.

Finally, under the title of "the practice of ICSID and Its Contribution to International Economic Law", this chapter explains the protection of shareholder rights through ICSID arbitration and the issue of contract claims v. treaty claims, and sovereign immunity. In particular, ICSID Convention acknowledged that diplomatic protection rights developed under international economic law will affect the execution of ICSID awards. This chapter also deals with the main substantive principles of international economic law such as most favoured nation, fair and equitable treatment and non-precluded measures in more detail. It should be noted that there are various inconsistent ICSID tribunal decisions regarding the scope and content of these principles.

---

[1] S. L. Caruba, "Resolving International Investment Disputes in a Globalised World", (2007) *New Zealand Business Law Quarterly* pp. 128–30.; E. Gottwald, "Leveling The Playing Field: "Is it Time for a Legal Assistance Center for Developing Nations in Investment Treaty Arbitrations?" ", (2007) *American University International Law Review*, pp. 246–7.

### 4.2. *The Growth and Impact of Bilateral Investment Treaties (BITs) on International Investment Law*

BITs are the main sources of international investment law. These treaties control investment relationships only between two countries. It should be noted that the main objective of signing BITs for capital importing countries is to attract foreign investment in the interest of development. On the other hand, the most important purpose of signing BITs for capital exporting countries is to obtain legal protection for investment and preclude non-commercial risks facing foreign investors in host countries.[2] If benefits can flow in both directions, both parties to a BIT may follow these two objectives simultaneously. In fact, BIT's original name is agreement signed between two countries concerning the reciprocal promotion and protection of investment. Most BITs do not stipulate which contracting party is the source of the investment or which is the recipient.[3] Hence, the objective of the promotion and the protection of investment are reciprocal. It should be noted that the first BIT was signed about fifty years ago between Germany and Pakistan in 1959. Recently, the number of BITs as well as the number of parties to these treaties have enormously increased.[4]

BITs consist of substantive and procedural rules that secure foreign investment and provide "investment neutrality" and "market facilitation".[5] Almost every BIT covers the same issues. Non-discrimination provision, expropriation and compensation provision, currency transfer provisions are examples of substantive provisions of most BITs that provide investment security and investment neutrality.[6]

It can be argued that signing BITs enhances the investor's confidence to make a decision to invest in a host country. BITs are the essential confidence-building measures that can be utilized to improve a host country's investment climate. Thus, the network of BITs extended considerably during the first half of the 1990s.[7]

---

[2] R. Dolzer and M. Stevens, *Bilateral Investment Treaties*, The Hague, Boston, London: Martinus Nijhoff Publishers, 1995, p. 12.

[3] J. L. Siquerios, "Bilateral Treaties on the Reciprocal Protection of Foreign Investment", (1994) 24 *California Western International Law Journal*, p. 255, p.257.

[4] UNCTAD, *Bilateral Investment Treaties 1995–2006: Trends in Investment Rulemaking*, New York and Geneva, 2007, pp. 1–2. (hereinafter UNCTAD, *Bilateral Investment Treaties 1995–2006*).; B. Tiryakioğlu, *Doğrudan Yatırımların Uluslararası Hukukta Korunması*, (Protection of Foreign Direct Investment in International Law), Ankara, 2003, pp. 160–4.

[5] K. J. Vandevelde, "Investment Liberalization and Economic Development: The Role of Bilateral Investment Treaties", (1998) 36 *Columbia Western Journal of Transnational Law*, p. 501, pp. 507–14.

[6] M. Sornarajah, *The International Law on Foreign Investment*, Second Edition, Cambridge University Press, 2004, p. 217; A. Newcombe and L. Paradell, *Law and Practice of Investment Treaties Standards of Treatment*, Kluwer Law International, 2009, p.1.

[7] S. W. Schill, *The Multileteralization of International Investment Law*, Cambridge University Press, 2009, p. 41.; Newcombe and Paradell, p. 47.

The impact of BITs on international investment law can be considerably recognized in three significant issues: the subject matter of international law, the protection of shareholder rights and the arbitral tribunals' decisions. Although international law does not recognize private companies as international subjects, it does, through BITs, allow States to bind themselves to agreements with such private companies and natural persons. Thus, under the BITs regime, private companies and natural persons can directly sue States. Furthermore, BITs create special regime for the protection of shareholders which do not have any protection in international law.[8] The dispute settlement provision of BITs can refer mainly ICSID arbitration and ICSID tribunals have interpreted the substantive principles of international investment law in various ways. Thus, through the utilization of the ICSID arbitration stipulated in BITs, the international investment law has developed in recent years.

It should be noted that most BITs do not prohibit States from enacting investment laws, but provide that any such laws should not interfere with any rights in the treaty. With respect to the interaction between BITs and national law, the BITs can affect national legislation. The countries have enacted or amended to their national laws so as to make them consistent with the BITs. For example, Professor Mutharika noted in his work on investment climate in Eastern and Southern Africa that in 1993 Zambia government revoked the 1991 code and enacted a new code that allows remittances similar to those provided in the Germany-Zambia BIT.[9]

BITs have also played an essential role as a source of inspiration in negotiations of recent regional and multilateral agreements. For instance, BITs were influential in the formulation of the World Bank Group Guidelines on the Treatment of Foreign Direct Investment, issued in September 1992 by the Joint Ministerial Development Committee of the World Bank and the IMF. Furthermore, Investment Chapter (Chapter 11) of the North American Free Trade Agreement includes provisions similar to those in most of the BITs.[10]

### 4.2.1. *The Dispute Settlement Provision of BITs*

BITs include provisions for settlement of disputes between the contracting parties and also between investor and the host State. The provision for dispute settlement is often provided in two separate articles in the BITs. Nevertheless, there is no uniformity with regard to dispute settlement provisions of the

---

[8] B. Kishoiyian, "The Utility of Bilateral Investment Treaties in the Formulation of Customary International Law", (1994) 14 *Northwestern Journal of International Law & Business*, p. 327, p. 350.

[9] A. P. Mutharika, "Creating an Attractive Investment Climate in the Common Market for Eastern and Southern Africa (COMESA) Region", (1997) *Foreign Investment Law Journal, ICSID Review*, p. 272.

[10] Dolzer and Stevens, p. Xii-Xiii.

numerous BITs. Due to the fact that dispute settlement provisions are different, it would be convenient to discuss them under separate title: State-State Dispute Settlement, and Investor-State Dispute Settlement.

#### 4.2.1.1. *State-State Dispute Settlement*

Under the dispute settlement between State and State provision, most BITs provide that parties should try to settle their dispute amicably before instituting formal proceedings. If they fail to do so, their disputes can be submitted at the request of either party to an ad hoc tribunal. With regard to the appointment of arbitrators, if the parties fail to reach an agreement for appointment of arbitrators, the President of the International Court of Justice will make the appointments.[11] It should be noted that many BITs set forth the same language and same procedure for State-State dispute settlement provision.

#### 4.2.1.2. *Investor—State Dispute Settlement*

BITs include dispute resolution provisions to settle disputes between an investor and the host government. These provisions provide investment security since investors will utilize the dispute settlement procedures of BITs without depending on diplomatic protection of their countries.[12] Through Investor-State dispute settlement provisions, investors can submit their dispute to the available forum that is stipulated in BITs. Most of the BITs refer cases to the ICSID. Nevertheless, a significant number of BITs refer cases to arbitration under the rules of the United Nations Commission on International Trade Law (UNCITRAL) or the court of arbitration of the Paris International Chamber of Commerce. It should be noted that significant variations exist among the agreements. For example, some BITs grant rights to parties to choose an arbitral forum from among arbitral proceedings. However, some agreements, for example Turkey-United Kingdom BITs, set forth that ICSID arbitration is the only acceptable dispute settlement mechanism for the Investor-State dispute settlement procedure.[13]

Most BITs contains general provision pertaining Investor-State dispute settlement mechanism. For example, providing different arbitration venues to investors, the appointment procedures for arbitrators, the obligation of the

---

[11] Z. Akgul, *The Development of International Arbitration on Bilateral Investment Treaties: Disputes Between States and Investor, ICSID Cases Against Turkey Regarding Energy Sector*, LLM Thesis, Boca Raton, Florida, USA: Dissertation.com, 2008, p. 13.

[12] UNCTAD, Bilateral Investment Treaties 1995–2006, p.100.

[13] Article 8 of Turkey-United Kingdom, Agreement for the Promotion and Protection of Investments states that: "...(2) Each contracting party hereby consents to submit to the International Centre for the Settlement of Investment Disputes (hereinafter referred to as "the Centre") for settlement by arbitration under the Convention on the Settlement of Investment Disputes between States and Nationals of other States, open for signature at Washington on 18 March 1965 any legal dispute arising between that Contracting party and national or company of the other Contracting party concerning an investment of the latter in the territory of the former..."

contracting parties with regard to the enforcement of arbitral awards are the limited provisions that are stipulated in most BITs.[14] Hence, various procedural aspects of arbitration are not regulated in the BITs. However, these unregulated issues can be clarified by the existing arbitration rules such as ICSID or UNCITRAL through referring these rules in the BITs.

It is essential to note that in recent years, most BITs have addressed Investor-State dispute settlement provisions in greater detail. New BITs provide guidance to the disputing parties regarding arbitration procedures and increase the strength of these adjudication mechanisms. It can be argued that not only Chapter 11 of the NAFTA but also the recent ICSID and other institutional and ad hoc arbitral awards have affected new BITs regime. For example, the USA and Canada BITs have incorporated new issues in Investor-State dispute settlement mechanism. This new BITs regime includes comprehensive and detailed provisions and even one chapter for Investor-State dispute settlement procedures. The following are the main purposes for this new trend: "to provide greater predictability and contracting parties' control over arbitration procedures"; "to promote the principle of judicial economy in investment-related disputes"; "to ensure consistence among arbitral awards and the development of sound jurisprudence on international investment law"; and "to promote the overall legitimacy of Investor-State arbitration."[15]

It is worthwhile to note that many BITs refer to numerous existing international arbitration conventions to prescribe the rules governing the arbitration. However, the most BITs provide for the possibility of settling the investment dispute under ICSID Convention. Taking into account the recent phenomenon of ICSID jurisprudence, this study will only analyze the ICSID arbitration proceedings and the practical impact of the ICSID awards to international investment law.

### 4.3. *The Role of the World Bank Group on the Development of International Investment Law*

The activities of the World Bank Group[16] have played an important role in the development of international legal framework on foreign direct investment. The World Bank Group have negotiated and adopted both binding and non-binding legal instruments dealing with foreign investment. Although legal instruments issued by the World Bank Group are generally considered "soft law", i.e. non-binding rules, they can be adopted by states and become legally binding. For example, the 1992 World Bank Guidelines on the Treatment of

[14] UNCTAD, Bilateral Investment Treaties 1995–2006, p. 100.
[15] Ibid. at 119.
[16] The term "World Bank" generally refers to the IBRD and IDA, whereas the World Bank Group is utilized to refer to the institutions collectively.

Foreign Direct Investment is considered as a "soft law" instrument.[17] Furthermore, the World Bank Group can provide technical information to promote investment and to enhance and revise national investment laws.

The World Bank Guidelines on the Treatment of Foreign Direct Investment stated the role of the World Bank Group on the development of foreign investment law through the following words: "that a greater flow of foreign direct investment brings substantial benefits to bear on the world economy and on the economies of developing countries in particular, in terms of improving the long term efficiency of the host country through greater competition, transfer of capital, technology and managerial skills and enhancement of market access and in terms of the expansion of international trade; that the promotion of private foreign investment is a common purpose of the International Bank for Reconstruction and Development, the International Finance Corporation and the Multilateral Investment Guarantee Agency; that these institutions have pursued this common objective through their operations, advisory services and research."[18]

The World Bank Group consists of five international institutions; the International Bank for Reconstruction and Development (IBRD), the International Development Association (IDA), the International Finance Corporation (IFC), Multilateral Investment Guarantee Agency (MIGA) and International Centre for Settlement of Investment Disputes (ICSID). IBRD and IDA provide loans, grants and development assistance to developing countries.[19]

### 4.3.1. *International Finance Corporation (IFC)*

International Finance Corporation (IFC) is one of the leading institutions of the World Bank Group for promoting sustainable private sector investment in developing countries. It has an essential role for the development of foreign investment flow in developing countries. In particular, it finances private sector projects in developing countries. Furthermore, it provides advice and technical assistance to developing countries and businesses. Although IFC is formally associated with the World Bank Group, it is legally and financially autonomous with its own Articles of Agreement and share capital.[20]

### 4.3.2. *Multilateral Investment Guarantee Agency (MIGA)*

The Multilateral Investment Guarantee Agency (MIGA) was established by an international convention on 12 May 1988 as one of the World Bank Group's

---

[17] T. Pollan, *Legal Framework for the Aadmission of fdi*, The Netherlands: Eleven International Publishing, 2006, p. 132; Newcombe and Paradell, p. 49.

[18] World Bank Group, "Guidelines on the Treatment of Foreign Direct Investment", *Legal Framework for the Treatment of Foreign Investment*, Volume 2: Guidelines (1992).

[19] www.worldbank.org (visited on 10.9.2009).

[20] About IFC, www.ifc.org (visited on 10.9.2009).

financial institutions to mitigate political risks and to support and provide information for foreign investors.[21] Even though MIGA is formally associated with the World Bank Group, it has financial autonomy.[22] The objective of the MIGA is to encourage the flow of private investments for productive purposes among member countries, in particular to developing countries. To accomplish this objective, the MIGA issues guarantees against non-commercial risks for foreign direct investment in member developing countries and provides technical assistance to governments of member developing countries to improve their ability to attract foreign investment.[23]

It can be argued that the MIGA is one of the striking international institutions that provide legal security for foreign investment. The MIGA is authorized under the convention to issue guarantees against specified non-commercial risk to foreign investment in developing countries. Under Article 11 (a) of the MIGA Convention, the following risks can be guaranteed to eligible investors: currency transfers restriction, expropriation, breach of contract, war and civil disturbance risk, and other non-commercial risks. The MIGA encourages foreign direct investment flows to developing countries by providing not only guarantee contracts, but also technical assistance activities. The technical assistance activities cannot be deemed as a secondary activity of MIGA because this activities' aim is also to promote foreign investment in developing countries. The technical assistance program consists of the following activities: a. organizing conferences and seminar concerning with investment and MIGA's role, b. supporting member countries to strength their institutional capacity to attract foreign investment. In particular, the MIGA will advise developing member countries to liberalize their foreign investment regulations.[24]

### 4.3.3. *The International Centre for the Settlement of Investment Disputes*

#### 4.3.3.1. *The Washington Convention*

As mentioned above, the number of Investor-State arbitration has been extensively grown in recent years. Most of the cases are administered by the ICSID. Thus, it is important to know the historical background and the structure of

---

[21] MIGA was established by the Convention Establishing the Multilateral Investment Guarantee Agency, opened signature (October 11, 1985, 24 *ILM* 1598 (entered into force April 12, 1988).

[22] I. Shihata, "Towards a Greater Depoliticization of Investment Disputes: The Roles of ICSID and MIGA" (1992) *ICSID Publication* p .20.

[23] I. Shihata, "The Multilateral Investment Guarantee Agency, (Symposium: Current Issues of International Financial Law, Part I International Organizations", (1986) 20 *International Law*, p. 485, p. 489.

[24] Y. Caliskan, *The Development of International Investment Law, Lessons From the OECD MAI Negotiations and Their Application to a Possible Multilateral Agreement on Investment*, JSD Dissertation, August 2002, Dissertation.com, USA, 2008, p. 262.

the ICSID. The ICSID was established in 1966 pursuant to the Convention on the Settlement of Investment Disputes between States and Nationals of Other States. Since it is executed in Washington, D.C, the ICSID Convention is also called as the Washington Convention.[25] The Executive Directors of the World Bank adopted the text of the Convention on the Settlement of Investment Disputes between States and Nationals of Other States on 18 March 1965. After its ratification by 20 States, the Washington Convention entered into force on 14 October 1966.[26]

The main goal of the Washington (ICSID) Convention is to facilitate foreign investment through creation of a favorable investment climate. In order to achieve this goal, the Convention provides a neutral international investment arbitration mechanism to resolve investment disputes between States and foreign investors. In fact, the Report of the Executive Directors on the Convention states this goal in the following terms:

> 9. *In submitting the attached Convention to governments, the Executive Directors are prompted by the desire to strengthen the partnership between countries in the cause of economic development. The Creation of an institution designed to facilitate the settlement of disputes between States and foreign investors can be a major step toward promoting an atmosphere of mutual confidence and thus stimulating a larger flow of private international capital into those countries which wish to attract it.*[27]

The ICSID Centre was established pursuant to the ICSID Convention so as to provide an effective dispute settlement mechanism for the international investment disputes between foreign investors and host States. The ICSID Convention is extensively ratified by developed as well as developing countries. Furthermore, recently the ICSID arbitration is broadly utilized by foreign investors and the ICSID plays an important role for the development of international investment law through its jurisprudence.

#### 4.3.3.2. *Structure of the ICSID*

The Organizational structure of ICSID is simple, consisting of an Administrative Council and a Secretariat.[28] However, it should be noted that a Panel of Arbitrators and Panel of Conciliators are also important organs of the ICSID

---

[25] L. Reed, J. Paulsson and N. Blackaby, *Guide to ICSID Arbitration*, Kluwer Law International, 2004, p. 1.

[26] UNCTAD, *Course on Dispute Settlement, International Centre For Settlement of Investment Disputes, (2.1. Overview)*, United Nations, New York and Geneva, 2003, p. 9. (hereinafter UNCTAD, 2.1. Overview)

[27] International Bank for Reconstruction and Development, Report of the Executive Directors on the Convention on the Settlement of Investment Disputes between States and Nationals of Other States (18 March 1965), paragraph 23, available at http://icsid.worldbank.org/ICSID/StaticFiles/basicdoc/CRR_English-final.pdf (visited on 20.2.2009).

[28] About ICSID, http://icsid.worldbank.org/ICSID/Index.jsp (visited on 20.2.2009).

for the facilitating arbitration proceedings. The Administrative Council is composed of one representative of each of the ICSID Contracting States and it is the governing body of the ICSID. Moreover, the President of the World Bank serves as the Chairman of the Council. As the governing body of the ICSID, the Council has various duties to implement the provisions of the ICSID Convention. For example, the adoption of regulations and rules for the institution and conduct of ICSID arbitration proceedings and the adoption of the ICSID budget are among the primary roles of the Council.[29]

The ICSID Secretariat consists of the Secretary-General, at least one Deputy Secretary-General, and Staff. Secretary-General and Deputy Secretary-General are elected by the Administrative Council. As the principle officer and legal representative of the ICSID Centre, the Secretary-General is responsible for the administration of the Centre. Moreover, the Secretary-General performs the function of Registrar and also has the power to appoint arbitrators in the absence of agreement between the parties. Providing institutional support for the initiation, conduct of ICSID proceedings and administering the proceedings are the main functions of the Secretariat.[30]

## 4.4. *ICSID Arbitration*

### 4.4.1. *Overview of ICSID Arbitration*

As noted above, the establishment of ICSID is the vital step for the development of arbitration in international investment disputes since the ICSID Convention focused on the settlement of investment disputes. The ICSID administers conciliation and arbitration process, but the ICSID does not carry out them.[31] This mission is left to the Conciliation Commission or Arbitral Tribunal whose members come from panels that the ICSID maintains with respect to the Convention. The ICSID Convention provides an effective dispute settlement system. In particular, under the Convention, ICSID awards are recognized as final in all States parties to the Convention.

### 4.4.2. *Practical Consideration: Jurisdiction of the ICSID*

It should be noted that Article 25 (1) of the ICSID Convention stipulates three preconditions which are personal jurisdiction, consent of the parties, and subject matter of jurisdiction for the ICSID jurisdiction.[32]

---

[29] Y. Kryvoi, *International Centre for Settlement of Investment Disputes*, Kluwer Law International, 2010, para. 37.

[30] Ibid. para. 40.

[31] UNCTAD, 2.1. Overview, p. 9.

[32] C. Şanlı, *Uluslararası Ticari Akitlerin Hazırlanması ve Uyuşmazlıkların Çözüm Yolları, (Drafting and Negotiating International Commercial Contracts and Dispute Settlement Mechanisms)*, İstanbul, 2005, p. 416.

#### 4.4.2.1. *Ratione Personae Jurisdiction*

Ratione Personae Jurisdiction is one of the essential elements required by the ICSID Convention to submit investment disputes to ICSID arbitration.[33] Ratione personae jurisdiction deals with the question of who may be a party to ICSID arbitration proceedings. Pursuant to the ICSID Convention, nationals of Contracting States can bring claims against other Contracting States. Moreover, Contracting States can bring claims against nationals of other Contracting States. In other words, in order to be eligible for ICSID jurisdiction, the dispute must be between a "Contracting State (or any constituent subdivision or agency of a Contracting State designated to the Centre by that State) and a national of another Contracting State." Article 25 (2) of the ICSID Convention defines "national of another Contracting State" as follows:"

> *(a) any natural person who had the nationality of a Contracting State other than the State party to the dispute on the date on which the parties consented to submit such dispute to conciliation or arbitration as well as on the date on which the request was registered pursuant to paragraph (3) of Article 28 or paragraph (3) of Article 36, but does not include any person who on either date also had the nationality of the Contracting State party to the dispute; and*
>
> *(b) any juridical person which had the nationality of a Contracting State other than the State party to the dispute on the date on which the parties consented to submit such dispute to conciliation or arbitration and any juridical person which had the nationality of the Contracting State party to the dispute on that date and which, because of foreign control, the parties have agreed should be treated as a national of another Contracting State for the purposes of this Convention.*

The ICSID Arbitral tribunals have addressed the issue of determining the nationality of a natural and legal person in numerous cases. With respect to natural persons, the ICSID Convention requires that the investor must be a national of a contracting State and investor must not be a national of the host country.[34] Moreover, investor must be a national of a contracting State from the date of the party's consent to ICSID arbitration, through the date on which the request for arbitration is registered at the ICSID Centre by the Secretary General. Thus, if the claimant investor changes citizenship to a State that is not party to the ICSID Convention before the dispute is submitted to the Centre, the ICSID will not have personal jurisdiction.[35]

The ICSID arbitration tribunals have determined the nationality of investors through applying the law of the country whose nationality is claimed. For example, in the *Soufraki v. UAE Case,*[36] the ICSID tribunal was faced with

---

[33] UNCTAD, *Course on Dispute Settlement International Centre For Settlement of Investment Disputes, 2.4. Requirements Ratione Personae*, New York and Geneva, 2003, p. 1. (hereinafter 2.4. Requirements Ratione Personae).

[34] C.H. Schreuer, *The ICSID Convention: A Commentary*, 2010, p. 263.

[35] Schreuer, pp. 274–7.

[36] *Soufraki v. UAE Case, (Hussein Nuaman Soufraki v. United Arab Emirates*, ICSID Case No. ARB/02/7, Award, 7 July 2004).

the determination of the nationality of the claimant. With respect to determination of the nationality of the claimant, the tribunal pointed out that:

> *It is accepted in international law that nationality is within the domestic jurisdiction of the State, which settles, by its own legislation, the rules relating to the acquisition (and loss) of its nationality…It will accord great weight to the nationality law of the State in question and to the interpretation and application of that law by its authorities.*[37]

It should be noted that a natural person who is dual national of the State Party to the investment dispute will not be able to submit a claim under the ICSID Convention. For example, in the *Champion Trading v. Egypt Case,*[38] applying the Egyptian law for determining the nationality of investors, the ICSID tribunal found that the investors had dual nationality, and hence it did not have jurisdiction over the claims. In particular, the Tribunal concluded that Article 25 (2) (a) includes a clear and precise rule pertaining to dual nationals who are excluded from invoking ICSID arbitration against the host country of the investment of which they are also citizens.

The determination of nationality of judicial persons is a crucial issue within the ICSID proceedings since most foreign investment are carried out by judicial persons. However, the term "judicial person" is not defined by the ICSID Convention. On the other hand, the ICSID tribunals have traditionally applied the criterion of incorporation when determining the nationality of judicial persons.[39] For example, in the *Kaiser Bauxite v. Jamaica Case,*[40] the ICSID tribunal found that the claimant is an American corporation since "Kaiser Bauxite" was a private corporation organized under the laws of the State of Nevada. In the *Tokios Tokeles v. Ukraine Case*, the ICSID arbitral tribunal had an interesting discussion regarding the nationality of the judicial person. In this case, a Lithuanian company owned and controlled by Ukrainian nationals requested arbitration against Ukraine claiming it breaches the Ukraine-Lithuania BIT. According to this BIT, investor means "any entity established in the territory of the Republic of Lithuania in conformity with its laws and regulations".[41] The majority of arbitrators in this case reached the conclusion based on the terms of the BIT and the ICSID Convention and it held that "Under the well established presumption *expressio unius est exclusio alterius,* the state of

---

[37] Ibid. para. 55.

[38] *Champion Trading v. Egypt Case*, (*Champion Trading Company, Ameritrade International, Inc.. James T. Wahba, John B. Wahba, Timothy T. Wahba v. Arab Republic of Egypt*, ICSID Case No. ARB/02/09, Decision on Jurisdiction, 21 October 2003).

[39] UNCTAD, *Investor-State Dispute Settlement and Impact on Investment Rulemaking*, New York and Geneva, 2007, p. 12.

[40] *Kaiser Bauxite v. Jamaica Case*, (*Kaiser Bauxite Company v. Jamaica*, ICSID Case No ARB/74/3, Decision on Jurisdiction, 6 July 1975).

[41] *Tokios Tokeles v. Ukraine Case, (Tokios Tokeles v. Ukraine,* ICSID Case No. ARB/02/18. Decision on jurisdiction, 29 April 2004), para. 28.

incorporation, not the nationality of the controlling shareholders or siège social, thus defines "investors" of Lithuania under Article 1(2) (b) of the BIT."[42]

Article 25 (2) (b) of the ICSID Convention stipulates two different solutions for determining *ratione personae* jurisdiction when the claimant is a judicial person. First part of this Article states that the judicial person must be of a contracting State other than the State party to the dispute on the date on which arbitration was consented. Second part of the Article 25 (2) (b) of the ICSID Convention states that the investor can also be a judicial person with the nationality of the contracting State on the date on which the parties consented to submit the dispute to arbitration, but because of foreign control, the parties agreed to treat it as a national of another contracting State for the purposes of the Convention. Therefore, in order to qualify as an investor for ICSID arbitration, judicial persons must be either (a) a national of a contracting State other than the host State on the date on which arbitration was consented to or, (b) a national of the host State, but which is under foreign control and the parties have agreed to such treatment.[43]

With respect to second solution, the ICSID Convention requires that parties to the dispute should agree to consider a legal entity constituted or having its seat in the host county as a foreign investor because of foreign control. Hence, two requirements must be met for this situation. First, there should be an agreement between the parties to the dispute to treat a legal entity of the host State as a foreign.[44] Second, such entity is effectively controlled by foreigners.[45] With respect to the first requirement, bilateral investment treaties generally include article regarding the definition of legal entities. When there was no agreement on this issue, the ICSID tribunals have decided whether the claimant is a legal person of the host country or not and whether the legal entity is under the foreign control or not on a case by case basis. The ICSID tribunals have looked for the "intention of the parties" in order to decide whether the legal entity is under the foreign control or not. The ICSID tribunals in *Liberian Eastern Timber Corporation (LETCO) v. Liberia*[46] and *Klöckner v. Cameron*[47] decided that the mere existence of an ICSID clause indicated an implicit agreement on foreign nationality.

Regarding the second requirement, it should be noted that the ICSID Convention does not include the definition of foreign control. Thus, the determining the foreign control is not an easy task for the ICSID tribunals.

---

[42] Ibid.para. 30.
[43] UNCTAD, 2.4. Requirements Ratione Personae, pp. 19–25.
[44] For detailed information, *see* Schreuer, pp. 299–312.
[45] For detailed information, *see* Schreuer, pp. 312–29.
[46] ICSID Case No. ARB/83/2, Award, March 31, 1986.
[47] *Klöckner v. Cameron Case*, (*Klöckner Industrie-Anlagen GmbH and Others v. United Republic of Cameroon and Société Camerounaise des Engrais*, ICSID Case No. ARB/81/2, Award, 21 October 1983).

Indeed, the ICSID tribunals have followed different approaches for determining the actual foreign control over legal entities. Numerous tribunals have recognized that if foreigners own a majority of the shares of the enterprise, that legal entity is deemed under foreign control. For example, in *Klöckner v. Cameron*, the tribunal found that the local company SOCAME was under the majority control of foreign interests since Klöckner and its European partners had subscribed to 51 percent of this company's capital. The ICSID jurisprudence has recognized that the effective foreign control may be "not only direct but also indirect."[48] Overall, it can be argued that the determination of nationality of a judicial person can be somewhat complex. Thus, the parties on BITs should explicitly provide that local companies of the host country are treated as foreign investors because of foreign control.

#### 4.4.2.2. *Consent to ICSID Arbitration*

Like in any form of international arbitration, the essential requirement for ICSID arbitration is the consent of the parties. In fact, in their 1965 Report on the ICSID Convention, the Executive Directors of the World Bank pointed out that "Consent of the parties is the cornerstone of the jurisdiction of the Centre."[49] Being a contracting party to the ICSID Convention does not mean that a contracting party grants its consent to the ICSID arbitration. Thus, in order to utilize the ICSID arbitration proceedings, host State and foreign investor must consent to the ICSID arbitration. Indeed, first sentence of Article 25 of the ICSID Convention stipulates in the following that the written consent of both parties are required for ICSID arbitration:

> *The Jurisdiction of the Centre shall extend to any legal dispute arising directly out of an investment, between a Contracting State (or any constituent subdivision or agency of a Contracting State designated to the Centre by that State) and a national of another Contracting State, which the parties to the dispute consent in writing to submit to the Centre.*

Under the ICSID Convention, consent must be in writing. However, there is no particular form of giving consent to ICSID arbitration.[50] Thus, the consent may take various forms. In practice, the consent can be given by three ways.[51] The first method to give consent to the ICSID arbitration is through a consent clause in a direct agreement between the parties. Dispute settlement

48 UNCTAD, *Investor-State Dispute Settlement and Impact on Investment Rulemaking*, p. 14.

49 International Bank for Reconstruction and Development, Report of the Executive Directors on the Convention on the Settlement of Investment Disputes between States and Nationals of Other States (18 March 1965), paragraph 23,available at http://icsid.worldbank.org/ICSID/StaticFiles/basicdoc/CRR_English-final.pdf (visited on 20.2.2009).

50 Schreuer, p. 191.

51 UNCTAD, *Course on Dispute Settlement International Centre For Settlement of Investment Disputes, (2.3. Consent to Arbitration)*, United Nations, New York and Geneva, 2003, p. 6.

provisions referring to the ICSID are very commonly used in contracts between host States and foreign investors.[52] The second method to give consent to ICSID arbitration is through a provision in the national legislation of the host State offering the ICSID arbitration to foreign investors.[53] Foreign investors simply accept that offer by filing a request to arbitration. The third method to give consent to ICSID arbitration is through bilateral and multilateral treaties. As mentioned before, most BITs include dispute settlement provisions referring to ICSID arbitration proceedings. The NAFTA and the Energy Charter Treaty also provide an opportunity for foreign investments to have recourse to the ICSID arbitration. Therefore, these treaties provide consent to the ICSID arbitration through "standing offer" and this offer must be accepted by foreign investors.[54]

It should be noted that consent to the ICSID arbitration has considerable consequences. In particular, the exclusion of other remedies, the prohibition of diplomatic protection, and the irrevocability of consent are important consequences of granting consent to the ICSID arbitration.

#### 4.4.2.3. *Ratione Materiae Jurisdiction*

With regard to *ratione matariae jurisdiction*, or subject matter jurisdiction, the ICSID Convention sets forth three requirements in Article 25 (1):

1. The dispute has to be of a legal nature,
2. The dispute must arise directly out of underlying transaction, and
3. Such underlying transaction must qualify as an investment.

In fact, Article 25 (1) of the ICSID Convention provides above mentioned requirements with the following words: "... Jurisdiction of the Centre shall extend only those legal disputes arising directly out of an investment..."

As to the first requirement, the ICSID Convention does not define the term "legal dispute". Thus, the ICSID jurisprudence and legal doctrine have delineated this term stating that "... if legal remedies such as restitution or damages are sought and if legal rights based on, for example, treaties or legislation are claimed", a dispute will qualify as a legal dispute.[55] It can be argued that the legal dispute requirement for ICSID jurisdiction is an easy one to meet. The report of the Executive Directors of the World Bank pointed out that "the expression "legal dispute" has been used to make clear that while conflicts of rights are within the jurisdiction of the Centre, mere conflicts of

---

[52] Even ICSID has published set of Model clauses to help the parties for drafting dispute settlement provisions.

[53] Schreuer, pp. 196–205.

[54] UNCTAD, 2.1. Overview, p. 16.

[55] UNCTAD, Investor-State Dispute Settlement and Impact on Investment Rulemaking, p.20.

interest are not. The dispute must concern the existence or scope of a legal right or obligation, or the nature or extent of the reparation to be made for breach of a legal obligation."[56]

With regard to the second requirement, the ICSID tribunals have addressed the requirement of "directness" in various cases. For example, in the *FEDAX v. Venezuela Case*, the ICSID Tribunal stated that: "... It is apparent that the term "directly" relates in this Article to the "dispute" and not the "investment". It follows that jurisdiction can exist even in respect of investments that are not direct, so long as the dispute arises directly from such transaction."[57] Hence, there must be a link between the covered investment and dispute. The legal dispute must be "reasonably closely connected" to the underlying investment transaction, so as to meet the requirement of directness.[58] It is worthwhile to note that the term directly does not mean that investment must be a foreign direct investment.[59]

With respect to the third requirement, the definition of investment is an essential characteristics of the ICSID arbitration system. On the other hand, even though the definition of investment is vital to the subject matter jurisdiction of ICSID arbitration, the ICSID Convention does not define the term of investment. Any definition of investment in the ICSID Convention is deliberately omitted, so as to avoid long-lasting jurisdictional discussions.[60] Namely, the ICSID Convention grants Contracting States a wide discretion to define what investment means. The flexibility for the determination of the term of investment is an important issue for the ICSID arbitration since foreign investment takes constantly new economic and legal forms. Therefore, most BITs and multinational investment treaties utilize open ended definition for the term "investment." Furthermore, in the ICSID practice, the term "investment" has been interpreted broadly. The ICSID tribunals have addressed the contracting parties' definition of investment in BITs. The following particular assets have been considered to be investments for the purposed of the ICSID Convention: "shares in companies, public concession agreements, corporations organized under domestic law, loans, promissory notes, construction

---

[56] Report of the Executive Directors on the Convention on the Settlement of Investment Disputes between States and Nationals of Other States, para. 26.

[57] *Fedax v. Venezuela Case, (Fedax N.V. v. Republic of Venezuela,* ICSID Case No. ARB/96/3, Decision on Jurisdiction, 11 July 1997), para. 24.

[58] UNCTAD, *Course on Dispute Settlement International Centre For Settlement of Investment Disputes, (2.5. Requirements Ratione Materiae),* United Nations, New York and Geneva, 2003, p. 12.

[59] Ibid. p. 12.

[60] With respect to the term "investment," paragraph 27 of the Report of the Executive Directors on the Convention on the Settlement of Investment Disputes between States and Nationals of Other States stated: "No attempt was made to define the term 'investment' given the essential requirements of consent by the parties, and the mechanism through which Contracting States can make known in advance, if they so desire, the classes of disputes which they would or would not consider submitting to the Centre (Article 25(4) )."

contracts, money spent in the renovation and development of a hotel, and the setting up of a law firm."[61]

It is vital to note that the parties do not have unrestricted discretion for determination of the term "investment" since, according to Article 41 of the ICSID Convention, a tribunal may examine on its own motion whether the jurisdictional requirements are met. Indeed, the ICSID arbitration tribunals have pointed out that the term "investment" as stipulated in Article 25 (1) of the ICSID Convention has certain objective limits. For example, in *Salini Costruttori S.p.A. and Italstrade S.p.A. v. Morocco*[62], the ICSID tribunal precisely recognized that for the subject matter of the ICSID jurisdiction the objective criteria must also be met if a particular asset is to be deemed an "investment." In particular, the Tribunal in this case noted that:

> *... ICSID case law and legal authors agree that the investment requirement must be respected as an objective condition of the jurisdiction of the Centre.... The doctrine generally considers that investment infers: contributions, a certain duration of performance of the contract and a participation in the risks of the transaction. In reading the Convention's preamble, one may add the contribution to the economic development of the host State of the investment as an additional condition.*[63]

Furthermore, the ICSID Tribunal in the *Joy Mining v. Egypt Case*, explicitly recognized the objective criteria for ICSID's subject matter jurisdiction. In particular, the Tribunal stated that:

> *The parties to a dispute cannot by contract or treaty define as investment for the purpose of ICSID jurisdiction, something which does not satisfy the objective requirements of Article 25 of the Convention. Otherwise Article 25 and its reliance on the concept of investment, even if not specifically defined, would be turned into a meaningless provision.*[64]

The ICSID arbitral tribunals have adopted objective criteria for the subject matter of jurisdiction. Thus for the ICSID's subject matter of jurisdiction, the existence of investment may have to be determined by objective criteria. The following four requirements have been developed by the ICSID tribunals for ascertaining whether a particular transaction constitutes an investment: 1. The project or transaction should have a certain duration; 2. The commitment involved would have to be substantial; 3. There should be a certain regularity of profit and return and an element of risk; 4. The operation should constitute a significant contribution to the host State's development.[65] For example, in *Bayindir Insaat Turizm Ticaret ve Sanayi A.S. v. Islamic Republic*

---

[61] UNCTAD, *Investor-State Dispute Settlement and Impact on Investment Rulemaking*, p. 22.

[62] *Salini v. Morrocco Case*, (*Salini Costruttori S.p.A. and Italstrade S.p.A. v. Kingdom of Morocco*, ICSID Case No. ARB/00/4, Decision on Jurisdiction, 23 July 2001).

[63] Ibid. para. 52.

[64] ICSID Case No. ARB/03/11, Decision on Jurisdiction, 6 August 2004,para. 50.

[65] UNCTAD, *Investor-State Dispute Settlement and Impact on Investment Rulemaking*, p. 25.

*of Pakistan*[66], an ICSID tribunal addressed the issue whether the highway construction agreement constitutes an investment under Article 25 of the ICSID Convention. The ICSID tribunal in this case followed the *Salini v. Morocco* decision, namely above mentioned four requirements, and held that it had jurisdiction over the dispute since *Bayindir* had "made a significant contribution, both in terms of knowhow, equipment, and personnel and in financial terms", and the project in this case have a certain duration and "*Bayindir*'s participation in the risks of the operation was significant" and finally this project was important for the development of the host country's road infrastructure.[67]

### 4.4.3. *Main Aspects of ICSID Arbitration*

#### 4.4.3.1. *Non-Interference by National Courts*

Unlike other international arbitration systems, the ICSID arbitration system has a unique and self-contained feature. ICSID arbitration proceedings are independent of the intervention of any State court. The non-interference by national courts principle stems from the interpretation of Article 26 of the ICSID Convention which sets forth that "Consent of the parties to arbitration under this Convention shall, unless otherwise states, be deemed consent to such arbitration to the exclusion of any other remedy."[68] According to this Article, submission of disputes to ICSID arbitration is considered to have excluded any other remedy, unless parties have agreed otherwise. Thus, national courts do not have power to stay and to influence ICSID proceedings. On the other hand, in other international arbitration systems, the arbitration proceeding is subject to interference from courts of the States within which the arbitration is seated. Even though national laws are different with regard to inference by local courts, local courts of the place of arbitration have power to rule on following issues: (a) determining the validity of an agreement to arbitrate, (b) designate the arbitral tribunal, (c) granting interim relief, (d) rule on applications to set aside awards.[69]

Pursuant to the ICSID Convention, the arbitration law of the place of arbitration has no effect on the arbitration proceedings. It is worthwhile to note that the *lex arbitri* of the ICSID arbitration is expressly "ICSID Convention and the ICSID arbitration rules and not the law of the seat of the arbitration."[70] Accordingly, the Convention and its related instruments provide precise and

---

[66] *Bayindir v. Pakistan Case*, (*Bayindir Insaat Turizm Ticaret ve Sanayi A.S. v. Islamic Republic of Pakistan*, ICSID Case No. ARB/03/29, Decision on Jurisdiction, 14 November 2005).

[67] Ibid. paras.122–38.

[68] K.V.S.K. Nathan, *The ICSID Convention, The Law of the International Centre For Settlement of Investment Disputes*, 2000, pp. 63–4.

[69] Reed, Paulsson and Blackaby, p. 8.

[70] C. Lawrence, C. G. J. Morse, D. McClean, A. Briggs, J. Harris, C. McLachlan, *Dicey, Morris&Collins on the Conflict of Laws*, 14th Edition, 2006, p.783.

comprehensive procedural rules for the conduct of ICSID arbitrations. Under Articles 41–44 of the ICSID Convention, ICSID arbitration tribunals have power to determine their own jurisdiction to hear a case and to decide all procedural issues. The ICSID tribunal has power to recommend provisional measures. Furthermore, Article 52 of the ICSID Convention provides internal annulment procedures. ICSID awards are not subject to any appeal or review by national courts. Hence, the ICSID arbitration proceeding is independent and insulated from interference of the national courts.

4.4.3.2. *Applicable Law*

Applicable law issue in the ICSID arbitration is an essential one since the ICSID Convention provides the possibility of annulling awards, if "the Tribunal has manifestly exceeded its powers". Failure to apply the proper law can be considered an excess of powers by the tribunal.[71] The ICSID Convention does not include any substantive rules. It provides a procedure for the settlement of investment disputes.[72] However, the ICSID Convention does contain a rule on applicable law. Article 42 of the ICSID Convention lays out a method for the tribunal to choose the applicable law for the particular dispute. First of all, Article 42 (1) of the ICSID Convention stipulates that contracting parties can choose the applicable law for the substance of the dispute. By granting this right to the parties, the ICSID Convention recognizes the party autonomy. The parties are free to choose the applicable substantive law that the tribunal should apply to solve the dispute. The parties generally choose the law of the host State as an applicable law. However, even though it is unusual, they can also select law of the investor's home county or of a third State. Article 42 of the ICSID Convention refers to "rules of law". Thus, it is generally accepted that parties are free to combine provisions from different domestic or international legal systems. Furthermore, the parties can also allow the tribunal to decide *ex aequo et bono*.[73]

In the absence of choice of law agreement, the tribunal should apply the law of the host State (including its rule on the conflicts of laws) and such rules of international law as may be applicable. Other international arbitration instruments generally grant powers to the arbitral tribunal to apply various tests to determine the applicable law for the substance of the dispute.[74] In contrast to other international arbitration rules, the ICSID Convention stipulates that the law of the host State is applicable. Moreover, the rules of international law will

---

[71] For detailed information, *see* Schreuer, pp. 954–77.

[72] UNCTAD, *Course on Dispute Settlement International Centre For Settlement of Investment Disputes, (2.5. Applicable Law)*, United Nations, New York and Geneva, 2003, p. 5. (hereinafter UNCTAD, *2.5. Applicable Law*); Schreuer, p. 550.

[73] Schreuer, p. 550.

[74] *Nathan*, p. 70.

prevail over other systems of law. The ICSID Tribunal in the *Santa Elena v. Costa Rica Case* held that: "...there may be any inconsistency between the two bodies of law, the rules of public international law must prevail."[75] Other international arbitral tribunal does not apply international law unless the parties agree its application.[76]

Pursuant to Article 42 (1) of the ICSID Convention, in the absence of an agreement governing applicable law, the ICSID tribunal should apply the law of host State (including its rules on the conflict of laws). This Article contains a renvoi provision so as to alleviate the reference to the law of host State.[77] Article 42 (1) second sentence stipulates that "...such rules of international as may be applicable..." Thus, the tribunal should also apply the international law. Article 38 of the ICJ Statute sets forth the sources of international law. Therefore, the ICSID tribunals have applied treaties, customary international law, general principles of law and judicial practice.

The relationship between international law and domestic law has played an essential role in the ICSID jurisprudence.[78] The ICSID tribunals have followed various versions of the role of international law. The international law plays supplemental and corrective role so as to fill the gaps or to remedy any violations of international law. As the Tribunal in the *Amco v. Indonesia Case* explained, "where there are applicable host State laws, they must be checked against international laws, which will prevail in case of conflict. Thus international law is fully applicable and to classify its role as 'only' 'supplemental and corrective' seems a distinction without a difference."[79] It is essential to consider that like the *Amco v. Indonesia Case*, most of the earlier cases in the ICSID arbitration was related to contract claims. However, recent cases concern treaty claims, especially bilateral investment treaty claims.[80] Therefore, the ICSID tribunals have applied the provisions of the bilateral investment treaties to the substance of disputes, as well as general international law rules. They also applied the law of host State concerned.

The BITs can include the applicable law provisions. On the other hand, most BITs do not contain a provision on applicable law. Even though BITs do not include a provision on applicable law, ICSID tribunals apply BITs provision.

---

[75] *Santa Elena v. Costa Rica Case*, (*Compania del Desarrollo de Santa Elena, S.A. v. Republic of Costa Rica*, ICSID Case No. ARB/96/1, Award, 17 February 2000) 15 ICSID Review- *Foreign Investment Law Journal* 169, 191. (2000).

[76] Ibid. at. 70.

[77] UNCTAD, *2.5. Applicable Law*, p.25.

[78] Antonio R. Parra, "Applicable Law in Investor-State Arbitration", in (Arthur Rovine, ed.) *Contemporary Issues in International Arbitration and Mediation*, 2008. This Article is also available at www.arbitration-icca.org/.../applicable_law_in_investor-state_arbitration.doc (visited on 10.11.2009).

[79] *Amco v. Indonesia Case*, (*Amco Asia Corporation and Others v. Republic of Indonesia*, ICSID Case No. ARB/81/1, Award in Resubmitted Case, 31 May 1990), 1 ICSID Reports 569, 580 (1993).

[80] Parra, p. 6.

By consenting to arbitration under investment-dispute settlement provisions, the parties also consented to the applicability of the provisions of the BITs. This approach is explicitly recognized in the *ADC v. Hungary Case*. The Tribunal in its awards pointed out that "...The consent must also be deemed to comprise a choice for general international law, including customary international law, if and to the extent that it comes into play for interpreting and applying the provisions of the Treaty."[81] The same approach has been followed by other ICSID tribunals. For example, in the *Azurix v. Argentina Case*, the ICSID Tribunal states that "...the Tribunal's inquiry is governed by the ICSID Convention, by the BIT and by applicable international law. While the Tribunal's inquiry will be guided by this statement, this does not mean that the law of Argentina should be disregarded. On the contrary, the law of Argentina should be helpful in the carrying out of the Tribunal's inquiry into the alleged breaches of the Concession Agreement to which Argentina's law applies, but it is only an element of the inquiry because of the treaty nature of the claims under consideration."[82]

One study regarding the applicable law on Investor-State arbitration points out that the ICSID tribunals in some BIT cases did not find an agreement on the applicable law issue.[83] Thus, the second sentence of Article 42 (1) of the ICSID Convention was cited in these cases.[84] However, one could rightly argue that there will be no problem in BIT cases whether the applicable rules of law derives from the provisions of the first sentence or the second sentence of Article 42 (1). Since the result will be the same for the application of these provisions. Namely, the arbitral tribunal should apply investment treaty and general international law, "with host State law rules also having a role."[85]

It should be noted the ICSID Convention includes a provision against an award of *non liquet* by ICSID tribunals. Article 42 (2) of the ICSID Convention provides that: "The Tribunal may not bring in a finding of *non liquet* on the ground of silence or obscurity of the law." In order to prevent denial of justice, the prohibition of *non liquet* is regulated in this article. According to this provision, the tribunal may not return a finding of *non liquet* if there is no rule of law applicable to any aspect of the dispute. Thus, the ICSID tribunals have power to make new rules of international law. In fact, the ICSID tribunals

---

[81] *ADC v. Hungary*, (*ADC Affiliate Limited and ADC & ADMC Management Limited v. Republic of Hungary*, ICSID Case No. ARB/03/16, 2 October 2006), para. 290.

[82] *Azurix v. Argentina Case*, (*Azurix Corp. v. Argentine Republic*, ICSID Case No. ARB/01/12, 14 July 2006), para. 67.

[83] Parra, p. 11.

[84] *Genin v. Estonia Case*, (*Genin, Eastern Credit Limited, Inc. And A.S. Baltoil v. Estonia*, ICSID Case No. ARB/99/2, Award, 25 June 2001).; *AIG v. Kazakhstan Case*, (*AIG Capital Partners, Inc. And CJSC Tema Real Estate Company v. Republic of Kazakhstan*, Case No. ARB/01/6).; *CMS v. Argentina Case*, (*CMS Gas Transmission Co. v. Argentine Republic*, Case No. ARB/01/8, Decision on Jurisdiction, 17 July 2003, Award, 12 May 2005).

[85] Parra, p. 13.

have great power of law making which is generally not available to other private arbitral tribunal.[86]

#### 4.4.3.3. *The Enforcement of ICSID Awards*

The ICSID arbitration mechanism is exceedingly effective compared to private international arbitration system. The binding character of an ICSID award and the enforceability of this award are the salient characteristics of the ICSID arbitration mechanism. According to the ICSID Convention, awards are binding, final and not subject to be challenged in national courts.[87] On the other hand, the ICSID award can be challenged internally by the annulment procedure stipulated in the ICSID Convention. Parties are obliged to comply with ICSID awards. In particular, most States willingly fulfill the obligation since they want to keep their good standing with the World Bank.[88]

Compared to other international arbitration system, the ICSID Convention provides a unique procedure for enforcement of ICSID awards. Pursuant to Article 54 of the ICSID Convention, ICSID awards are to be recognized and enforced in all contracting States to the Convention like final judgments of the contracting States' court.[89] The ICSID awards consist pecuniary obligations are to be enforced like final judgments of the local courts in all States parties to the ICSID Convention.[90] Thus, a party to ICSID arbitration may seek recognition and enforcement in any State party to the ICSID Convention. The ICSID Convention provides an automatic enforcement system that domestic courts do not have power to review ICSID awards in the enforcement stage.[91] Even though ICSID awards must be recognized and enforced without any review of the award at the stage of enforcement, State law still governs the execution stage. Therefore, sovereign immunity on execution will still apply.[92] In fact, Article 55 of the Convention explicitly states that the rules on immunity from execution will remain unaffected.

### 4.4.4. *Improving the ICSID Arbitration Practice*

#### 4.4.4.1. *Amendments of the ICSID Rules*

It should be noted that to complement the provisions of the ICSID Convention, according to Article 6 (1) (a)-(c) of the Convention, the Administrative

---

[86] Nathan, p. 71.

[87] ICSID awards only subject to remedy stipulated in the ICSID Convention. These remedies are: supplementation and rectification (Art. 49(2), interpretation (Art. 50), revision (Art. 51) and annulment (Art. 52).

[88] Nuray Ekşi, *ICSID Hakem Kararlarının Tanınması Tenfizi ve İcrası*, (*Recognition Enforcement and Execution of ICSID Awards*), 2009, p. IV.

[89] Schreuer, p. 1117–1119. It should be noted that awards rendered under the Additional Facility are not subject to the ICSID Convention's provisions on recognition and enforcement.

[90] Schreuer, p. 1139.; Reed, Paulsson, and Blackaby, pp. 105–6.

[91] Schreuer, p. 1139; Ekşi, p. 91

[92] Sovereign Immunity issue will be explained in more detailed in 4.5.3.

Council of ICSID adopted Regulations and Rules. These Regulations and Rules comprise Administrative and Financial Regulations, Rules of Procedure for the Institution of Conciliation and Arbitration Proceedings, Rules of Procedure for Conciliation Proceedings, and Rules of Procedure for Arbitration Proceedings.[93] Moreover, the Administrative Council has adopted Additional Facility Rules, which allow the ICSID Secretariat to administer certain types of proceedings between States and nationals of other States that fall outside the scope of the ICSID Convention.[94]

Pursuant to Article 66 (1) of the ICSID Convention, the Convention may only be amended by unanimous ratification of all contracting States. Therefore, amending the ICSID Convention is practically impossible. However, ICSID Regulations and Rules may be amended by a two-thirds majority vote of the Administrative Council. Indeed, over the years, ICSID Regulations and Rules and the Additional Facility Rules have been amended several times by the Administrative Council.[95]

The dramatic increase in ICSID case load in the last ten years and the proliferation of bilateral investment treaties led ICSID to change its arbitration rules. Thus, through consultations with its contracting States, civil society, arbitrators, legal scholars, and other relevant institutions, ICSID amended its rules on April 10, 2006. These amendments include non-party participation in ICSID arbitration proceedings, disclosure requirements for arbitrator, expedited preliminary procedures, and publication of awards.[96] According to Article 44 of the ICSID Convention, any ICSID arbitration to which the parties consented after this date will be conducted in accordance with the new ICSID rules.

#### 4.4.4.2. *New Rules on Preliminary Procedures*

Under Article 47 of the ICSID Convention, an arbitral tribunal may recommend any provisional measures that should be taken to preserve respective rights of either party. Moreover, Article 39 of the ICSID Arbitrational Rules has explicitly regulated the power of ICSID Tribunal to order provisional relief. According to these two articles, the ICSID Tribunal's jurisdiction to

---

[93] http://icsid.worldbank.org/ICSID/StaticFiles/basicdoc/CRR_English-final.pdf (visited on 12.12.2009)

[94] http://icsid.worldbank.org/ICSID/StaticFiles/facility/AFR_English-final.pdf (visited on 12.12.2009)

[95] *See* detailed other amendments: A. R. Parra, "The Development of the Regulations and Rules of the International Centre for Settlement of Investment Disputes", (2007) 22/1 *ICSID Review: Foreign Investment Law Journal*, pp. 55–68.

[96] A. P. Tuck, "Investor-State Arbitration Revised: A Critical Analysis of the Revisions and Proposed Reforms to the ICSID and UNCITRAL Arbitration Rules", (2007) *Law and Business Review of the Americas*, p. 892.

order provisional relief is an exclusive jurisdiction.[97] Since pursuant to the ICSID Arbitration Rules, provisional measures may only be sought from national courts, if this is stipulated in the consent to arbitration of the parties. Thus, to protect the parties' interest through granting provisional measures is based on the decision of the ICSID tribunals, unless parties agrees that they can seek provisional measures from national courts.

The 2003 version of ICSID Arbitration Rule 39 allowed a party to request provisional measures only "during the proceedings." Therefore, the parties must await the constitution of the arbitral tribunal even they need an urgent provisional measures to protect their rights. In order to solve the problem and improve a tribunal's ability to grant provisional measures on an expedited basis, the 2006 amendment of ICSID Arbitration Rule 39 now allows parties to request provisional measures "at any time after the institution of the proceedings."[98] Thus, under the new version of the ICSID Arbitration Rules, a party may request for provisional measures even before the tribunal is constituted. However, the tribunal still has power to decide on request for provisional measures. The 2006 amendment of ICSID Arbitration Rule 39 also imposes an obligation on the ICSID Secretary General to fix time limits for the parties to present observations on request so that the tribunal may decide the issue "promptly upon its constitution."[99] It can be argued that the 2006 amendments to ICSID's rules governing provisional measures will help the parties to obtain interim relief in a timely manner so that they can successfully protect their rights.[100]

Under Article 36 (3) of the ICSID Convention, the Secretary General of ICSID will have screening power to refuse registering the arbitration request if the dispute is manifestly outside the scope of Centre's jurisdiction. The screening power of the Secretary General does not extend to the merits of the dispute. Therefore, it is essential to grant a special procedure for preliminary objections that the tribunal may at an early stage of the case dismiss frivolous claims. Indeed, the new ICSID Arbitration Rule 41 allows parties to raise preliminary objection that a claim is "manifestly without legal merit."

---

[97] L. Yves and C. C. Fortier,, "Interim Measures: An Arbitrator's Provisional Views", Fordham Law School Conference on International Arbitration and Mediation, Investor-State Arbitration, June 16, 2008.

[98] L. Malintoppi, "Provisional Measures in Recent ICSID Proceedings: What Parties Request and What Tribunals Order" in C. Binder, U. Kriebaum, A. Reinisch, S. Wittich (eds.), *International Investment Law For The 21st Century*, Oxford University Press, 2009, p. 159. *See* Rule 39 of the ICSID Rules of Procedure for Arbitration Proceedings (Arbitration Rules).

[99] *See* Rule 39 (5) of the ICSID Rules of Procedure for Arbitration Proceedings (Arbitration Rules).

[100] Tuck, pp. 893–4.; S. P. Finizio, J. Davis Mortenson and E. G. Shenkman, "Recent Developments in Investor-State Arbitration: Effective Use of Provisional Measures", (2007) *The European Arbitration Review*, p. 15.

Thus, it is now possible to utilize a fast-track procedure to seek the dismissal of claims that are without legal merit.[101] According to Arbitration Rule 41, a party can file an objection within 30 days after the tribunal is constituted arguing that the claim is "manifestly without merit." This rule also requires that the party making the objection must specify as precisely as possible the basis for that objection. The tribunal is required to rule on that objection at its first session or promptly thereafter. It is worthwhile to note that the expedited procedure does not affect the right of a party to file a jurisdictional objection under the ordinary procedure for such filings or to file an objection during the proceedings that "a claim lacks legal merit."[102] These amendments create an opportunity for parties with an expedited mechanism for dismissing frivolous claims.

4.4.4.3. *Transparency and Third Party Participation in ICSID Arbitration*

Transparency is an important subject matter in investment treaty arbitration proceedings due to the fact that Investor-State disputes often involve public interest issues which are not so common in international commercial arbitration.[103] Indeed, investment treaty disputes have essential public interest implications since these disputes often involve environmental and socio-political issues as well as human rights violations. NGOs and other civil society organizations are demanding to intervene in investment treaty disputes on this basis. On the other hand, investors seek a high level of privacy and confidentiality in arbitration procedure. The balance between the confidentiality available in arbitration and transparency in the process of investment treaty arbitrations should be well provided in order to consider these different interests. Thus, ICSID rules were amended in 2006 to provide efficient and effective transparency in investment treaty arbitration proceedings. Arbitration Rules 32, 37, and 48 are the amendments regarding the transparency and third party participation in an ICSID Arbitration.

The ICSID Arbitration Rule 37 regulates the tribunal's power to accept *amicus curiae* submissions. Literally "a friend of the court," *amicus curiae* means that "a person who is not a party to a law suit but who petitions courts or is requested by the court to file a brief in the action because that person has a strong interest in the subject matter."[104] Arbitration Rule 37 specifies procedures for the tribunal to decide whether to allow amicus submissions

[101] A. L. McDougall and A. Santens, "ICSID Amends its Arbitration Rules" (2006) *International Arbitration Law Review*, p. 121.

[102] McDougall and Santens, p. 121.

[103] OECD Investment Committee, "Transparency and Third Party Participation in Investor-State Dispute Settlement Procedures", Working Papers on International Investment, Number 2005/1, para. 1.; R. P. Buckley and P. Blyschak, "Guarding the Open Door: Non-Party Participation Before the International Centre for Settlement of Investment Disputes", (2007) *Banking & Finance Law Review*, p. 353.

[104] Black's Law Dictionary, 8 th Edition, Thomson West, 2004, p. 93.

from third parties. Rule 37 stipulates the circumstances in which an amicus submission might be accepted by the tribunal. It should be taken into account that a tribunal can decide to accept *amicus curiae* submissions even if the parties object. However, the tribunal is required to consult both parties when deciding whether to allow *amicus curiae* submissions.

The role of an amicus is to help the tribunal by providing information with regard to an important public interest issue affected by the investment-treaty arbitration proceedings. In determining whether to accept third party participation in ICSID arbitration, the tribunal must consider, among other things: "(a) the non-disputing party submission would assist the tribunal in the determination of a factual or legal issue related to the proceeding by bringing a perspective, particular knowledge or insight that is different from that of the disputing parties; (b) the non-disputing party submission would address a matter within the scope of the dispute; (c) the non-disputing party has a significant interest in the proceeding."[105] Furthermore, the tribunal must ensure that the *amicus curiae* submission does not "disrupt the proceeding or unduly burden or unfairly prejudice either party."[106] Although both parties are granted an opportunity to present their comment on *amicus curiae* submission, they do not have a veto right.[107] This provision empowers tribunals to accept *amicus curia* submission by non-parties with an interest in an investment disputes. Thus, Arbitration Rule 37 promotes transparency through granting an opportunity to allow *amicus curiae* submission.

It is worthwhile to note that non-parties can submit *amicus curiae* briefs in accordance with the above mentioned Arbitration Rule 37. This provision will not give non-parties a right to attend hearings in the arbitration proceedings. Rule 32 addresses this issue and stipulates that the tribunal can allow non-parties to attend the arbitration hearings subject to procedures to protect proprietary information and appropriate logistical arrangements. The tribunal has a discretionary power to allow non-parties to attend or observe all or part of the arbitration hearings unless either party objects. It should be noted that the 2003 ICSID Arbitration Rules authorized tribunals to allow third parties to attend the arbitration hearing in ICSID arbitration only with the consent of the parties. Thus, before the 2006 ICSID Arbitration Rules, explicit consent of the parties was necessary to allow non-parties to attend or observe hearings.[108]

Another way of providing transparency in ICSID arbitration is public disclosure of awards which is stipulated in Rule 48 of the ICSID Arbitration

---

[105] The ICSID Arbitration Rule 37, available at http://icsid.worldbank.org/ICSID/StaticFiles/basicdoc/partF-chap04.htm (visited on 12.12.2009).

[106] Ibid.

[107] McDougall and Santens, p. 120.

[108] Ibid. at 120.

Rules. Rule 48 states that "the centre shall, however, promptly include in its publication excerpts of the legal reasoning of the tribunal." In other words, to improve transparency and to promote a more consistent application of international investment law, this Rule requires ICSID to promptly publish excerpts of the legal reasoning of every award.[109]

It is essential at this point to look at the development of ICSID jurisprudence after the amendments on the issue of transparency. The first ICSID Tribunal that accepted *amicus curiae* submission was in the *Suez v. Argentina Case.* On 8 January 2005, five NGOs submitted to the ICSID a "Petition for Transparency and Participation as Amicus Curiae". The ICSID tribunal ruled on the First Suez Petition in its "Order in Response to a Petition for Transparency and Participation as Amicus Curiae" on 19 May 2005. At the time of this order, the ICSID Arbitration Rules did not include a provision on *amicus curiae* submissions. However, the tribunal held that it had the power to allow *amicus curiae* submissions under the last sentence of Article 44 of the ICSID Convention, which provides in relevant part: "if any question of procedure arises which is not covered by this Section or the Arbitration Rules or any rules agreed by the parties, the Tribunal shall decide the question."[110] According to the tribunal, in determining whether to accept a third party submission, three basic criteria must be met: "(a) the appropriateness of the subject matter of the case; (b) the suitability of a given non-party to act as amicus curiae in that case; and (c) the procedure by which the amicus curiae submission is made and considered."[111]

The Suez Tribunal's May 2005 decision is fundamental precedent, since it is the first ICSID case in which a tribunal decides to accept the non-disputing party as *amicus curiae* even at that time the ICSID Arbitration Rules did not provide *amicus curiae* submissions. In particular, the Tribunal in this case pointed out that "the acceptance of amicus submission would have the additional desirable consequence of increasing the transparency of Investor-State arbitration. Public acceptance of the legitimacy of international arbitral processes, particularly when they involve States and matters of public interest is strengthened by increased openness and increased knowledge as to how these processes function."[112]

There is also second Suez Tribunal's Order regarding *amicus curiae* submissions. The same five NGOs filed with the Suez Tribunal a "Petition for Permission to Make an Amicus Curiae Submission" on 1 December 2006.

---

[109] Ibid.

[110] Suez, Order in Response to a Petition for Transparency and Participation as Amicus Curiae, May 19, 2005. Paras. 8–16.

[111] A. L. McDougall and A. Santens, "ICSID Tribunals Apply New Rules on Amicus Curiae", White & Case, http://www.whitecase.com/publications_02012007_3/ (visited on 12.12.2009).

[112] Suez, Order in Response to a Petition for Transparency and Participation as Amicus Curiae, May 19, 2005. para. 22.

On 12 February 2007, the ICSID Tribunal in the *Suez Case* decided to a joint *amicus curiae* submission. This decision can be deemed a landmark precedent since it recognized the third party participation in ICSID arbitration. The Tribunal stated that: "… because of the high stakes in this arbitration and the wide publicity of ICSID awards, one cannot rule out that the forthcoming decision may have some influence on how government and foreign investor operators of the water industry approach concessions and interact when faced with difficulties."[113]

The *Biwater Gauff v. Tanzania Case* was the first ICSID decision permitting *amicus curiae* submission under the 2006 Amendment Rules.[114] The dispute arose over a concession to operate the water and sewerage services of Tanzania's capital, Dar es Salaam. *Biwater Gauff* filed a claim against the Republic of Tanzania under the UK- Tanzania BIT. Five NGOs filed a "Petition for Amicus Curiae Status" claiming that the case involved issued related to sustainable development, environment, human rights and governmental policy in which they hold expertise. It should be noted at the outset that the arbitration procedure was started before the amendments to the ICSID Arbitration Rules which came into effect in April 2006. However, the parties had agreed on the application of the ICSID Arbitration Rules adopted on 10 April 2006, which as mentioned above includes provisions on submissions of non-disputing parties. The NGOs requested the following orders: "(i) status as amicus curiae in the arbitration; (ii) access to the key arbitration documents; (iii) permission to attend any hearings and to reply to any specific questions of the Tribunal on the written submission."[115] The NGOs argued the following reasons for their petition: "This arbitration raises a number of issues of vital concern to the local community in Tanzania, and a wide range of potential issues of concern to developing countries (and indeed all countries) that have privatized, or are contemplating a possible privatization of, water or other infrastructure services. The arbitration also raises issues from a broader sustainable development perspective and is potentially of relevance for the entire international community."[116]

The involvement of the NGOs in this case was allowed by the Arbitral Tribunal notwithstanding Claimant's objections. As set out in Procedural Order No. 5, the Arbitral Tribunal acknowledged that "this arbitration raises a number of issues of concern to the wider community in Tanzania." Thus, it is important that information and submissions on the issues in dispute from all relevant sources can be obtained. On the other hand, the Arbitral Tribunal

---

[113] Ibid. para. 18.

[114] *Biwater Gauff v. Tanzania Case, (Biwater Gauff Tanzania Lmt. v. United Republic of Tanzania*, ICSID Case No. ARB/05/22, Award, 24 July 2008), (hereinafter *Biwater Gauff Case*).

[115] Biwater Petition available at http: http://ita.law.uvic.ca/documents/investment_petition _arb0522.pdf (visited on 14.12.2009).

[116] Ibid. p. 7.

noted that the ICSID Arbitration does not grant "amicus curiae status," "in so far as this might be taken to denote a standing in the overall arbitration akin to that of a party, with the full range of procedural privileges that that might entail."[117] Furthermore, the Tribunal addressed that the ICSID Arbitration Rules explicitly provide two specific and narrow types of non-parties participation: (a) the filing of a written submission (Rule 37 (2)) and (b) the attendance at hearing (Rule 32 (2)). The Tribunal also noted that participation of non-disputing parties in the ICSID arbitration is decided on a case-by-case basis at the Tribunal's discretion.[118]

The Tribunal carefully considered each of the conditions stipulated in Arbitration Rule 37 (2). In particular, the Tribunal found that: "(a) …a written submission by the Petitioners appears to have the reasonable potential to assist the Arbitral Tribunal by bringing a perspective, particular knowledge or insight that is different from that of the disputing parties (Rule 37(2)(a)); (b) …the Petitioners indication that their submissions would address matters within the scope of the dispute, and obviously reserves the right to disregard any submission that does not do so (Rule 37(2)(b)); (c)…each of the Petitioners has a sufficient interest in this proceeding (Rule 37(2)(c))."[119]

The Tribunal granted the NGO's request to file a written submission in the arbitration proceedings according to Rule 37 (2). However, to ensure that the parties were not unduly burdened, the Tribunal proposed a number of procedural safeguards, including that a single joint submission of a maximum length of 50 pages double-spaced and this submission should not attach any evidence or documentation.[120] The Tribunal's decision regarding the procedural safeguard is in line with Arbitration Rule 37 (2) since, as we mentioned above, it provides that the tribunal can decide certain procedural safeguards so as not to disrupt the proceeding or unduly burden any party.

The NGOs also requested to have an access to key arbitration documents that had been produced by the parties for the purpose of the arbitration proceeding. With regard to this request, the Tribunal noted that it was essential to be clear as to the proper role of a non-disputing party or *amicus curiae* in any given case. It envisaged that the NGOs would address broad policy

---

[117] *Biwater Gauff Case*, para. 361.

[118] Paragraph 46 of the Procedural Order No.5 of the *Biwater Gauff Case* states that: "Each of these types of participation is to be addressed by a tribunal on an ad hoc basis, rather than by the granting of an overall "amicus curiae status" for all purposes. Indeed, Rule 37(2) is specifically drafted in terms of the discretion of a tribunal to accept "a" written submission, rather than all submissions from a particular entity. It follows that there may be some written submissions from any given non-disputing party that are accepted as qualifying under the terms of Rule 37(2), and some that are not. It also follows that a "non-disputing party" does not become a party to the arbitration by virtue of a tribunal's decision under Rule 37, but is instead afforded a specific and defined opportunity to make a particular submission."

[119] Ibid. para. 50.

[120] Ibid. para. 60.

issues concerning sustainable development, environment, human rights, and government policy, all of which are within the ambit of Arbitration Rule 37 (2). Nevertheless, the Tribunal did not expect the NGOs to consider "themselves as simply in the same position as either party's lawyers," or to suggest "to the Arbitral Tribunal how issues of fact or law as presented by the parties ought to be determined."[121] The Tribunal held that this dispute was a very public and widely reported one with which each NGO was already well acquainted. Therefore, the Tribunal denied the request for access to key arbitration documents.

The NGOs also requested to attend the hearing and to reply to any specific questioned of the Tribunal on their written *amicus curiae* submission. As indicated earlier, ICSID Arbitration Rule 32 (2) explicitly states that "Unless either party objects, the Tribunal is empowered to allow a non-disputing party to attend or observe all or part of the hearings." The Tribunal in this case by quoting this Rule, denied NGOs request to attendance at hearing. Nevertheless, the tribunal reserved the right to ask the NGOs specific questions in relation to their written submission.[122]

It is essential to note that the Tribunal in the *Biwater Gauff v. Tanzania Case* determined that NGO's *amicus curiae* submissions offered "expertise and perspective that have been demonstrated to materially differ from those of the two contending parties, and as such have provided a useful contribution to the proceedings."[123] The Tribunal found that "the *Amici's* observations useful."[124] Therefore, it can be argued that the 2006 amendments regarding the transparency and non-party participation in ICSID arbitration proceedings promote transparency and assist the ICSID tribunals in resolving disputes.

Another important case regarding the non-parties participation in arbitration was the *Piero Foresti, Laura de Carli and others v. Republic of South Africa Case.*[125] In this case, the Tribunal decided to allow the NGOs to participate in arbitration proceeding in accordance with Arbitration (Additional Facility) Rule 41(3). Unlike the *Biwater Gauff v Tanzania Case*, the Tribunal in the *Piero Foresti v. South Africa Case*, allowed NGOs to access to those papers submitted to the Tribunal by the Parties that are necessary to enable them to focus their submissions upon the issues arising in the case and to see what positions the Parties have taken on those issues.[126] This can be considered "an innovative step" in the involvement of NGOs in the ICSID arbitration proceedings since

---

[121] Ibid. para. 64.
[122] Ibid. para. 72.
[123] *Biwater Gauff Case*, para. 359.
[124] Ibid., para. 392.
[125] *Piero Foresti, Laura de Carli and others v. Republic of South Africa Case, (Piero Foresti, Laura de Carli and others v. Republic of South Africa*, ICSID Case No. ARB(AF)/07/1).
[126] The Tribunal Decision on non-disputing parties participation: http://ita.law.uvic.ca/documents/ForestiNon-DisputingPartiesOrder.pdf, (Visited on 5.12.2009)

it is the first time that any ICSID tribunal has decided to obtain comment from the NGOs and the disputing parties on its non-disputing party's procedure and has also ordered the disclosure of Parties' key filing to the non-disputing parties.[127] The Tribunal recognized the fairness and efficacy of non-disputing parties' participation in ICSID arbitration.

### 4.5. *The Practice of the ICSID and Its Contribution to International Economic Law*

#### 4.5.1. *The Protection of Shareholder Rights through ICSID Arbitration*

The rights of shareholders to bring claims against host State before the ICSID is one of the most essential issues that ICSID tribunals have dealt with. Before analyzing the ICSID jurisprudence regarding the issue of standing in terms of shareholder, it is important to briefly explain the implication of *Barcelona Traction Case*[128] in order to understand the development of international investment law. Belgian nationals were shareholders in the *Barcelona Traction, Light and Power Company* (hereinafter *Barcelona Traction* or Company), which was incorporated in Toronto, Canada. The Company produced and distributed electric service in Spain through its Spanish subsidiaries. After the unlawful acts committed by Spanish government caused injury to the financial interest of its national shareholders in the Company, Belgium filed a case against Spain to the International Court of Justice (ICJ). The ICJ held that the *Barcelona Traction* was a Canadian corporation since it was incorporated there. Furthermore, the ICJ concluded that foreign shareholders in foreign investment had no right under customary international law to submit a damage claim on their own behalf.

The Court, however, recognized remedies for shareholders in two exceptional situations. First, if the direct rights of shareholder are infringed, "the shareholder has an independent right of action." The Court granted some examples of "direct rights": "the right to any declared dividend, the right to attend and vote at general meetings, the right to share in the residual assets of the company on liquidation."[129] Second, the ICJ recognized that if the case involved breach of an international treaty, the Belgium government could be entitled to bring a claim on behalf of its national shareholders.

---

[127] Elizabeth Whitsit, An ICSID Tribunal Introduces Innovative Steps into Non-Disputing Party Procedure, http://www.investmenttreatynews.org/cms/news/archive/2009/10/10/an-icsid-tribunal-introduces-innovative-steps-into-non-disputing-party-procedure.aspx, (visited on 5.12.2009).

[128] *Barcelona Traction Case, (Case Concerning the Barcelona Traction, Light and Power Company, Limited (Belgium v. Spain),* 5 February 1970 (1970), *ICJ Reports*, 9. ILM 227.

[129] Excerpts from the opinion of the ICJ, H. J. Steiner, D. F. Vagts and H. H. Koh, *Transnational Legal Problems*, (1994), p.47.

The *Barcelona Traction Case* has influenced the development of the new perspectives on the protection of shareholder rights since the ICJ recognized the importance of investment treaties for the protection of shareholders' rights in foreign investment. The Court stated that:

> *Thus, in the present state of the law, the protection of shareholders requires that recourse be had to treaty stipulations or special agreements directly concluded between the private investor and the State in which the investment is placed. States ever more frequently provide for such protection, in both bilateral and multilateral relations, either by means of special instruments or within the framework of wider economic arrangements.*[130]

The ICJ decision encouraged countries to negotiate and conclude international investment treaties, in particular bilateral investment treaties that expand the right of their nationals as shareholders in foreign investment. In fact, in ICSID jurisprudence, most of the disputes addressing the issue of shareholders' standing have involved bilateral investment treaties. The ICSID tribunals -in recent ICSID cases against Argentina- had to answer the question whether minority, non-controlling or indirect shareholders have *jus standi* before the ICSID tribunals. In these cases, respondent Argentina challenged the ICSID jurisdiction through referring to the *Barcelona Traction Case* and claimed that shareholders were not entitled to resort to ICSID arbitration separately from the company directly owning the investment.[131]

The ICSID tribunals in these cases have decided in favor of the right of minority, non-controlling and indirect shareholders to be accepted as claimants in ICSID arbitration. In other words, the ICSID tribunals held that nothing in international law prohibited investment claims submitted by all kind of shareholders independently from those of the corporation concerned. In particular, in the *CMS v. Argentina Case*, the ICSID Tribunal pointed out:

> *The Tribunal therefore finds no bar in current international law to the concept of allowing claims by shareholders independently from those of the corporation concerned, not even if those shareholders are minority or non-controlling shareholders. Although it is true, as argued by the Republic of Argentina, that this is mostly the result of lex specialis and specific treaty arrangements that have so allowed, the fact is that lex specialis in this respect is so prevalent that it can now be considered the general rule, certainly in respect of foreign investments and increasingly in respect of other matters. To the extent that customary international law or generally the traditional law of international claims might have followed a different approach- a proposition that is open to debate- then that approach can be considered the exception.*[132]

---

[130] Ibid. p. 215.

[131] UNCTAD, Investor-State Dispute Settlement and Impact on Investment Rulemaking, p. 16.

[132] *CMS v. Argentina Case*, (*CMS Gas Transmission Co. v. Argentine Republic*, Case No. ARB/01/8, Award, 12 May 2005), para. 48.

The ICSID tribunals analyzed the issue of shareholders' *jus standi* in the light of the ICSID Convention and specific provisions of the applicable treaty. As we already discussed before, the ICSID Convention deliberately does not define "investment" in order to extend comprehensive protection to investors. Hence, there is no requirement that an investment "must necessarily be made by shareholders controlling a company or owning the majority of its shares." Not only the majority shareholder but also the minority ones can resort to ICSID arbitration. Alexandrov explicitly points out that "the question whether investors holding shares in local companies have made an investment in the host State and therefore have standing to submit claims to ICSID arising directly out of that investment should not pose significant obstacles to ICSID jurisdiction."[133] Furthermore, the ICSID tribunals concluded that indirect, minority, and non-controlling investors were covered investors under the applicable bilateral investment treaties. For example, in the *Lanco v. Argentina Case*, the ICSID Tribunals for the first time precisely recognized a minority shareholder's right to bring claims under bilateral investment treaty. In this case, Lanco owned only about 18% of the capital stock of the local consortium.[134]

Most BITs include definitions of investment that stipulate shares of participation in companies as forms of investment. For example, the BIT between Argentina and the United States precisely provides that investment includes "a company or shares of stock or other interest in a company or interests in the assets thereof." For example, in the *Enron Case*, the Tribunal concluded that:

> *The Tribunal must accordingly conclude that under the provisions of the Bilateral Investment Treaty, broad as they are, claims made by investors that are not in the majority or in the control of the affected corporation when claiming for violations of their rights under such treaty are admissible.*[135]

To sum up, the ICSID practice in the issue of shareholders' standing grants broad protection to shareholders. Most BITs define shareholdings or participation in a company as a form of investment. Thus, minority, indirect, and non-controlling shareholders are entitled to submit claims to the ICSID since their shares constitute the investment.[136]

---

[133] S. A. Alexandrov, "The "Baby Boom" of Treaty-Based Arbitrations and the Jurisdiction of ICSID Tribunals: Shareholders as "Investors" and Jurisdiction Ratione Temporis", (2005) 4 *The Law and Practice of International Courts and Tribunals*, p. 28.

[134] *Lanco v. Argentina Case*, (*Lanco International Inc. v. Argentine Republic*, ICSID Case No. ARB/97/6).

[135] *Enron Corporation and Ponderosa Assets, L.P. v. Argentine Republic* (ICSID Case No. ARB/01/3), Decision on Jurisdiction of January 14, 2004, http://www.asil.org/ilib/Enron.pdf, para. 49.

[136] C. Schreuer, "Shareholder Protection in International Investment Law", 23 May 2005, http://www.arbitration.fr/resources/shareholder+protection+in+international+investment+law+by+chirstoph+shreuer+2005.pdf (visited on 20.12.2009), p. 6.

### 4.5.2. *Contract Claims v. Treaty Claims*

#### 4.5.2.1. *Breach of Contract and Breach of Treaty Claims in ICSID Arbitration*

One of the most debated issues in ICSID Jurisprudence is breach of contract versus breach of treaty claims. In fact, many international investment disputes deal with the jurisdiction of the arbitral tribunal in terms of whether the jurisdiction can be extended to address breach of investment contract claims. The jurisdictional issues in investment treaty arbitration are difficult due to the existence of two different dispute resolution mechanisms: investment treaty and investment contract dispute resolution mechanisms.[137] Investment contracts have provided their own dispute settlement mechanism under the domestic law of the host State. Therefore, when foreign investors submit contract claims to international arbitration tribunals, in our case, ICSID tribunals, respondents argued that the ICSID tribunal does not have jurisdiction on this issue since the tribunals have jurisdiction only related to breaches of the investment treaty.[138]

The ICSID tribunals have recognized that a breach of contract and breach of treaty form separate causes for action. For example *Vivendi* annulment decision shows the importance of the differences between breach of contract and breach of treaty claims in ICSID arbitration. The tribunal held that:

> *A state may breach a treaty without breaching a contract, and vice versa, and this is certainly true of these provisions of the BIT... Whether there has been a breach of the BIT and whether there has been a breach of contract are different questions. Each of these claims will be determined by reference to its own proper or applicable law-in the case of the BIT, by international law; in the case of the Concession contract, by the proper law of the contract...*[139]

The distinction between contract and treaty claim is mainly important if the investment contract includes an exclusive choice of court or arbitration clause. In this particular situation, the question will be raised as to whether foreign investors can submit treaty claims to investment arbitration. The answer of this particular question is simple. Since the ICSID tribunals have recognized the distinction between treaty and contract claims, foreign investors can submit treaty claims to investment arbitration.[140] For example, the ICSID Tribunal in the *CMS v. Argentina Case* held that:

> *As contractual claims are different from treaty claims, even if there had been or there currently was recourse to the local courts for breach of contract, this would not have prevented submission of the treaty claims to arbitration.*[141]

---

137 L. A. Mistelis and J. D.M. Lew QC, *Pervasive Problems in International Arbitration*, 2006, p. 262.

138 UNCTAD, Investor-State Dispute Settlement and Impact on Investment Rulemaking, p. 27.

139 ICSID Case No. ARB/97/3, Decision on annulment, July 3, 2002, para. 96.

140 Mistelis and Lew QC, p. 263.

141 ICSID Case No. ARB/01/8, Decision on jurisdiction, July 17 2003, para. 80.

It is essential to note that even though the ICSID tribunals have recognized the distinction between contract claims and treaty claims, the ICSID tribunals still can deal with breach of contract claim. There are various situations in which arbitral tribunals should deal with a breach of contract claim. In particular, there are situations in which a breach of contract amounts to breach of investment treaty. Indeed, when the host State breaches an investment contract, this may also be a violation of obligations stipulated in most international investment agreements, such as the fair and equitable treatment principle, non-discriminatory treatment, or expropriation. For example, the ICSID tribunals held that States' measures for nullifying rights under an investment contract may amount to an expropriation.[142]

#### 4.5.2.2. *The Interpretation of "Umbrella Clauses"*

As mentioned above, ICSID tribunals can deal with contract claims in various situations. Situation in which the international investment treaty provides an "umbrella clauses" is one of the important and highly debated issues in terms of whether the ICSID tribunal has jurisdiction to decide foreign investor's contract-based claims or not. Many BITs include "umbrella clauses" that require States to respect all obligations with regard to investment. Even though umbrella clauses take many forms, they require each contracting State party to observe all obligations incurred with regard to the covered investments.[143] For example, the umbrella clause in the Belarus-the Republic of Korea BIT provides: "Each Contracting Party shall observe any other obligation it may have entered into with regard to investments in its territory by investors of the other Contracting Party."[144]

Although many BITs include umbrella clauses, the scope and the effect of these umbrella clauses can vary and they have been construed differently by ICSID tribunals. Due to the fact that international investment treaties provide umbrella clauses, foreign investors argue that the ICSID has jurisdiction over the contract claim. Thus, ICSID tribunals face the question of whether these clauses transform breaches of a contract to breaches of the treaty. It should be noted that many legal scholars agreed that due to the effect of an umbrella clause, a breach of contract becomes a breach of treaty.[145] For example, F. A. Mann recognized that the umbrella clause "protects the investors against any interference with his contractual rights, whether it results from a mere breach

[142] UNCTAD, Investors-State Dispute Settlement and Impact on Investment Rulemaking, p. 26.

[143] Y. Shany, "Contract Claims vs. Treaty Claims: Mapping Conflicts Between ICSID Decision on Multisourced Investment Claims", (2005) 99 *American Journal of International Law*, p. 837.

[144] http://www.unctad.org/sections/dite/iia/docs/bits/korea_belarus.pdf (visited on 21.12.2009).

[145] OECD; Working Papers on International Investment, Interpretation of the Umbrella Clause in Investment Agreements, No:2006/3 (October 2006), pp. 7–8.

of contract or a legislative or administrative act, and independently of the question whether or no such interference amounts to expropriation."[146]

The ICSID tribunals have different approaches as to the precise scope and effect of umbrella clauses. Some ICSID tribunals have recognized most of the legal scholars' view that these clauses transform breach of a contract to treaty violation. On the other hand, other ICSID tribunals did not agree that umbrella clauses have the effect of elevating breaches of contract to breaches of treaty.[147] We can divide the ICSID tribunals' interpretions of the umbrella clauses into three categories: a narrow interpretation, a broad interpretation, and a balance approach.

The first ICSID Tribunal that evaluated the legal effect and the scope of an umbrella clause was in the *SGS v. Pakistan Case*.[148] SGS, a Swiss company, filed a request for arbitration with ICSID pursuant to the Switzerland-Pakistan BIT after the government terminated its services contract with SGS. Companies' request contained both breach of contract and breach of treaty claims. SGS's breach of contract claim is based on Article 11 of the Switzerland-Pakistan BIT, which stated: "Either Contracting Party shall constantly guarantee the observance of the commitments it has entered into with respect to the investments of the investors of the other Contracting Party." The ICSID Tribunal ruled that it did not have jurisdiction over SGS's contract claims. In particular, the Tribunal noted that: "The Text itself of Article 11 does not purport to state that breaches of contract alleged by an investor in relation to a contract it has concluded with a State (widely considered to be a matter of municipal rather than international law) are automatically 'elevated' to the level of breaches of international treaty law."[149] The Tribunal asserted that the effects of an umbrella clause were so far reaching and evidence was needed to show that contracting parties intended those effects.[150]

Like in the *SGS v Pakistan Case*, some ICSID tribunals have adopted a narrow interpretation approach. In the *Joy Mining v. Egypt Case*,[151] the ICSID tribunal construed the umbrella clause in similar way to the *SGS v. Pakistan* Tribunal. It pointed out that:

> *In this context, it could not be held that an umbrella clause inserted in the treaty, and not very prominently, could have the effect of transforming all contract disputes*

[146] F.A. Mann, "British Treaties for the Promotion and Protection of Investments", (1981) 52 *British Yearbook of International Law*, p. 241, p. 246.

[147] UNCTAD, Investors-State Dispute Settlement and Impact on Investment Rulemaking, p. 29.

[148] *SGS v. Pakistan Case*, (*SGS Société Générale de Surveillance, S.A. v. Islamic Republic of Pakistan*, ICSID Case No ARB/01/13, Decision on Jurisdiction, 6 August 2003).

[149] Ibid. para. 166.

[150] UNCTAD, Investors-State Dispute Settlement and Impact on Investment Rulemaking, p. 29.

[151] *Joy Mining v. Egypt Case*, (*Joy Mining Machinery Limited v. Egypt*, ICSID Case No. ARB/03/11, Decision on Jurisdiction, 6 August 2004).

> *into investment disputes under the Treaty, unless of course there would be a clear violation of Treaty rights and obligations or a violation of contract rights of such a magnitude as to trigger the Treaty protection, which is not the case...*[152]

The ICSID Tribunal in the *Salini Construttori S.p.A. and Italstrade S.p.A. v. The Hashemite Kingdom of Jordan Case* narrowly interpreted the umbrella clause of the Italy-Jordan BIT which provides that: "each Contracting Party shall create and maintain in its territory a legal framework apt to guarantee the investors the continuity of legal treatment, including the compliance, in good faith, of all undertakings assumed with regard to each specific investor." The Tribunal concluded that, pursuant to the wording of the umbrella clause in question, it did not have jurisdiction over breach of contract claims.[153]

In contrast to above mentioned tribunals' decisions, some other ICSID tribunals have adopted broad interpretation approach. The first ICSID case in which the tribunal adopted this approach was the *SGS v. Philippines Case.*[154] The dispute concerned a comprehensive import supervision agreement which provided a dispute resolution clause granting exclusive jurisdiction on the courts of the Philippines. SGS's breach of contract claims was based on the Switzerland-Philippines BIT's umbrella clause, which stated in Article X(2) that: "Each Contracting Party shall observe any obligation it has assumed with regard to specific investments in its territory of the other Contracting Party." The Tribunal pointed out that the umbrella clauses must be interpreted in its plain and ordinary meaning.[155] After criticizing the *SGS v. Pakistan* decision, the Tribunal in *SGS v. Philippines* concluded that:

> *Interpreting the actual text of Article X(2), it would appear to say, and to say clearly, that each Contracting Party shall observe any legal obligation it has assumed, or will in the future assume, with regard to specific investments covered by the BIT.*[156]

In addition to the *SGS v. Philippines Case*, the ICSID tribunal in *Sempra Energy International v. Argentina*[157] acknowledged that contractual claims were also treaty claims. Furthermore, the ICSID tribunals have followed the analysis of the tribunal in *SGS v. Philippines*. For example, the partial award in *Eureko B. V. v. Poland*[158] analyzed the question of the umbrella clause included in the

---

152 Ibid. para. 81.

153 H. Seriki, "Umbrella Clauses and Investment Treaty Arbitration: All Encompassing or a Respite for Sovereign States and State Entities?", (2007) *Journal of Business Law*, p. 579.

154 *SGS v. Philippines Case*, (*SGS Société Générale de Surveillance, S.A. v. Republic of the Philippines*, ICSID Case No. ARB/02/6, Decision on Jurisdiction, 29 January 2004), (hereinafter *SGS v. Philippines*).

155 Seriki, p. 576.

156 *SGS v. Philippines*, para. 115.

157 *Sempra v. Argentina Case*, (*Sempra Energy International v. Republic of Argentina*, ICSID Case No ARB/02/16, Decision on Jurisdiction, 11 May 2005).

158 *Eureko v. Poland Case*, (*Eureko B.V. v. Poland, Partial Award*, 19 August 2005). http://ita.law.uvic.ca/documents/Eureko-PartialAwardandDissentingOpinion.pdf (visited on 24.12.2009).

Netherlands-Poland BIT in greater detail. The Tribunal broadly interpreted the Netherlands-Poland BIT's umbrella clause, which provides that "Each Contracting Party shall observe any obligations it may have entered into with regard to investments of investors of the other Contracting Party." The Tribunal construed this provision in accordance with its ordinary meaning. The Tribunal held that the umbrella clause "means what it says."[159]

The ICSID tribunal in the *Noble Ventures v. Romania Case*[160] also widely interpreted the umbrella clause in the US-Romania BIT in light of considering the object and purpose of the clause. In particular, the tribunal noted that "the Parties had as their aim to equate contractual obligations governed by municipal law to international treaty obligations as established in the BIT." Moreover, the ICSID tribunal in the *LG&E v. Argentina Case*[161] described the umbrella clause as one which "creates a requirement by the host State to meet its obligations toward foreign investors, including those that derive from a contract; hence such obligations receive extra protection by virtue of their consideration under the bilateral treaty". In line with these decisions, the ICSID Tribunal in the *Consorzio Groupement L.E.S.I.-DIPENTA v. Republic of Algeria Case*[162] explicitly explained the effect of the umbrella clause stating that "the effect of such clauses is to transform the violations of the State's contractual commitments into violations of the treaty umbrella clause and by this to give jurisdiction to the Tribunal over the matter..."[163]

Overall, following the broad analysis and interpretation of the umbrella clause in *SGS v. Philippines*, in the above mentioned cases, the ICSID tribunals agreed that the scope of the umbrella clause and its effect are so extensive that by virtue of this clause host State's breach of contract becomes a breach of treaty. For example, the ICSID tribunal in the *Siemens v. Argentina Case*[164] found that the umbrella clause "has the meaning that its terms express, namely, that failure to meet obligations undertaken by one of the Treaty parties in respect to any particular investment is converted by this clause into a breach of the Treaty."[165]

---

[159] Ibid. para. 256.

[160] *Noble Ventures v. Romania Case*, (*Noble Ventures, Inc. v. Romania*, ICSID Case No ARB/01/11, Award, 12 October 2005).

[161] *LG&E v. Argentina Case*, (*LG & E Energy Corp., LG & E Capital Corp. and LG & E International Inc. v. Argentine Republic*, ICSID Case No. ARB/02/01, Decision on Liability, 3 October 2006, Award, 25 July 2007). Decision on Liability, paras. 169–75.

[162] *L.E.S.I.-DIPENTA v. Algeria Case*, (*Consortium Groupement L.E.S.I.-DIPENTA v. Democratic Republic of Algeria*, ICSID Case No. ARB/03/08, Award, 10 January 2005).

[163] OECD, p. 21.

[164] *Siemens A.G. v. Argentine Republic*, ICSID Case No. ARB/02/8, Award, 6 February 2007.

[165] E. G. Shenkman, D. Jason File, Recent Developments in Investment Treaty Jurisprudence: Arbitrating Contract Claims Under Umbrella Clauses, http://www.wilmerhale.com, ICGL To: International Arbitration 2007, (visited on 20.2.2009).

The latest development on the interpretation of the umbrella clauses is the balance approach which has been adopted by the ICSID tribunals. For example, in the *El Paso v. Argentina Case*[166] the Tribunal adopted balanced approach to investment treaty interpretation and it stated that: "both State sovereignty and State's responsibility to create an adopted and evolutionary framework for the development of economic activities, and the necessity to protect foreign investment and its continuing flow."[167] The Tribunal pointed out that the broad interpretation of umbrella clauses would have "far reaching consequences, quite destructive of the distinction between national legal orders, and international legal order."[168] Thus, the Tribunal did not agree that contractual breaches amounted to treaty breaches. On the other hand, the Tribunal clearly stated that the umbrella clause will cover some contracts: "... the umbrella clause read in conjunction with Article VII (the Umbrella clause in the US-Argentina BIT), will not extend the Treaty protection to breaches of an ordinary commercial contract entered into by the State or a State-owned entity, but will cover additional investment protections contractually agreed by the State as a sovereign- such as stabilization clause-inserted in an investment agreement."[169]

The ICSID Tribunal in the *Pan American v. Argentina Case*[170] followed the same balanced approach adopted in the *El Paso v. Argentina Case*.[171] The tribunal concluded that an umbrella clause cannot transform any contract claim into treaty claim. However, the Tribunal agreed that certain kinds of contract breaches will be covered under the scope of the umbrella clause. Thus, there is a distinction between contract with the "State as a merchant" and the "State as a sovereign".[172] Similarly, the ICSID Tribunal in the *CMS Gas Transmission co. v. Argentina Case*[173] decided that "not all contract breaches result in breaches of the Treaty. The standard of protection of the Treaty will be engaged only when there is a specific breach of treaty rights and obligations or a violation of contract rights under the treaty. Purely commercial aspects of a contract might not be protected by the treaty in some situations, but the protection is likely to

---

166 *El Paso v. Argentina Case*, (*El Paso Energy International Company v. Argentine Republic*, ICSID Case No. ARB/03/15, Decision on Jurisdiction, 27 April 2006). (hereinafter *El Paso v. Argentina Case)*.

167 Ibid. para. 70.

168 OECD, p. 17.

169 *El Paso v. Argentine Case*, para. 81.

170 *Pan American v. Argentina Case*, (*Pan American Energy LLC and BP Argentina Exploration Company v. Argentine Republic*, ICSID Case No. ARB/03/13), and *BP America v. Argentina Case, (BP American Production Co. and Others v. Argentine Republic*, ICSID Case No. ARB/04/8, Decision on Jurisdiction, 27 July 2006).

171 It should be noted that in the *Pan American v. Argentina Case*, the tribunal consisting of two of the same three arbitrators of the *El Paso v. Argentina Case*.

172 Shenkman and File, p. 5.

173 *CMS v. Argentina*, ICSID Case No. ARB/01/8, Award, 12 May 2005.

be available when there is significant interference by governments or public agencies with the rights of the investor."[174]

It should be noted that umbrella clause can play an important role in securing foreign investment. However, there are significant divergences among ICSID tribunals as to the scope and effect of umbrella clauses. It is a well-known rule that the BITs should be interpreted pursuant to Article 31 of the Vienna Convention on the Law of Treaties. According to Article 31, BITs should be interpreted in good faith in accordance with the ordinary meaning of the clause in the treaty. Thus, the wording utilized in umbrella clauses should be the main point for evaluation of the effect and the scope of the umbrella clauses. In other words, whether an umbrella clause is interpreted as transforming breach of contract claims to the level of breach of treaty claims will eventually be based on the precise wording of the clause in question.[175] It is essential to note that BITs should also be interpreted "in the light of its object and purpose." Therefore, balanced approach should be adopted by ICSID tribunals since this approach is taking into account not only the protection of foreign investor, but also the host State's responsibility to "create and adapt a framework for the development of economic activities and the necessity to protect foreign investment and its continuing flow."[176] It is worthwhile to note that due to the existence of different approaches adopted by ICSID tribunals for the interpretation of umbrella clauses, contracting parties should incorporate them with a clear language in BITs.

### 4.5.3. *Sovereign Immunity*

As mentioned in "the enforcement of ICSID Awards" section, a party to ICSID arbitration may seek recognition and enforcement of ICSID awards in any State party to Convention. Indeed, once the ICSID award is issued, defaulting party, in particular the host state, is under a public international law obligation to comply with it. In the case of non-compliance, winning party has a right to seek enforcement of the award in all contracting parties of ICSID Convention.[177] This is the main difference and influential aspects of ICSID arbitration compared with other international arbitration proceedings. Articles 54, 55 and 56 are the provisions for the enforcement of ICSID awards. Article 54 stipulates that each contracting State must recognize and enforce ICSID awards as if they were final judgments of local courts.

Although Article 54 of the ICSID Convention provides that all contracting States must recognize and enforce ICSID awards, the question is still raised

---

[174] Ibid. para. 299.
[175] Seriki, p. 580.
[176] Seriki, p. 573.
[177] Dolzer and Schreuer, p. 288.

whether the above mentioned provisions of the ICSID Convention grant effective enforcement mechanism for ICSID arbitral awards. The particular problem is that even though the procedure for enforcement of ICSID award is simple and effective, a winning party of a recognized ICSID awards has only an executory title.[178] Article 54 (3) provides that "execution of the award shall be governed by the laws concerning the execution of judgments in the State in whose territories such execution is sought." Furthermore, Article 55 emphasized that execution of an ICSID award against a state is subject to the rules on State immunity. Article 55 provides States immunity for execution of awards in the following terms: "Nothing in Article 54 shall be construed as derogating from the law in force in any Contracting State relating to immunity of that State or of any foreign State from execution."

It should be noted that the execution of ICSID awards depend on the national laws on sovereign immunity.[179] Thus, holder of recognized ICSID awards will seek out the more favorable forum which facilities execution of ICSID awards. In other words, the winning party in ICSID arbitration proceedings will choose the place that State's assets are not protected by sovereign immunity from execution.[180] Article 54(3) states that execution of an ICSID award is subject to national law of the forum States. Article 55 is a specification of this Article and provides that sovereign immunity will apply to the execution of ICSID award. Thus, the execution of ICSID awards will not be possible in various jurisdictions since sovereign immunity laws are different from one State to another.[181]

Even though the State immunity law was developed by domestic courts, State immunity is also accepted and regulated under customary international law. Numerous countries have specific regulations on State immunity. In particular, United States and the United Kingdom have laws on State immunity. Furthermore, there are treaties on the issue of State immunity. The European Convention on State Immunity of 1972 and the International Law Commission's Draft Articles on Jurisdictional Immunities of States and Their Property in 1991 are the examples to international treaties on State immunity.[182]

The national laws and international treaties on State immunity regulate immunity from jurisdiction and immunity from execution. With respect to

---

[178] O. Vincent and O. Nmehielle, "Enforcing Arbitration Awards Under the International Convention for the Settlement of Invesment Disputes (ICSID Convention)," (2001) *Annual Survey of International and Comparative Law*, p. 31.

[179] A. Blane, "Sovereign Immunity as a Bar to the Execution of International Arbitral Awards", (2009) 41/2 *New York University Journal of International Law and Politics* pp. 461–4.

[180] A. Boralessa, "Enforcement in the United States and United Kingdom of ICSID Awards Against The Republic of Argentina: Obstacles that Transnational Corporations May Face," (2004) *New York International Law Review*, p. 78.

[181] Reed, Paulsson and Blackaby, p. 107.

[182] UNCTAD, Dispute Settlement, ICSID, 2.9. Binding Force and Enforcement, New York and Geneva, 2003, p.17.

ICSID awards, the distinction between the immunity from execution and immunity from jurisdiction should be made. Article 55 of the ICSID Convention can be applicable only to sovereign immunity from execution. This Article does not apply to immunity from jurisdiction since jurisdiction is stipulated in Article 25 of the ICSID Convention. Furthermore, Article 55 is related to execution and not for enforcement of an ICSID award. Thus, the State immunity cannot be applied in the recognition and enforcement procedure of ICSID awards.[183]

The jurisprudence relating the enforcement of ICSID awards also try to differentiate between immunity from enforcement and immunity from execution. In *Liberian Eastern Timber Co. v. Government of Liberia (Letco v. Liberia),*[184] the United States District Courts for the Southern District of New York recognized an ICSID award rendered against Liberia and declared it enforceable.[185] Letco's demand for the execution of the judgment was denied on the basis of immunity from execution. The court examined whether the property in question was utilized for commercial activity in the United States or not. The court concluded that the assets in question are not commercial nature. Registration fees and other taxes are revenues for the support and maintenance of government functions.[186] The immunity of execution is applicable for the ICSID awards and the immunity of assets based on whether they are utilized for commercial and governmental purposes. Therefore, immunity from execution is granted if the property attached was intended to be utilized for governmental purposes. In the *SOABI v. Senagal Case,*[187] the French court also made this distinction. The Court of Cassation held that consent to arbitration by France constitutes an implicit waiver of immunity from suit. However, it did not grant immunity from execution.[188] Therefore, the Court of Cassation acknowledged that Article 53 and 54 of the ICSID Convention creates a simple and independent system of recognition, enforcement and the State of immunity that can prevent the execution of an ICSID award against assets of the State party to the dispute. Furthermore, commercial assets are subject to execution. But, assets that are used for governmental activities would enjoy sovereign immunity.[189]

[183] Ibid. p. 18.

[184] *LETCO v. Liberia Case, (Liberian Eastern Timber Co. v. Republic of Liberia,* Award, 31 March 1986, ICSID Case No. ARB/83/2, ICSID Reports 343).

[185] District Court, S. D. N. Y., 5 September 1986, 2 *ICSID Reports* 384.

[186] District Court, S. D. N. Y., 12 December 1986, 2 *ICSID Reports* 385.

[187] *SOABI v. Senagal Case, (Société Quest Africaine des Bétons Industriels v. Senegal,* Award, 25 February 1988, 2 ICSID Reports 190).

[188] *See* detailed information regarding this case: K. Highet, G. Kahale III and G. R. Delaume, "France-Recognition of ICSID Awards- Sovereign Immunity", (1992) 86 *American Journal of International Law,* pp. 138–42.

[189] UNCTAD, 2.9. Binding Force and Enforcement, pp. 20–1.

Recognition of ICSID awards and execution are two separate issues. Thus, the sovereign immunity defense can only be applied for the execution of ICSID awards. However, there might be some solutions for the immunity problem. "Forum shopping for execution" is one of the practical solutions for possible execution of ICSID awards. The winning party of ICSID awards will seek to execute this award in a country that the losing party has assets in and that follows restrictive doctrine of immunity.[190] The other solution for the execution of ICSID awards is to include a contract clause explicitly waiving immunity from execution.[191] However, a waiver of immunity from execution is subject to the law of the county in where execution is sought. Thus, the validity and the scope of such a waiver will be interpreted differently by the courts.[192]

It is worthwhile to note that relying on State immunity from execution does not change the fact that non-compliance with an ICSID award is a violation of the ICSID Convention. In other words, the impossibility of enforcing an ICSID award due to the law on sovereign immunity does not have effect on the binding nature of the award. Thus, the States' obligation to comply with an award has remained. States which successfully rely on State immunity still comply with an award since this is a treaty obligation.[193] The ICSID Convention provides two possible remedy for the compliance of ICSID award even debtor State successfully plea its right to immunity. The first remedy is diplomatic protection stipulated under Article 27 (1). Article 27(1) provides that the right to diplomatic protection can be applicable if a State does not comply with the award. This Article grants rights to the contracting State espousing its nationals' claims directly against losing State.[194] Granting the diplomatic protection rights as a remedy for the immunity problems, this Article also acknowledges the basic principles of diplomatic protection under international economic law. Nonetheless, the diplomatic protection is a political remedy and depends on the policy of the contracting State.[195] The second remedy is submitting a dispute to the International Court of Justice provided in Article 64 of the Convention. The non-compliance of ICSID award constitutes to a dispute regarding the interpretation of the ICSID Convention.[196] In this case, State may refer the dispute to the ICJ. However, like the first remedy, the application

---

[190] G. Cane, "The Enforcement of ICSID Awards: Revolutionary or Ineffective", (1994) 15 *American.Review of International Arbitration*, p. 439, p. 457.

[191] The ICSID recommends the following model clause for the purpose of waiving immunity: "

"The (Name of Contracting State) hereby irrevocably waives any claim to immunity in regard to any proceedings to enforce any arbitral award rendered by a Tribunal constituted pursuant to this agreement, including immunity from service of process, immunity from jurisdiction of any court, and immunity of any of its property from execution."

[192] Reed, Paulsson and Blackaby, p. 109.

[193] Nmehielle, p. 40.

[194] Boralessa, p. 111.

[195] Boralessa, pp. 111–2.: Nmehielle, p. 41.

[196] Cane, p. 458.

of this provision also has political implications. Overall, even though the above mentioned remedies for the sovereign immunity problem have political nature and implications, the ICSID Convention recognized that granting diplomatic protection rights which are developed under international economic law will affect the enforcement and execution of ICSID awards.

### 4.5.4. *Main Substantive Principles of International Law Applied and Redefined by ICSID Tribunals*

#### 4.5.4.1. *Most Favoured Nation Treatment*

MFN treatment has been a part of international trade law for centuries and became an important feature of international investment law in recent years.[197] Indeed, most bilateral investment treaties include MFN clause. Thus, it is essential to analyze the ICSID Jurisprudence regarding MFN clauses to understand the development of main substantive principles of international economic law.

As mentioned above, bilateral investment treaties are the main sources of international investment law. Most BITs provides investment security through including non-discrimination provisions. In fact, most BITs contain provisions that each contracting party ensures that investments and investments activities of nationals and companies of the other party receive MFN treatment. Generally, clauses require each contracting State to accord to investors of the other contracting State treatment that is no less favourable than that accorded to investors of the third State. Consequently, according to these clauses, host country will provide foreign investor with the highest standard of treatment available to an investor from any other foreign country that signed BITs with host country. It should be noted that MFN clauses not only provide investment security, they also promote investment neutrality. Due to the fact that the MFN clause is a non-discrimination provision, the host country is obliged not to discriminate among investments and investors based on nationality.[198] Furthermore, most BITs provide some exceptions to MFN obligations. For instance, regional economic integration agreement such as customs union is the most significant exception that undermines the non-discrimination provisions.[199]

It is worthwhile to note that even though most BITs include MFN clauses, they are not addressing these clauses in the same manner. In other words,

---

[197] Schill, pp. 129–50.; P. Baklacı, *Uluslararası Yatırım Hukukunda En Çok Gözetilen Ulus Kaydı, (MFN Clauses in International Investment Law)* 2009.; Newcombe and Paradell, pp. 195–204.

[198] Vandevelde, p. 512.

[199] *See* Article 2 of the Turkey-Tunisia BITs, Agreement between The Republic of Tunisia and The Republic of Turkey Concerning The Reciprocal Promotion and Protection of Investments, http://www.unctad.org/sections/dite/iia/docs/bits/TurkeyTunisia.pdf (visited on 20.6.2007).

the wording of the MFN clauses is different from treaty to treaty. Thus, the scope of the MFN treatment and the protection provided by the clauses varies from one treaty to another treaty.[200] Some BITs provide that MFN treatment applies to all matters covered by the treaty; others provide that it applies to all investments of investors. Furthermore, some BITs state that MFN applies with respect to the management, maintenance, use, enjoyment, and disposal of investments. For example Article 3 of the Turkey -United Kingdom BITs stated that:

> *... 2-Neither Contracting party shall in its territory subject nationals or companies of the other Contracting party, as regards the management, maintenance, use, enjoyment or disposal of their investments, to treatment less favourable than that which it accords to its own nationals or companies or to nationals or companies of any third State.*

Due to the fact that various approaches are utilized in BITs regarding MFN treatment, there is no uniformity on interpreting the scope of MFN clauses. In fact, host State and investors have different interests over the scope of MFN treatment. Host States claim for the least possible protection. On the other hand, investors want to get the best possible protection for their investments in host States. The ICSID tribunals reach different conclusions with respect to the scope of MFN treatment. In particular, the problem will arise whether the scope of MFN clauses in a BIT apply to dispute resolution provisions or not.[201] In other words, it can be possible for investors to utilize MFN clause to establish jurisdiction over their investment disputes with host States. The MFN clause can be a powerful tool for investors, for example, if the claimant investor fails to fulfill requirement in the Investor-State dispute settlement provisions of the applicable BIT.

The scope of the MFN clauses has been a controversial issue in recent ICSID arbitration cases. In particular, recent ICSID tribunals have delt with the question whether the MFN clause should apply to dispute settlement procedures. The problem was addressed in numerous ICSID decisions.[202] Legal scholars working on this issue generally examine these following four cases:

---

[200] S. Fietta, "Most Favoured Nation Treatment and Dispute Resolution Under Bilateral Investment Treaties: A Turning Point", (2005) *International Arbitration Law Review*, p. 131.

[201] Ibid. pp. 131–8.

[202] The following ICSID decisions are the examples for the issue of application of most-favored-nation clauses to dispute resolution provisions in BITs: Gas *Natural v. Argentina*, Decision on Jurisdiction, 17 June 2005.; *Suez et al v. Argentina Case*, (*Suez Sociedad General de Aguas de Barcelona S.A., and Inter Aguas Servicios Integrales del Agua S.A. v. Argentine Republic*, ICSID Case No. ARB/03/17, Decision on Jurisdiction 16 May 2006).; *Suez and AWG v. Argentina Case, (Suez Sociedad General de Aguas de Barcelona S.A., and Vivendi Universal S.A. v. Argentine Republic*, ICSID Case No. ARB/03/19, Decision on Jurisdiction, 3 August 2006).; Telenor Mobile Communications A.S. v. The Republic of Hungary, ICSID Case No. ARB/04/15, September 13, 2006.

*Maffezini*[203], *Siemens*[204], *Salini*[205] and *Plama*[206] cases. The ICSID arbitral tribunals expansively interpret the MFN clauses in first two cases. On the hand, the tribunals narrowly interpret the applicability of MFN to dispute settlement procedures in *Salini* and *Plama* cases.

The first BIT case addressing the question of the applicability of MFN to dispute settlement procedures was *Maffezini v. Spain*. In this case, investors successfully argued that the MFN clauses should be interpreted broadly. In particular, the investors claimed that the MFN clause in the BIT that applied to their dispute entitled them to the favourable procedures that were provided in one of host State's other BITs.

The *Maffezini Case* concerned an investment dispute arising out of the alleged treatment by Spanish authorities of *Emilio Agustin Maffezini*, an Argentine national who invested in an enterprise for the production and distribution of chemical products in Spain. In his request for ICSID arbitration, Mr. *Maffezini* invoked the provisions of the BIT between Argentina and Spain. Pursuant to Article 10 of this BIT, the investor had to submit the claim first to domestic courts. In the absence of any agreement to the contrary, the possibility of settling the dispute through international arbitration existed only if domestic tribunals had failed to resolve the dispute on its merits within an 18-month period. Mr. *Maffezini* did not follow the dispute resolution provisions of this BIT. He directly requested for arbitration in the ICSID. However, Spain objected to the jurisdiction of the arbitration tribunal, arguing that Mr. *Maffezini* had failed to fulfill the requirements of the dispute resolution provision of BIT between Argentina and Spain.[207]

Mr. *Maffezini* asserted that the MFN clause in Article 4 of the Argentina-Spain BIT allowed him to invoke the dispute settlement provisions in the BIT between Chile and Spain, which allows the investors to submit the dispute to ICSID arbitration without having to submit it first to domestic courts. Article 4 of the Argentina-Spain BIT provides that:

> *[...]*
>
> *2. In all matters subject to this Agreement, this treatment shall be no less favourable than that extended by each Party to the investments made in its territory by investors of a third country. [...] (non-official translation from Spanish, emphasis added)*

---

[203] *Maffezini v. Spain Case*, (*Emilio Augustin Maffezini v. Kingdom of Spain*, ICSID Case No. ARB/97/7, Decision on Jurisdiction, 25 January 2000). (hereinafter *Maffezini v. Spain Case*).

[204] *Siemens v. Argentina Case*, (*Siemens A.G. v. Argentine Republic*, ICSID Case No ARB/02/8, Decision on Jurisdiction, 3 August 2004), (hereinafter *Siemens v. Argentina Case*).

[205] *Salini v. Jordan Case*, (*Salini Construttori S.p.A. and Italstrade S.p.A. v. Hashemite Kingdom of Jordan*, ICSID Case No. ARB/02/13, Decision on Jurisdiction, 29 November 2004), (hereinafter *Salini Case*).

[206] *Plama v. Bulgaria Case*, (*Plama Consortium Limited v. Bulgaria*, ICSID Case No. ARB/03/24, Decision on Jurisdiction, 8 February 2005), (hereinafter *Plama Case*).

[207] *Maffezini v. Spain Case*, paras. 19–37.

Mr. *Maffezini* argued that Chilean investors in Spain were treated more favourably than Argentine investors in Spain. Therefore, the MFN provision in the Argentina-Spain BIT granted him the option of submitting the dispute to the ICSID tribunal without initiation of the domestic proceedings in Spain. On the other side, Spain objected to Maffezini's claim regarding the applicability of MFN clause to dispute settlement provision. In particular, Spain argued that "under the principle ejusdem generis the most favored nation clause can only operate in respect of the same matter and cannot be extended to matters different from those envisaged by the basic treaty."[208] Spain argued that the MFN clauses apply to substantive matters of treatment granted to investor. These clauses cannot be applicable to dispute settlement provisions.

After examining both claimant's and respondent's arguments, the ICSID Tribunal agreed with claimant's request. Thus, it granted itself jurisdiction over the disputed case. The Tribunal concluded that

> *Notwithstanding the fact that the basic treaty... does not refer expressly to dispute settlement as covered by the most favored nation clause, the Tribunal considers that there are good reasons to conclude that today dispute settlement arrangements are inextricably related to the protection of foreign investors*[209]

After examining the wording of the Argentina-Spain BIT, the Tribunal found that the MFN clause could extend to dispute resolution provision because the MFN clause in this BIT explicitly refers to "all matters subject to this Agreement".[210] The *Maffezini Case* illustrates that the MFN standard cannot be automatically applied. Thus, the Tribunal set important limitations to the application of the MFN clause to the dispute resolution provisions. The first limitation is regarding the applicable treaty for MFN treatment. The Tribunal stated that the scope of the MFN treatment has to be based on the text of the applicable treaty. The second limitation is regarding the *ejusdem generis* principle. Pursuant to this principle, the MFN treatment can cover only matters belonging to the same subject matter or the same category of subject to which the clause relates. The third limitation is pertaining to public policy consideration. The investors should not be able to utilize an MFN clause to override public policy considerations envisaged by the contracting parties as fundamental to their acceptance of the agreement. In the words of the Tribunal:

> *Notwithstanding the fact that the application of the most favored nation clause to dispute settlement arrangements in the context of investment treaties might result in the harmonization and enlargement of the scope of such arrangements, there are*

---

[208] Ibid. paras. 38–40.

[209] Ibid. para. 54.

[210] J. Wong, "The Application of Most-Favored-Nation Clauses to Dispute Resolution Provisions in Bilateral Investment Treaties", (2008) *Asian Journal of WTO & International Health Law and Policy*, p. 182.

> *some important limits that ought to be kept in mind. As a matter of principle, the beneficiary of the clause should not be able to override public policy considerations that the contracting parties might have envisaged as fundamental conditions for their acceptance of the agreement in question, particularly if the beneficiary is a private investor, as will often be the case. The scope of the clause might thus be narrower than it appears at first sight.* [211]

The Tribunal pointed out four situations where its ruling regarding MFN clauses might not apply. For example, a requirement to exhaust domestic remedies could not be sidestepped by invoking an MFN clause since this condition reflects a "fundamental rule of international law." If BITs includes "fork in the road" provision, "provision for a particular forum such as ICSID" and "a highly institutionalized system of arbitration that incorporates precise rules of procedure" the Tribunal concluded that MFN treatment should not be applicable to dispute settlement provisions since "...these very specific provisions reflect the precise will of the contracting parties."[212] One might rightly argue that these public policy exceptions to the findings of the Tribunal regarding the scope of MFN treatment create a confusion and difficulty in ICSID jurisprudence.[213]

Like in the *Maffezini Case*, the ICSID Tribunal expansively interpreted the scope of MFN clause in the *Siemens v. Argentina Case*. The *Siemens Case* concerned a dispute relating to the alleged treatment by Argentina authorities of Siemens for the development of a system of migration control and personal identification.[214] Siemens invoked the BIT between Argentina-German BIT and initiated an international arbitral procedure before the ICSID. Pursuant to the provision of this BIT, the investor had to submit the claim first to domestic courts. However, to avoid long litigation in Argentina, Siemens argued that the MFN clause in the Argentina-Germany BIT allowed it to receive the most favorable treatment available in the Argentina-Chile BIT, which did not require a submission to local courts prior to ICSID arbitration.[215]

Argentina objected to the jurisdiction of the ICSID tribunal, arguing that Siemens had failed to comply with the BIT between Argentina-Spain. In particular, Argentina claimed that reliance squarely upon the *Maffezini Case* was improper since the MFN clause in the *Maffezini Case* is broader than Argentina-Germany Case. Argentina also argued that Siemens's interpretation of the scope of the MFN clause is incompatible with generally accepted principles of treaty interpretation.[216] However, the ICSID Tribunal held that the BIT

---

[211] *Maffezini v. Spain Case*, para. 62.
[212] Ibid. paras. 62–3.
[213] Fietta, p. 133.
[214] *Siemens v. Argentina Case*, paras. 23–7.
[215] Ibid. para. 32.
[216] G. Egli, "Don't Get BIT: Addressing ICSID'S Inconsistent Application of Most Favored-Nation Clauses to Dispute Resolution Provisions", (2007) *Pepperdine Law Review*, p. 1071.

should be interpreted in accordance with the Vienna Convention; "in good faith in accordance with the ordinary meaning to be given to the terms of the treaty in their context and in the light of its object and purpose."[217] The ICSID tribunal concluded that:

> *...Access to these mechanisms is part of the protection offered under the Treaty. It is part of the treatment of foreign investors and investments and of the advantages accessible through a MFN clause. This conclusion concurs with the findings of the arbitral tribunal in Maffezini.*[218]

It is interesting that Argentina also argued that if Siemens was entitled to import the advantageous aspects of the dispute settlement provisions of the Argentina-Chile BIT, then it should also be required to import the disadvantageous aspects of those provisions. In particular, Argentina-Chile BIT includes "fork in the road provision" which is not stipulated in the Argentina-Germany BIT. The ICSID Tribunal agreed that "the disadvantages may have been a trade off for the claimed advantages." Nevertheless it concluded that MFN clauses "relates only to more favorable treatment".[219]

Unlike *Maffezini* and *Siemens* cases, in the following two cases, the ICSID tribunals construed the scope of the MFN clauses narrowly. The first of these cases was the *Salini Case*, concerned of alleged failure to pay amounts owed to the Italian investors in connection with a dam project in Jordan.[220] Italian investors, Sallini and Italstrade, relied on the provisions of the Italy-Jordan BIT, in their request for arbitration. The BIT clearly provided that disputes arising from contract should be governed by the dispute settlement provisions of the contract. To avoid this issue, Italian investors invoked the MFN clause in the Italy-Jordan BIT as the BITs that Jordan signed with United Kingdom and United States permitted investors to refer a contract based claim to ICSID arbitration.[221] Thus, Italian investors argued that the MFN clause in the Italy-Jordan BIT should be applied to dispute settlement provisions as was decided in the *Maffezini Case*. On the other hand, Jordan claimed that the MFN clause could not apply to dispute settlement provisions since the intent of the parties is essential for the application of dispute settlement procedures.[222]

The ICSID Tribunal dismissed the MFN argument raised by the Italian investors. It followed a narrow approach for the application of the MFN treatment to dispute settlement. In particular, the following four factors were determined by the Tribunal to support its decision: 1. The Italy-Jordan BIT

---

[217] J. W. Boscariol, "The Widening of the MFN Obligation and Its Impact on Investor Protection", (2005) *International Trade Law &Regulation,* p. 63.
[218] *Siemens v. Argentina Case,* paras.102–3.
[219] Ibid. para. 120.
[220] *Salini Case*, paras. 14–7.
[221] Ibid. para. 102.
[222] Ibid. para. 103.

did not clearly stipulate that the MFN clause would apply to dispute settlement; 2. The wording of this treaty was narrower than the one in *Maffezini* since it did not provide "all rights or all matters covered by the agreement"; 3. There was no indication of parties' intent to apply MFN clause to dispute settlement; 4. Italian investors had not cited any Jordanian or Italian practice in support of their situation.[223]

It should be noted that the ICSID Tribunal in the *Salini Case* examined the impact of the *Maffezini* decision. In particular, the Tribunal pointed out that "the precautions taken by authors of the award may in practice prove difficult to apply, thereby adding more uncertainties to the risk of "treaty shopping."[224] In fact, the broad interpretation of the MFN clauses can cause treaty shopping and it is against the intention of the parties of the treaty.

The Tribunal decision is irreconcilable with the *Maffezini* decision as the Tribunal rightly interpreted the scope of the MFN clauses narrowly. In particular, the ICSID Tribunal points out that:

> *The Tribunal observes that the circumstances of this case are different. Indeed, Article 3 of the BIT between Italy and Jordan does not include any provision extending its scope of application to dispute settlement. It does not envisage "all rights or all matters covered by the agreement." Furthermore, the Claimants have submitted nothing from which it might be established that the common intention of the Parties was to have the most-favored nation clause apply to dispute settlement. Quite on the contrary, the intention as expressed in Article 9 (2) of the BIT was to exclude from ICSID jurisdiction contractual disputes between an investor and an entity of a State party in order that such disputes might be settled in accordance with the procedures set forth in the investment agreements. Lastly, the Claimants have not cited any practice in Jordan or Italy in support of their claims.*[225]

Another important case regarding the applicability of the MFN treatment to dispute settlement procedures was the *Plama Consortium Limited (Plama) v. Bulgaria Case. Plama*, a Cypriot company, bought an equity interest in a Bulgarian company that owned an oil refinery. In this case, *Plama* asserted that the Republic of Bulgaria deliberately created numerous problems which caused material damages to operations of the refinery.[226] *Plama* filed a request for arbitration with ICSID relied on the Energy Charter Treaty and the Bulgaria-Cyprus BIT. The Bulgaria-Cyprus BIT provided a restrictive dispute settlement provision that allowed *ad hoc* arbitration only in cases regarding the "amount of the compensation."[227] In order to avoid the dispute settlement provision of this BIT, *Plama* asserted that the MFN provision set out in Article 3 of the BIT provided means of incorporating the more favourable dispute

---

[223] Egli, pp. 1074–5.; Silva, p. 65.
[224] *Salini Case*, para. 115.
[225] Ibid. para. 118.
[226] *Plama Case*, paras. 19–21.
[227] Ibid. para. 26.

settlement provisions of the Bulgaria-Finland BIT. The wording of the relevant MFN provision was as follows:

> *Each Contracting Party shall apply to the investments in its territory by investors of the other Contracting Party a treatment which is not less favourable than that accorded to investments by investors of third states...*[228]

The ICSID Tribunal rejected *Plama*'s argument. It concluded that the MFN provision could not be construed as providing consent to submission of a dispute under the Bulgaria-Cyprus BIT to ICSID arbitration. In reaching its decision, the Tribunal addressed that an agreement to arbitrate must be "clear and unambiguous." In other words, the parties' agreement to arbitrate is the main requirement for arbitration.[229] The Tribunal pointed out that:

> *It is a well-established principle, both in domestic and international law, that such an agreement should be clear and unambiguous. In the framework of a BIT, the agreement to arbitrate is arrived at by the consent to arbitration that a state gives in advance in respect of investment disputes falling under the BIT, and the acceptance thereof by an investor if the latter so desires. Doubts as to the parties' clear and unambiguous intention can arise if the agreement to arbitrate is to be reached by incorporation by reference.*[230]

The Tribunal also observed that there was a difficult situation for the application of an objective test to determine which dispute settlement provision is more favorable. With respect to this issue, the Tribunal stated:

> *The Claimant argues that it is obviously more favorable for the investor to have a choice among different dispute resolution mechanisms, and to have the entire dispute resolved by arbitration as provided in the Bulgaria-Finland BIT, than to be confined to ad hoc arbitration limited to the quantum of compensation for expropriation. The Tribunal is inclined to agree with the Claimant that in this particular case, a choice is better than no choice. But what if one BIT provides for UNCITRAL arbitration and another provides for ICSID? Which is more favorable?*[231]

Recent decision of an ICSID tribunal in the *Wintershall v. Argentina Case*[232] is also important one for the issue of application of MFN clauses to dispute settlement provisions. The claimant argued that Argentina violated the Argentina-Germany BIT. The dispute settlement provisions of this BIT requires an 18month waiting period before submitting the dispute to ICSID arbitration. Thus, the claimant relied on the MFN clause in the Argentina-Germany BIT and invoked the dispute settlement mechanism in Article VII of Argentina-United States BIT. On the other hand, the respondent argued that

---

[228] Ibid. para. 26.

[229] UNCTAD, Investor-State Dispute Settlement and Impact on Investment Rulemaking, p. 54.

[230] *Plama Case*, paras. 198–9.

[231] Ibid. para. 208.

[232] *Wintershall v. Argentina Case*, (*Wintershall Aktiengesellschaft v. Argentine Republic*, ICSID Case No. ARB/04/14, Award, 8 December 2008).

the MFN clause under the Argentina-Germany BIT cannot be applied to dispute settlement provisions.[233] After considering the previous ICSID decisions on the issue, the Tribunal adopted *Plama*'s approach.[234] It is important to construe the ambit of the State's consent strictly. In particular, the Tribunal refused to apply the interpretative approach to MFN clauses in *Maffezini* and it stated that:

> *The precautions mentioned by the authors of the decision in Maffezini have proved difficult of application, resulting in much uncertainty, as to how to distinguish in a given case between "the legitimate extension of rights and benefits by means of the operation of the (MFN) clause" on the one hand, and how to avoid the use of the MFN clause for purposes plainly of "disruptive treaty shopping", on the other hand*[235]

It is essential to evaluate all these cases in order to find out a settled approach to MFN treatment concerning with dispute settlement procedure. In the *Maffezini Case*, the Tribunal held that Mr. *Maffezini* was allowed to use the dispute settlement provisions of the BIT between Chile and Spain because the MFN clause of the BIT between Argentina and Spain is broad and precisely refers to "all matters subject to this agreement".[236] In the *Siemens Case*, the ICSID Tribunal applied the principles made in the *Maffezini Case* in a narrowly drafted MFN provision. On the other hand, in the *Salini* and *Plama* cases, the ICSID Tribunals found that the MFN clauses of the applicable BITs were not intended to extend to dispute settlement provisions.[237] This new approach taken by ICSID Tribunals was summarized in the *Plama Case*. Paragraph 223 of the *Plama Case* points out that:

> ... *the principle with multiple exceptions as stated by the tribunal in the Maffezini case should instead be a different principle with one, single exception; an MFN provision in a basic treaty does not incorporate by reference dispute settlement provisions in whole or in part set forth in another treaty, unless the MFN provision in the basic treaty leaves no doubt that the Contracting Parties intended to incorporate them.*

After analyzing these ICSID cases' outcomes, it can be inferred that the claimant investor can only utilize MFN clauses to apply for the more favourable dispute resolution provisions of BITs with third States, if the Contracting Parties had an intention for this possibility. Thus, the wording of MFN clauses is the crucial factor to determine the applicability of MFN clauses to dispute settlement provisions. For example, the UK Model BIT illustrates the

---

233 Ibid. para 18.2

234 Schill, p.171.

235 Ibid. para. 182.

236 UNCTAD, Investor-State Dispute Settlement and Impact on Investment Rulemaking, p. 39.

237 C. McLachlan QC, L. Shore and M. Weiniger, *International Investment Arbitration Substantive Principles*, 2008, pp. 256–7.

intention of the parties to incorporate Investor-State dispute settlement provisions into a BIT through MFN clauses. Indeed, Article 3 (3) of the UK Model BIT states that:

> *For avoidance of doubt it is confirmed that the treatment (MFN) provided for in paragraphs (1) and (2) above shall apply to the provisions of Articles 1 to 11 of this Agreement (It should be noted that Articles 8 and 9 of the UK Model BIT set out dispute settlement provisions)*[238]

It should also be noted that the parties' intention regarding the applicability of MFN treatment to dispute settlement provision must be clear and unambiguous. In fact, ascertaining the intention of the parties is consistent with the basic rules of treaty interpretation at international law.[239] Furthermore, such an intention may be ascertained by reference to any factors stipulated in Articles 31 and 32 of the Vienna Convention on the Law of Treaties.

The ICSID jurisprudence regarding the MFN and dispute settlement procedure affects the international investment law. To avoid the problem of the applicability of MFN treatment to dispute settlement procedures, contracting parties clearly include or exclude MFN provisions regarding this issue in new BITs and other international investment instruments. For instance, Article 3 of the BIT between Armenia and Egypt (1995) makes explicit reference to the provisions to which MFN treatment applies: "…*3) In the avoidance of doubt it is confirmed that the treatment provided for the paragraphs (1) and (2) above shall apply to the provisions of Articles 1 to 11 of this Agreement.*"[240] Because of this fact Article 8 of the Armenia- Egypt BIT provides dispute settlement provision. Therefore, the MFN standard would apply to dispute settlement procedures. Overall, if the Contracting parties do not want to extend MFN treatment to dispute settlement procedures, they should explicitly exclude this issue in their agreement. Thus, the drafting of MFN clauses in BITs is an extremely important for the scope of MFN clauses in terms of its application to dispute settlement procedures. Furthermore, Stephan W. Schill argues that the MFN clauses in BITs "influence the multilateralization of bilateral investment relations between States" through application of MFN clauses to substantive and procedural provisions.[241]

#### 4.5.5.2. *Fair and Equitable Treatment*

The most debated and analyzed issue under the ICSID Jurisprudence is the concept of fair and equitable treatment (FET), which was first found in the

238 Fietta, p. 136.

239 Fietta, p. 137.; S. Vesel, "Clearing A Path Through A Tangled Jurisprudence: Most-Favored-Nation Clauses and Dispute Settlement Provisions in Bilateral Investment Treaties", (2007) *Yale Journal of International Law*, pp. 137–8.

240 UNCTAD, Bilateral Investment Treaties 1995–2006, pp. 40–1.

241 Schill, pp. 193–6.

Havana Charter of 1948. Article 11 (2) of the Charter states that foreign investments should be assured "just and equitable treatment".[242] Today, most BITs and multilateral agreements have provided the fair and equitable treatment standard. For example, Article 3 (1) of the BIT between Turkey and Lebanon says: "Each Contracting Party shall ensure fair and equitable treatment within its territory of the investments of the other Contracting Party."[243] FET is a general standard whose scope and content are to be deemed independent of treatment of host State nationals or third country nationals. It derives from customary international law on the protection of the property of aliens and includes a basic standard, "detached from the host country's domestic law, against which the behavior of the host country vis-à-vis foreign investment can be assessed."[244]

Most BITs and other international investment instruments have utilized the FET standard in a numerous ways. While some agreements provide only fair and equitable treatment, others combine this standard with non-discrimination principles. Furthermore, some BITs links the FET standard to international law. For example, the BIT between USA and Turkey in II (3) states that: "Investments shall at all times be accorded fair and equitable treatment and shall enjoy full protection and security in a manner consistent with international law."[245] It should be noted that UNCTAD studies on bilateral investment agreement addressed that there are seven different categories of BITs providing various content of the FET standard.[246] Thus, the wording of the FET standard is an essential factor to determine the scope and the content of the FET standard.

Even though there is no general agreement on the precise meaning of the FET, nearly all BITs provide that investment and investors covered under the treaty receive fair and equitable treatment. Moreover, this standard has been recently considered an essential ground by foreign investors for a finding of violations of the investment agreement by the host country. Indeed, the majority of the awards that are issued in international investment arbitration procedure found that host countries violated the FET standard.[247]

In international arbitration practice, the content and the scope of the FET standard are highly debated since this standard lacks a precise meaning. There are two different views that have emerged in international legal doctrine for the precise meaning of the term fair and equitable treatment: a) the plain meaning approach; b) equating fair and equitable treatment with the

---

[242] http://www.worldtradelaw.net/misc/havana.pdf (visited on 28.12.2009).
[243] http://www.unctad.org/sections/dite/iia/docs/bits/lebanon_turkey.pdf (visited on 28.12.2009)
[244] UNCTAD, Investor-State Dispute Settlement and Impact on Investment Rulemaking, p. 40.
[245] http://www.unctad.org/sections/dite/iia/docs/bits/us_turkey.pdf (visited on 28.12.2009).
[246] UNCTAD, Bilateral Investment Treaties 1995–2006, p. 30.
[247] Dolzer and Schreuer, p. 119.

international minimum standard. According to some scholars, the FET standard is different from the international minimum standard. Pursuant to this view, the term fair and equitable treatment should be given its plain meaning. F.A. Mann is a prominent supporter of this view and points out that:

> *The terms "fair and equitable treatment" envisage conduct which goes far beyond the minimum standard and afford protection to a greater extent and according to a much more objective standard than any previously employed form of words. A Tribunal would not be concerned with a minimum, maximum or average standard. It will have to decide whether in all circumstances the conduct in issues is fair and equitable or unfair and inequitable. No standard defined by other words is likely to be material. The terms are to be understood and applied independently and autonomously.*[248]

It is worthwhile to note that this approach is consistent with the rules of interpretation in international law. In fact, FET clauses have to be construed in accordance with Article 31 of the Vienna Convention on the Law of Treaties, duly taking into account its text and, if appropriate, its history.

According to some other scholars, the FET is no more than the international minimum standard, as contained in customary international law. Pursuant to this view, FET has been recognized as one of the elements of the minimum standard of treatment of foreigners and of their property required by customary international law since this law grants a certain level of treatment to foreign investors.[249] The utilization of this approach to find out the scope and content of the FET standard will be problematic. Most international investment instruments do not make a clear connection between the international minimum standard and FET standard. Thus, if the contracting States accept that the FET standard is tantamount to international minimum standard, they could specify this explicitly in their international investment instruments. Furthermore, even though the international minimum standard has been strongly supported by developed countries, the standard is debated among developing countries regarding whether this standard is a part of customary international law.[250]

With respect to jurisprudence relating to the fair and equitable treatment, NAFTA has been very fruitful and evolutionary since the scope of the fair and equitable treatment standard has been challenged in NAFTA's Chapter 11 arbitrations. Almost every claim in NAFTA arbitration includes violation of Article 1105 of the NAFTA, which provides fair and equitable treatment. The Article concerned states the following:

---

[248] F.A. Mann, "British Treaties for the Promotion and Protection of Investments", (1981) 52 *British Year Book of International Law*, p. 241, p. 244.

[249] OECD, "Fair and Equitable Treatment Standard in International Investment Law", Working Papers on International Investment, Number 2004/3, September 2004, p. 9.

[250] UNCTAD, *Fair and Equitable Treatment*, New York and Geneva, 1999, pp. 12–3.

> *...Each Party shall accord to investments of investors of another Party treatment in accordance with international law, including fair and equitable treatment and full protection and security*[251]

There were three important cases for the interpretation of Article 1105 of the NAFTA: *Metalclad v. Mexico,*[252] *S.D. Myers v Canada*[253] and *Pope & Talbot v. Canada.*[254] All three cases construed the said Article in a different way.

In the *Metalclad Case*, the Tribunal interpreted Article 1105 (1) of the NAFTA in a broad manner to include a transparency obligation found in NAFTA. The Tribunal concluded that "Mexico failed to ensure a transparent and predictable framework for Metalclad's business planning and investment",[255] thus Mexico violated Article 1105. Mexico sought judicial review of the award in British Columbia, the place of arbitration. The Supreme Court of British Columbia found that the Tribunal in this case had exceeded its jurisdiction by basing its decision on treaty obligations. The Court found that the Tribunal had broadly interpreted Article 1105 (1) of the NAFTA. The Supreme Court also stressed that the reference to "international law" in Article 1105 was to "customary international law".[256]

In the *S.D. Myers Inc. v. Canada Case*, S.D. Myers argued that the promulgation of the export ban by Canada issued in a discriminatory and unfair manner. The Tribunal found that the breach of National Treatment standard stipulated in Article 1102 essentially create a breach of Article 1105. According to the Tribunal, a violation of a conventional international rule is equivalent to a violation of Article 1105.

In the *Pope & Talbot Inc. v. Government of Canada Case*, the Tribunal has expansively interpreted Article 1105. The Tribunal recognized that "fair and equitable treatment" and "full protection and security" are elements which are included within the requirements of international law. Nevertheless, the Tribunal construed that provision as the follows:

> *Another possible interpretation of the presence of the fairness elements in Article 1105 is that they are additive to the requirements of international law. That is, investors under NAFTA are entitled to the international law minimum, plus the fairness elements. It is true that the language of Article 1105 suggests otherwise, since it states that the fairness elements are included in international law*[257]

As mentioned above, the arbitral tribunals in NAFTA cases differently interpreted the fair and equitable provision of the NAFTA. To elucidate the

[251] http://www.nafta-sec-alena.org/en/view.aspx?conID=590 (visited on 12.12.2009).

[252] *Metalclad v. Mexico Case (AF), (Metalclad Corporation v. United Mexican States,* ICSID Case No. ARB/AF/97/1, Award, 30 August 2000). (hereinafter *Metalclad Case*).

[253] UNCITRAL, First Partial Award, 13 November 2000.

[254] UNCITRAL, Award on the Merits, 10 April 2001.

[255] *Metalclad Case*, para.101.

[256] UNCTAD, *Investor-State Dispute Settlement and Impact on Investment Rulemaking*, p. 41.

[257] UNCITRAL, Award on the Merits, 10 April 2001, para. 110.

interpretation of Article 1105(1), the NAFTA Free Trade Commission (FTC) issued official interpretation. Pursuant to this interpretation:

> *Article 1105 (1) prescribes the customary international law minimum standard of treatment of aliens as the minimum standard of treatment to be afforded to investments of investors of another Party.*
>
> *The concepts of "fair and equitable treatment" and "full protection and security" do not require treatment in addition to or beyond that which is required by the customary international law minimum standard of treatment of aliens.*
>
> *A determination that there has been a breach of another provision of the NAFTA, or of a separate international agreement, does not establish that there has been a breach of Article 1105 (1).* [258]

NAFTA tribunals have accepted and followed the FTC interpretation. Moreover, after the FTC interpretation, there are two important factors that are followed by NAFTA tribunals. First, it is acknowledged that the fair and equitable treatment standard has considerably evolved since the *Neer* decision. Second, bad faith was not a required element for breach of fair and equitable standard.[259]

In the *Mondev v. United States Case,*[260] the Tribunal broadly construed the fair and equitable treatment standard by referring to the relationship between "fair and equitable" and "minimum standard of treatment" in customary international law. Furthermore, it recognized the evolutionary character of the minimum standard. The award sets out that "the Tribunal need not pass upon all the issues debated before it as to the Free Trade Commission's interpretations of 31 July 2001."[261]

In the *ADF v. United States Case*, the Tribunal followed the *Mondev Case* decision. The Tribunal explicitly stated its view on the evolutionary character of the minimum standard:

> *...what customary international law projects is not a static photograph of the minimum standard of treatment of aliens as it stood in 1927 when the Award in the Neer case was rendered. For both customary international law and the minimum standard of treatment of aliens it incorporates, are constantly in a process of development.* [262]

In the *Loewen v. United States Case*, the Tribunal recognized the obligatory nature of the FTC's interpretation on Chapter 11 and said:

---

[258] Note of Interpretation of the NAFTA Free Trade Commission, 31 July 2001. http://www.sice.oas.org/tpd/nafta/Commission/CH11understanding_e.asp (visited on 12.12.2009).

[259] UNCTAD, *Investor-State Dispute Settlement and Impact on Investment Rulemaking*, p. 42.

[260] *Mondev v. United States Case (AF)*, (*Mondev International Ltd. v. United States of America*, ICSID Case No. ARB (AF)/99/2, Award, 11 October 2002).

[261] Ibid. para. 125.

[262] *ADF v. United States Case* (AF), (*ADF Group Inc. v. United States of America*, ICSID Case No. ARB (AF)/00/1, 9 January 2003), para. 179.

> *The effect of the Commission's interpretation is that 'fair and equitable treatment' and 'full protection and security' are not free-standing obligations. They constitute obligations only to the extent that they are recognised by customary international law. Likewise, a breach of Article 1105(1) is not established by a breach of another provision of NAFTA. To the extent, if at all, that NAFTA Tribunals in Metalclad, S.D. Myers and Pope & Talbot, may have expressed contrary views, those views must be disregarded.*[263]

The tribunal in this case concluded that bad faith was not a requirement for breach of the fair and equitable standard. The Tribunal expressly stated that:

> *Neither State practice, the decisions of international tribunals nor the opinion of commentators support the view that bad faith or malicious intention is an essential element of unfair and inequitable treatment or denial of justice amounting to a breach of international justice.*[264]

It should be noted that the view of BIT tribunals is generally different from NAFTA tribunals with respect to the interpretation of FET standard. Unlike Article 1105 of the NAFTA Agreement, most BITs include FET clause in various ways and the vagueness of the standard cause interpretation problems. Thus, there is no uniformity and consistency with regard to the application of the fair and equitable treatment standard in international arbitration awards. According to the UNCTAD study, the BIT Tribunal decisions concerning this issue can be classified into three groups.[265]

In the first group of awards, the tribunals followed a semantic approach. Therefore, the arbitral tribunals broadly construe the scope of the FET standard. In particular, these decisions do not cite customary international law so as to determine the applicability of the standard. The Tribunals in the following awards utilize a semantic approach: *Emilio Agustin Maffezini v. Spain and Middle East Cement Shipping and Handling Co. S.A. v. Egypt.*[266] In the *Maffezini Case*, the Tribunal held that:

> *[...] the lack of transparency with which this loan transaction was conducted is compatible with Spain's commitment to ensure the investor a fair and equitable treatment in accordance with Article 4(1) of the [...] treaty between Argentina and Spain].*[267]

In the second group of awards, the tribunals followed a restricted approach when applying the FET standard. The tribunals acknowledge and follow the reasoning of *Neer* decision and connecting the standard to customary international law. *Alex Genin, Eastern Credit Limited. Inc. v. Estonia Award* is an

---

[263] *Loewen v. United States Case (AF), (Loewen Group, Inc. and Raymond L. Loewen v. United States of America*, ICSID Case No. ARB (AF)/98/3, Award, 26 June 2003). para. 128.

[264] Ibid. para. 132.

[265] UNCTAD, *Investor-State Dispute Settlement and Impact on Investment Rulemaking*, p. 43.

[266] Ibid. p. 43.

[267] *Maffezini v Spain Case*, para. 83.

example of this group.[268] In this case, the Tribunal did engage how the FET standard had been generally understood under international law. The ICSID Tribunal in this case linked the FET standard under Article II (3) (a) of the US-Estonia BIT to the minimum standard and explained its elements as follows:

> *Acts that would violate this minimum standard would include acts showing a willful neglect of duty, an insufficiency of action falling far below international standards, or even subjective bad faith.*[269]

The third group of awards connects the fair and equitable standard to evolving content of customary international law. In particular, recent awards regarding the applicability of FET standard such as *CMS Gas Transportation Company v. Argentina and Azurix Corp. v. Argentina awards* follow the evolving customary international law concept.[270] The Tribunal in the *Azurix Case* spelled out as follows:

> *The question whether fair and equitable treatment is or is not additional to the minimum treatment requirement under international law is a question about the substantive content of fair and equitable treatment and, whichever side of the argument one takes, the answer to the question may in substance be the same.*[271]

*The Tecmed v. Mexico Case*[272] is one of the leading cases that follow the textual interpretation with the general expectations of the foreign investors when making investment and evolving international law. The ICSID Tribunal pointed out:

> *the scope of the undertaking of fair and equitable treatment under Article 4(1) of the Agreement...is that resulting from an autonomous interpretation, taking into account the text of Article 4(1) of the Agreement according to its ordinary meaning (Article 31(1) of the Vienna Convention), or from international law and the good faith principle, on the basis of which the scope of the obligation assumed under the Agreement and the actions related to compliance therewith are to be assessed.*[273]

To sum up, the tribunals demonstrate that there are several factors can be utilized for determining the scope and content of the FET standard. The fair and equitable standard clauses may be interpreted "as no longer applicable solely to what would be considered egregious abuses of government power, or disguised uses of government powers for untoward purposes, but to any open and deliberate use of government powers that fails to meet the requirements of good governance, such as transparency, protection of the investor's legitimate

---

[268] ICSID Case No. ARB/99/2, Award, 25 June 2001.

[269] Ibid. para. 367.

[270] UNCTAD, *Investor-State Dispute Settlement and Impact on Investment Rulemaking*, p. 44.

[271] ICSID Case No. ARB/01/12, Final Award, 14 July 2006, para. 364.

[272] *Tecmed v. Mexico Case (AF)*, (*Técnicas Medioambientales Tecmed, S.A. v. United Mexican States*, Award, 29 May 2003, (2004) 43 ILM 133).

[273] Ibid. para. 155.

expectations, freedom from coercion and harassment, due process and procedural propriety and good faith."[274]

4.5.5.3. *Non-Precluded Measures*

Many BITs include non-precluded measures (NPM) provisions that preclude liability for actions in exceptional circumstances. In other words, even though BITs are signed to encourage foreign investment, many BITs providing NPM provisions in reality limit investment protections in exceptional circumstances. These NPM provisions allow host country to take actions in consistent with treaty obligations when necessary for protection of essential security, maintenance of public order, national security, and public health.[275] According to Kenneth Vandevelde, NPM clauses are included in many BITs since "some public policy concerns of the State were deemed sufficiently compelling that they justified State interference with market-based allocations of capital."[276]

It should be noted that NPM provisions are not only included in BITs, these provisions are also stipulated in the World Trade Organization Agreements, in particular, the GATT Agreement. Thus, it is essential to determine the applicability and scope of the NPM clauses in order to find out its implications for the development of international economic law. As mentioned before, BITs are the main sources of international investment law and in particular they are signed for the promotion and reciprocal protection of investments. Therefore, most of the BITs have a number of provisions that provide security and protection to foreign investment.[277] However, the existence of NPM clauses in BITs means that investment security and investment protections do not apply in exceptional situations. In other words, the NPM provision has "a risk-allocation function, transferring the costs of harming an investment from host states to investors in exceptional circumstances."[278] If host country is able to claim that its actions taken falls under the exceptional circumstances, the State will not be liable for actions that would normally breach the BIT.[279]

Although there is a growing use of NPM clauses in BITs, NPM clauses can be drafted in different ways. In particular, these clauses can be included to apply to an entire BIT or can be drafted in a more limited manner to apply

[274] UNCTAD, *Investor-State Disputes Arising From Investment Treaties: A Review*, 2005, p. 39.

[275] W. W. Burke-White and A. von Staden, "Investment Protection in Extraordinary Times: The Interpretation and Application of Non-Precluded Measures Provision in Bilateral Investment Treaties", (2008) *Virginia Journal of International Law*, p.311.; Newcombe and Paradell, pp. 483–4.

[276] K. J. Vandevelde, "Of Politics and Markets: The Shifting Ideology of the BITs", (1993) 11 *International Tax & Business Law*, p. 159, p. 164

[277] Caliskan, pp .40–1.

[278] Burke-White and Von Staden, pp. 313–4.

[279] C. L. Goodman, "Uncharted Waters: Financial Crisis and Enforcement of ICSID Awards in Argentina", (2007) 28/2 *University of Pennsylvania Journal of International Economic Law*, p. 476.; Burke-White and Von Staden, p. 314.

to some parts of the substantive provisions of the treaty. The U.S.A., Canada and India frequently utilize broad scope approach to apply NPM clauses to the treaty as a whole. For example, Article XIV of the US-Mozambique BIT provides that: "This treaty shall not preclude a Party from applying measures that it considers necessary...."[280] Limited scope NPM clauses are also used by countries such as Germany and Turkey in order to restrict the application of NPM clauses only to specified provisions of the treaty. For example, Article 2 (2) of Turkey-Morocco BIT stipulates that: "Each Contracting party shall ensure fair and equitable treatment and subject to the strictly necessary measures to maintain the public order provide full protection and security for investments of investors of the other Contracting Party."[281]

It should be noted that like many BITs, customary international law also provides some legal defenses in extraordinary circumstances. Thus, the question will be raised as to whether the NPM clauses should be treated as equivalent to the defenses in customary international law used in exceptional circumstances. Customary international law provides some exemptions from substantive protection in extraordinary situations. Force majeure and necessity are among these situations in which States are immune from international liability. According to William W. Burke-White and Andreas von Staden, the NPM clauses are different from these customary defenses "in terms of their substantive content, their theoretical justification, their source of legal authority, and their scope of applicability."[282]

Jurisprudence regarding as to whether the NPM clauses are distinguished from defenses in customary international law has also recognized that NPM clauses are distinct from customary defenses. "Reading an NPM clause as equivalent to the customary defense of necessity would render the clause pointless because the customary defense of necessity would be available to states irrespective of the inclusion of the NPM clause in a BIT. In order to satisfy the principle of effectiveness in treaty interpretation, NPM clauses must be read as distinct rules that states create in their treaty relationships, independent of the necessity defense in customary international law."[283] However, it should be noted that the NPM clauses do not replace the customary defenses, unless the treaty specifies that it replaces customary rules. Thus, the BIT NPM provisions and customary rules are applicable independently. These provisions can also coexistent with customary defenses.[284]

---

280 http://www.unctad.org/sections/dite/iia/docs/bits/us_mozambique.pdf (visited on 29.12.2009).

281 http://www.unctad.org/sections/dite/iia/docs/bits/turkey_morocco.pdf (visited on 29.12.2009).

282 *See* the detailed information regarding the distinguishing treaty based NPM clauses from defenses in customary international law: Burke-White and Von Staden, pp. 321–4.

283 Appellate Body Report, United States-Standards for Reformulated and Conventional Gasoline, WT/DS2/AB/R (April 29, 1996).

284 Burke-White and Von Staden, p. 324.

The application and interpretation of NPM clauses become an important debated issue in ICSID Jurisprudence. In particular, there are four *Argentina Cases* regarding the applicability of NPM provisions: *CMS v. Argentina,*[285] *Enron v. Argentina,*[286] *Sempra v. Argentina,*[287] *LG&E v. Argentina.*[288] While these cases brought against Argentina, Argentina has claimed its rights under the NPM provision of the United States-Argentina BIT. Argentina asserted that the NPM clause in this treaty allow Argentina to claim a defense for violation of its treaty obligations. The four tribunals have followed different approaches to the NPM clause of the US-Argentina BIT. The Tribunal in the *LG& E v. Argentina Case* found that Argentina was not liable for harms to investors caused during the economic crisis since the NPM clause in the United States-Argentina BIT justified Argentina's position. On the other hand, the other three tribunals found that the NPM clauses are inapplicable, thus Argentina is liable for damages to investors.[289]

The four tribunals find the NPM clauses applicable to economic emergency. Moreover, the tribunals find NPM clause in the US-Argentina BIT is not "self-judging."[290] However, there was an essential disagreement between four tribunals regarding the applicability of the NPM clauses. In particular, the relationship between the NPM clause in the treaty and the customary law defense of necessity is the main discrepancy among the decisions. In the *CMS v. Argentina, Enron v. Argentina, Sempra v. Argentina cases,* the tribunals found that the NPM clause in BIT did not applicable in light of the customary international law defense of necessity. Nevertheless, the Tribunal in the *LG&E v. Argentina Case* applied NPM clause in US-Argentina BIT independently from the customary international law defense of necessity.[291]

It is worthwhile to note that with respect to NPM clauses there has been a problematic treaty interpretation made by ICSID Tribunals. The tribunals should follow a fundamental rule of treaty interpretation. This rule has received its most authoritative and concise expression in Article 31 of the Vienna Convention on the Law of Treaties which provides in relevant part:

> *1. A treaty shall be interpreted in good faith in accordance with the ordinary meaning to be given to the terms of the treaty in their context and in the light of its object and purpose.*

---

[285] ICSID Case No. ARB/ 01/08, Award, May 12, 2005.

[286] *Enron v. Argentine Case,* (*Enron Corporation and Ponderosa Assets, L. P. v. Argentine Republic,* ICSID Case No. ARB/01/03, Award, 22 May 2007).

[287] ICSID Case No. ARB/02/06, Award, September 28, 2007.

[288] ICSID Case No. ARB/02/01, Award, July 25 2007.

[289] Burke-White and Von Staden, p. 337.; Goodman, pp. 476–7.

[290] Burke-White and Von Staden, p. 394.

[291] Ibid. p. 395.

The ICSID tribunals should apply the basic principle of interpretation that the words of a treaty are to be given their ordinary meaning in their context and in the light of the treaty's object and purpose.[292] Furthermore, the tribunals should take into account the intent of States entering into BITs.[293] Overall, the drafting NPM clause is an important task for the States to protect its public health and safety and public order.

### 4.6. *Conclusion*

The proliferation of international investment arbitration through bilateral investment treaties has impacted the development of international investment law. In particular, international investment arbitration practice has created either new procedural and substantive issues or tried to solve existing problems in international investment law and international investment arbitration. It should be noted that there is no system of binding precedent in international law.[294] However, previous ICSID tribunals' decisions influence later decision and even though the ICSID tribunals are not bound by earlier decisions, they will definitely consider such decisions.

The ICSID tribunals have construed the substantive principles of international investment law in numerous and different ways. Therefore, utilizing the ICSID arbitration procedure set out in most BITs, the international investment law has developed in recent years. In particular, the ICSID tribunals have considered various problems on procedural and substantive issues. With regard to procedural issues, the ICSID jurisprudence has concentrated on some of the jurisdictional problems. For example, under the protection of bilateral investment treaties, private companies and shareholders have a right to invoke investment arbitration procedure. Thus, BITs create special regime for the protection of shareholders. Furthermore, with respect to the issue of subject matter jurisdiction, the ICSID tribunals have adopted objective criteria for the existence of investment. The ICSID award has also impacted the amendments of the ICSID rules. In particular, non-party participation in ICSID arbitration proceedings is one of the essential amendments of ICSID Rules. These amendments provide transparency and third party participation in ICSID arbitration which is an important subject matter in investment treaty arbitration proceedings since international investment arbitration have essential public interest implications. It can be argued that by granting rights to tribunals to accept *amicus curiae* submissions, the amendments of ICSID rules

---

[292] Ibid. p. 316.

[293] *See* detailed analysis of the interpretation problems of NPM Provisions: Burke-White and Von Staden, pp. 337–41.

[294] McLachlan QC, Shore and Weiniger, p. 71.

promote effective and efficient transparency which is a crucial issue for the development of international economic law.

With respect to substantive issues, the ICSID tribunals have decided the scope and effect of main substantive principles of international law such as MFN clauses and fair and equitable treatment clauses. It should be noted that there are significant discrepancies among ICSID awards as to the scope, content, and effect of these principles. It is a well-known rule that the BITs should be interpreted in accordance with Articles 31 and 32 of the Vienna Convention on the Law of Treaties. Therefore, the wording of the clauses should be the main point for evaluation of the effect and the scope of the main substantive principles that utilized in BITs. It is also worthwhile to note that due to inconsistent decisions of ICSID tribunals on the interpretation of these principles, contracting parties should incorporate them in a precise and clear langue in their future BITs or other international investment instruments. In fact, considering previous decisions and problematic procedural and substantive issues in ICSID arbitration practice, many developed countries incorporate comprehensive dispute settlement provision in their new BITs practice in order to provide predictability and "to ensure consistence among arbitral awards and the development of sound jurisprudence on international investment law."[295]

[295] UNCTAD, Bilateral Investment Treaties 1995–2006, p. 119.

# TOWARDS GLOBAL DISPUTE SETTLEMENT MECHANISMS IN INTERNATIONAL ECONOMIC LAW

Yusuf Aksar

International economic law is a sub-branch of international law and has interdisciplinary features. As has been explained above, it has close relationship with other branches of law including private international law, business law, environmental law, and human rights law. It is also important to realise that international economic law, as can be inferred from its name, is intrinsically bound up with international economics and international relations. However, the substantive content of international economic law, for the purpose of this work, is limited to the areas of international economic law which govern the relations between the subjects of international law. The main reasons why international economic law is to be limited to the mentioned fields are as follows: First, being basically developed from general international law, the subjects of international law, and the governance of economic relations among them are taken into account. In other words, the concept of international economic law is examined from the more general international law perspective. Second, though each sub-branches of international economic law establishes its own legal regimes and institutions that enable and enhance international economic activities, a functioning international economic law may become possible when international finance law, international trade law, and international investment law work together. The practice of the institutions operating in the field of international economic law such as the IMF, the World Bank, and the WTO also supports this point.

International economic law and its institutions have been playing a major role in meeting the needs of the international community of the 21st century. Since World War II, particularly after the end of the 'cold war era', the rapid increase in the number of international economic activities and of international treaties raised a number of legal, economic, and political issues. In the early days of the 21st century, it became clear that the institutions created right after World War II were not sufficient to deal with the problems and crises that the international community has faced. The 2008 financial crisis in general and the ongoing crisis in the European Union (in Greece, Spain, Portugal, Ireland and Italy etc.) in particular, once more affirmed the fact that the international community has to work harder on improving the global economic system and its legal instruments.

As indicated by Bantekas, the international financial institutions have failed the developing world and have done little to alleviate the financial woes of the developed world in the aftermath of the 2008 crisis. International community has been witnessing a radical change from a robust and uncompromising neo-liberalism to State ownership in banks, automobile industries, and others. Perhaps this will be the practice of the developed countries in tackling the crisis to come for the next few decades, until the global economy stabilises. Not to witness such crisis again, it is imperative to restructure and reshape the international financial institutions. In this context, new financial resources should be provided for the IBRD and the IMF in lending to countries in desperate need, in particular to the developing countries. The policy of lending must not only seek to build necessary infrastructures but should also lead to the creation of meaningful employment and sustainable development, something that is currently escaping the impoverished parts of our planet. It is true that affirmations to this end were not highlighted in the recent G20 declarations, but at least they were given some prominence. Moreover, political and social reforms of international financial institutions have to be done.

In international economic law, the establishment of the WTO and its dispute settlement system should be considered as one of the most important developments of the international community since the establishment of international financial institutions at the Bretton Woods Conference. This is because, one of the gaps of international economic law was able to be filled by the WTO and its agreements consisting of major rules for international trade for more than 150 States. As Ms. Baklaci discussed in detail above, the dispute settlement of the WTO certainly is the biggest contribution to international trade law on the ground that dispute settlement system provides security and predictability to the multilateral trading system, which is the *sine qua non* requirement of international trade law in particular, and of globalisation in general. It is also important to note that the dispute settlement system of the WTO does not require the recognition of its jurisdiction by member States. In other words, its jurisdiction is compulsory once a State becomes party to the WTO. As mentioned earlier, the adjudicative bodies of the WTO has been widely used. This fact should be regarded as an evidence supporting the credibility of the system. Of course, it does not mean that the WTO dispute settlement system is a perfect system. Like any other system, it is still open for improvement and there are proposals for changes on the shortcomings of the system. Some of them could be indicated as follows: the need to make the system more transparent; the establishment of permanent panels and permanent panelists from qualified individuals; the introduction of the remand authority to the Appellate Body; third party rights; and prompt implementation.

As Mr. Caliskan concluded, the proliferation of international investment arbitration through bilateral investment treaties has significantly contributed to the development of international investment law. In particular, the ICSID tribunals had to consider different types of problems on procedural and substantive issues. Concerning procedural issues, the ICSID jurisprudence has focused on some of the jurisdictional matters that needed to be solved. For example, private companies and shareholders have a right to invoke investment arbitration procedure under the protection of bilateral investment treaties; thus, BITs set out special regime for the protection of shareholders. Furthermore, in relation to the issue of subject matter jurisdiction, the ICSID tribunals have adopted objective criteria for the existence of investment. The contribution of ICSID awards may be examined in the amendments of the ICSID rules. For instance, non-party participation in ICSID arbitration proceedings is one of the essential amendments of ICSID Rules. This amendment provides transparency and third party participation in ICSID arbitration. Based on these facts, it can be argued that granting rights to tribunal to accept *amicus curiae* submissions, the amendments of ICSID rules promote effective and efficient transparency. With regard to substantive issues, the ICSID tribunals have contributed on the determination of the scope and interpretation of major principles of international law such as MFN clauses and fair and equitable treatment clauses. When the fact that there are significant discrepancies among ICSID awards as to the scope, content, and effect of these principles are taken into consideration, the real impact of ICSID tribunals becomes obvious in implementing international economic law in a predictable and secure way. Furthermore, the principle that treaties including the BITs should be interpreted in accordance with Articles 31 and 32 of the Vienna Convention on the Law of Treaties and its significance in international investment arbitration in terms of the wording of the clauses to be the main point for evaluation of the effect and the scope of the main substantive principles that utilized in BITs should be once more noted here. It is also worthwhile to note that due to inconsistent decisions of the ICSID tribunals for the interpretation of these principles, contracting parties should incorporate them in a precise and clear langue in their future BITs or other international investment instruments. In fact, considering previous decisions and problematic procedural and substantive issues in the ICSID arbitration practice, many developed countries incorporate comprehensive dispute settlement provision in their new BITs practice in order to provide predictability and sound jurisprudence on international investment law.

To sum up from the point of view of a general international economic law perspective, although the age of globalisation is the main feature of the world, it seems that regionalisation will challenge it so long as the trend in interpreting and applying the rules of international economic law is taken into consideration. The international community, on the one hand, has the EU, the AU, the NAFTA, and the MERCUSOR as regional organisations, and the WTO that may be seen as the equivalent of the United Nations for the world trading system on the other. However, the rules and their implementation within the same regional international organization may be different when similar situations occur at the international level. For instance, the EU law by the European

Court of Justice is differently interpreted and applied when the case is only concerned with Member States as has been witnessed in the creation of the direct effect doctrine. As is known from the practice of EU law, individuals can bring cases arising from the rules of Community law before their own national and EU courts through the application of direct effect doctrine. In a sense, private enforcement of the EU law by way of adopting individual/citizen approach becomes possible. By contrast, the same approach was not employed by the Court when the WTO agreements were in question. The basic reason for such a practice is to protect the interests of the EU in the first place. In other words, the European Court of Justice adopts the state/international organisation centred approach in defining the interests of the Community and settling the disputes when it faces with disputes between the EU and any other international organisation. Similarly, the legal relationship between the NAFTA and the WTO is not clearly defined and it is ambiguous that whether the NAFTA or the WTO law will prevail in cases of inconsistency. That is also true when the judicial organs of the WTO face with the ruling of a regional organisation which is conflicting with WTO agreements. Based on these facts, the international community should create new rules and mechanisms governing the relations between international organisations, through which different international regional organizations and international/universal organizations can co-operate and operate side by side.

As has been witnessed in the EU practice, one of the most effective methods of providing a dispute settlement mechanism for finding solutions to the issues between/among international organisations and regional organisations is to establish a supra-national/global judicial institution which has power to implement individual-centred approach to the cases. Putting individuals in the centre for the purpose of implementing international economic law is also in conformity with the development of subjects of international law. As is well-known, individuals have become one category subjects of international law (in addition to States, international organisations) enjoying international personality since World War II. In light of these facts, individuals (either as natural persons or legal persons like companies) should have the right to bring cases against their own governments in cases of violations of their own rights deriving from international economic law at the international level. The right of bringing cases by investors against the host State through ICSID in international investment law clearly constitutes one of the implementations of this understanding. Furthermore, to achieve a similar goal in international trade law, the establishment of an International Trade Court by way of conclusion of a treaty should be seriously taken into consideration. The creation of International Trade Court can be considered as the most convenient response to proposed changes for the WTO dispute settlement system on the ground that the Court will be a permanent international organisation composed of qualified judges and respecting third party rights, providing prompt implementation. This is exactly the point in where general international law and international economic law interrelate. Undoubtedly, the sources of international law and the successful practice of the European Court of Justice can provide the needed guideline in this regard. The practice of the international community also supports this point: The International Criminal Court in international criminal law, the International Tribunal for the Law of the Sea in international law of the sea, the European Court of Human Rights (as a regional judicial institution) in international human rights law as operating organisations on the one hand, and the International Human Rights Court and the International Court for the Environment as proposed global judicial institutions on the other could be indicated here since they basically focus on individuals.

# INDEX